ZEW Economic Studies

Publication Series of the Centre for European Economic Research (ZEW), Mannheim, Germany

ZEW Economic Studies

Further volumes of this series can be found at our homepage:
springeronline.com

Vol. 6: B. Fitzenberger
Wages and Employment Across Skill Groups
An Analysis for West Germany
1999. XII, 251 pp. ISBN 3-7908-1235-8

Vol. 7: K. Rennings et al. (Eds.)
Social Costs and Sustainable Mobility
Strategies and Experiences in Europe and the United States
1999. VI, 212 pp. ISBN 3-7908-1260-9

Vol. 8: H. Legler et al.
Germany's Technological Performance
2000. X, 191 pp. ISBN 3-7908-1281-1

Vol. 9: O. Bürgel
The Internationalization of British Start-up Companies in High-Technology Industries
2000. XIV, 230 pp. ISBN 3-7908-1292-7

Vol. 10: J. Hemmelskamp et al. (Eds.)
Innovation-Oriented Environmental Regulation
Theoretical Approaches and Empirical Analysis
2000. VI, 348 pp. ISBN 3-7908-1313-3

Vol. 11: K.L. Brockmann, M. Stronzik (Eds.)
Flexible Mechanisms for an Efficient Climate Policy
Cost Saving Policies and Business Opportunities
2000. VIII, 130 pp. ISBN 3-7908-1314-1

Vol. 12: W. Smolny
Endogenous Innovations and Knowledge Spillovers
A Theoretical and Empirical Analysis
2000. VIII, 277 pp. ISBN 3-7908-1320-6

Vol. 13: M. Lechner, F. Pfeiffer (Eds.)
Econometric Evaluation of Labour Market Policies
2001. X, 242 pp. ISBN 3-7908-1372-9

Vol. 14: M. Beise
Lead Markets
Country-Specific Success Factors of the Global Diffusion of Innovations
2001. XVI, 305 pp. ISBN 3-7908-1430-X

Vol. 15: O.H. Jacobs, C. Spengel
Effective Tax Burden in Europe
Current Situation, Past Developments and Simulations of Reforms
2002. X, 131 pp. ISBN 3-7908-1470-9

Vol. 16: U. Kaiser
Innovation, Employment, and Firm Performance in the German Service Sector
2002. X, 164 pp. ISBN 3-7908-1481-4

Vol. 17: J. Köke
Corporate Governance in Germany
An Empirical Investigation
2002. VIII, 184 pp. ISBN 3-7908-1511-X

Vol. 18: E. Wolf
What Hampers Part-Time Work?
An Empirical Analysis of Wages, Hours Restrictions and Employment from a Dutch-German Perspective
2003. X, 174 pp. ISBN 3-7908-0006-6

Vol. 19: P. Cecchini et al. (Eds.)
The Incomplete European Market for Financial Services
2003. XII, 255 pp. ISBN 3-7908-0013-9

Vol. 20: C. Böhringer, A. Löschel (Eds.)
Empirical Modeling of the Economy and the Environment
2003. VI, 326 pp. ISBN 3-7908-0078-3

Vol. 21: K. Rennings, T. Zwick (Eds.)
Employment Impacts of Cleaner Production
2003. VIII, 322 pp. ISBN 3-7908-0093-7

Vol. 22: O. Bürgel, A. Fier, G. Licht, G. Murray
The Internationalisation of Young High-Tech Firms
An Empirical Analysis in Germany and the United Kingdom
2003. XII, 291 pp. ISBN 3-7908-0120-8

Felix Hüfner

Foreign Exchange Intervention as a Monetary Policy Instrument

Evidence for Inflation Targeting Countries

With 32 Figures
and 23 Tables

ZEW
Zentrum für Europäische
Wirtschaftsforschung GmbH
Centre for European
Economic Research

Springer-Verlag Berlin Heidelberg GmbH
A Springer-Verlag Company

Series Editor
Prof. Dr. Wolfgang Franz

Author

Dr. Felix Hüfner
Centre for European Economic Research (ZEW)
L7, 1
68161 Mannheim
Germany

ISBN 978-3-7908-0128-6 ISBN 978-3-7908-2672-2 (eBook)
DOI 10.1007/978-3-7908-2672-2

Cataloging-in-Publication Data applied for
A catalog record for this book is available from the Library of Congress.
Bibliographic information published by Die Deutsche Bibliothek
Die Deutsche Bibliothek lists this publication in the Deutsche Nationalbibliografie; detailed bibliographic data is available in the Internet at <http://dnb.ddb.de>.

springeronline.com

Originally published by Physica-Verlag Heidelberg in 2004

Cover design: Erich Dichiser, ZEW, Mannheim

SPIN 10957905 88/3130-5 4 3 2 1 0 – Printed on acid-free paper

Preface

This book was written while I was a PhD student at University of Würzburg and a research fellow at the Zentrum für Europäische Wirtschaftsforschung (ZEW) (Centre for European Economic Research) in Mannheim. It was accepted as a doctoral dissertation in March 2003 under the title *"Sterilized Foreign Exchange Intervention as a Monetary Policy Instrument in Inflation Targeting Countries – Evidence for Australia, Canada, New Zealand, Sweden and the United Kingdom"*. I owe a particular debt of gratitude to my supervisor, Professor Peter Bofinger, for his steady support and many helpful discussions. I would also like to thank my second advisor, Professor Martin Kukuk. Furthermore, I would like to thank the ZEW and in particular Professor Wolfgang Franz for supporting this dissertation.

During the preparation of this book I benefited from fruitful discussions with my colleagues, Friedrich Heinemann, Volker Kleff, Jens Köke, Matthias Meitner, Michael Schröder and Martin Schüler from the ZEW financial markets department. Furthermore, I received many helpful comments from participants of the doctoral seminars in Würzburg. In particular, I would like to thank Timo Wollmershäuser from University of Würzburg for several comments and suggestions.

Finally, I would like to thank my parents, my brother Max as well as Sandra for their support and encouragement over the past years.

Mannheim, June 2003 *Felix Hüfner*

Table of Contents

1 Introduction

"I see no reason why a transparent inflation-targeter should undertake foreign-exchange interventions."
(Svensson, 2001e: 48)

1.1 Background

The above statement by Lars Svensson exemplifies that up to now foreign exchange interventions are not recognised as an instrument for central banks that pursue inflation targeting. This contrasts with the observation that intervention operations are actually undertaken in reality, also by inflation targeting countries, as is evident from news reports (see appendix for a list). The Swedish Riksbank, for example, writes: "Interventions play a role in a central bank's range of instruments." (Riksbank, 2001b: 19). Obviously, there is a discrepancy between academics and practitioners concerning the use of interventions in inflation targeting.

In economic research sterilised foreign exchange intervention[1] by central banks has long been kept separate from the actual conduct of monetary policy (i.e. interest rate policy). Studies have mostly focussed either on conventional interest rate policy or analysed foreign exchange interventions. There exists basically no theory for the use of interventions. One reason for this neglect might be the scepticism of economists regarding the effectiveness of sterilised interventions. Indeed, for a long time the consensus among economists was that sterilised interventions are not effective in regimes of floating exchange rates. Despite this prevailing view, central banks around the world intervened frequently and there are several examples of successful intervention operations in the last 25 years of floating exchange rates, the most prominent being the Plaza and Louvre accords in the 1980s.[2] Furthermore, many central banks in floating exchange rate regimes keep intervening in foreign exchange markets as pointed out in a range of recent studies (see e.g. Calvo and Reinhart, 2000; Levy-Yeyati and Sturzenegger, 2000) and as

---

1 In the following we will always refer to foreign exchange intervention as sterilised (i.e. interventions that do not alter the monetary base) by central banks unless indicated otherwise.

2 A report in the early 1980s (the so-called Jurgensen study) found that sterilised interventions have little impact on exchange rates. However, only a few years later with the apparent success of the Plaza Accord in 1985 this view became increasingly challenged.

can be seen in the increase and variation in world-wide foreign exchange reserves after the breakdown of the Bretton Woods system. This stands in obvious contrast to the above mentioned consensus among economists so far.

Nevertheless, it is seldom asked what implications interventions have for monetary policy.[3] One reason for this is that most countries with floating exchange rates were operating a monetary strategy of money growth targeting. Officially, monetary policy thus had to set interest rates so that excessive growth in monetary aggregates was avoided. Controlling the intermediate target of monetary aggregates was the key to achieving price stability. Since the exchange rate is not explicitly part of such a strategy foreign exchange interventions were not needed in theory. A further aspect is that yet still many economists believe that exchange rates do follow paths that can be described with fundamental theories. If this was the case, there would be no need to intervene in foreign exchange markets.

The advent of inflation targeting in the beginning of the 1990s has changed the environment of monetary policy and led to a decline in the use of monetary targeting. Inflation targeting is foremost characterised by the lack of an explicit intermediate target. Instead, all variables that might serve to forecast future inflation are taken into consideration when setting the stance of monetary policy rather than restricting the attention to a single variable like in money growth targeting or exchange rate targeting. In such a framework the only goal of the central bank is to achieve the inflation target. Among the variables used for monetary policy the exchange rate is important since the majority of inflation targeting countries are small and open economies which are typically characterised by a high degree of exchange rate pass-through to domestic prices. Thus, central banks have to incorporate exchange rate movements in their decision process insofar as future inflation is affected. However, if exchange rate developments are important for future inflation then foreign exchange intervention might be a useful tool for the central bank.

Traditional models of inflation targeting point out the importance of the exchange rate in influencing the inflation rate, as the pass-through of exchange rate changes to inflation occurs faster than the effects of interest rate changes on inflation. These models (see e.g. Svensson, 2000b; Ball, 1999) assume the validity of uncovered interest parity, i.e. the efficiency of the foreign exchange market. In such an environment central banks can influence exchange rates with their interest rate policy. Still, it is a well-known fact in economics that uncovered interest parity does not hold in reality – at least not for floating exchange rates (see e.g. Flood and Rose, 1996). Consequently, the exchange rate can be influenced only insufficiently with the interest rate as the sole operating target. However, as pointed out by Bofinger and Wollmershäuser (2001) a central bank has a further instrument at hand, namely foreign exchange intervention, with which the exchange rate can be controlled much more effectively. As long as foreign exchange interventions are sterilised, i.e. do not alter the monetary base and thus leave short-term interest rates unchanged, they provide an independent instrument for monetary policy.

---

[3] As Baillie et al. (1999) state: "[...] very few studies have looked at the role of intervention within the overall macro-policy mix." (p. 20).

Thereby, foreign exchange intervention is not viewed as a means by itself but rather presents an instrument to achieve the goal of monetary policy, namely to achieve the published inflation target.

While there exists extensive research on the conduct of monetary policy in inflation targeting countries (see e.g. Bernanke et al., 1999; Leiderman and Svensson, 1995), the use of foreign exchange interventions as a monetary policy tool has not been studied so far (at least not for industrial countries). It is the main goal of this thesis to close this gap and to analyse whether inflation targeting central banks actually use interventions as an additional monetary policy tool. Hereby, we focus on five industrial countries (Australia, New Zealand, Canada, Sweden and the United Kingdom) who were the first countries to adopt inflation targeting. Using changes in foreign exchange reserves as a proxy for intervention activity we perform a detailed analysis to find out to what extent foreign exchange intervention is prevalent. Furthermore it is asked what repercussions interventions have on the operation of conventional interest rate policy.

Specifically, we aim to achieve the following goals:

- to analyse the assumptions of the existing literature on inflation targeting by testing empirically for uncovered interest parity and by pointing out the lack of sterilised interventions;
- to show that sterilised interventions are actually already pursued by analysing sterilisation behaviour and changes in foreign exchange reserves in five inflation targeting countries; and
- to analyse to what extent sterilised interventions are used as an additional policy tool besides conventional interest rate policy by estimating policy reaction functions and looking at interest rate volatility.

The results will provide further insight into the actual conduct of monetary policy under inflation targeting in practice. They will contribute to the discussion on whether interventions provide a suitable instrument of monetary policy besides interest rate policy.

1.2 Approach to the Problem and Research Strategy

In order to illustrate the main idea of this thesis, its connection to the traditional thinking about monetary policy and the structure of our analysis, Figure 1 displays a very simple, stylised model of monetary policy in an open economy.

Usually, interest rate policy is seen as the only policy tool of a central bank, i.e. the central bank engages in open market operations to control a short-term interest rate as operating target.[4] As this interest rate affects aggregate demand, this in turn influences inflation (this is the mechanism as described by the conventional IS

---

4 While a central bank may also opt to control the monetary base in contrast to a short-term interest rate, 'interest rate targeting' is the prevalent strategy among central banks today.

curve: With price stickiness an increase in nominal interest rates leads to an increase in real interest rates; as a consequence consumption is postponed and investment spending reduced, thus leading to a decline in aggregate demand).[5] A further channel in an open economy works through the exchange rate: Fluctuations in the external value of the currency translate into changes in inflation through the so-called exchange rate pass-through.[6] It is traditionally assumed that by controlling the interest rate, both the exchange rate (via uncovered interest parity) and aggregate demand can be influenced. Thus, only one instrument – open market operations to control short-term interest rates – is needed. This is what can be called the *conventional* view on inflation targeting with only one policy instrument.

We introduce sterilised interventions as a second monetary policy instrument and thereby aim to expand the conventional view. Similar as open market operations in the domestic money market influence interest rates, foreign exchange interventions influence the exchange rate which then becomes a second operating target. If these interventions are sterilised, they do not alter the money supply and hence have no influence on domestic interest rates. Therefore, sterilised foreign exchange interventions provide an *additional* monetary policy tool.

What is new about our approach is the addition of sterilised foreign exchange interventions as an independent policy instrument (upper left circle in Figure 1). Our aim is to offer a rationale for the use of such a second instrument, to analyse to what extent this additional tool is already used in inflation targeting countries and what repercussions this has for their conventional interest rate policy. We start with a summary of the traditional inflation targeting models and then proceed to tackle several issues related to sterilised interventions for five inflation targeting countries (Australia, Canada, New Zealand, Sweden and the United Kingdom).

Our analysis can be divided into six subsequent subjects of inquiry that will be analysed empirically (the numbers refer to the illustration in Figure 1):

1: Uncovered interest parity – evidence for inflation targeting countries
As will be seen in our summary of the existing literature on open economy inflation targeting, uncovered interest parity is one of the main building blocks of theoretical models. We analyse empirically for inflation targeting countries whether uncovered interest parity (UIP) holds, i.e. whether there is a close link between exchange rate changes and interest rate differentials. If UIP holds in practice there is no need for a further policy instrument to control exchange rate changes.

5 For a detailed and recent illustration of the monetary transmission channel see Kuttner and Mosser (2002).

6 As will be discussed in more detail in later chapters, the exchange rate also has an effect on aggregate demand (via the competitiveness of the economy). Thus, exchange rate pass-through and aggregate demand channel cannot be separated completely in practice. However, for illustrative purposes we divide both channels in the stylised model presented in Figure 1.

Figure 1: Stylised model of monetary policy

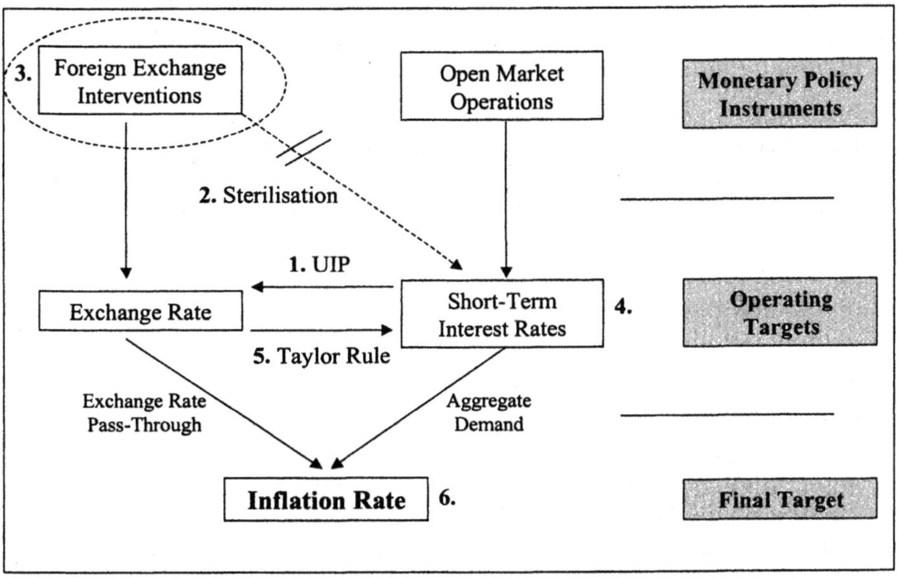

Note: UIP denotes uncovered interest parity.

2: Sterilisation of foreign exchange operations
In order to understand foreign exchange interventions as an independent and thus additional policy instrument these interventions need to be sterilised. Only if this condition holds, the money supply and hence interest rates are not affected by interventions. An empirical investigation of the relationship between domestic and foreign central bank assets will show whether interventions are indeed sterilised.

3: The extent of foreign exchange interventions in inflation targeting
Comparing changes in foreign exchange reserves as well as news reports about interventions across inflation targeting countries we explore to what extent these central banks actually make use of foreign exchange interventions. A result of this analysis will be a rough 'intervention ranking' of inflation targeting countries.

4: Foreign exchange interventions and the volatility of short-term interest rates
Having analysed to what extent countries actually intervene to influence the exchange rate, the next step of our analysis is to examine the consequences for interest rate policy. The first hypothesis is that countries that intervene more heavily than others exhibit a smaller volatility of short-term interest rates because they do not have to tackle both domestic and external factors with the same instrument. In other words, the use of interventions should lead to lower interest rate volatility.

5: Exchange rate fluctuations and interest rate policy: differences across countries
A further analysis will examine the link between interventions and policy reaction functions across countries. By estimating an open-economy Taylor rule it will be

inquired if countries that make relatively more use of the intervention tool focus their interest rate policy more on domestic factors. Vice versa, it will be inquired if countries that intervene less can be expected to give a greater weight to exchange rate developments in setting interest rates.

6: Performance comparison across inflation targeting countries
At last we compare the performance of monetary policy across inflation targeting countries and try to detect whether interventions have a positive influence. In doing this we calculate different forms of loss functions over different time periods.

1.3 Structure of the Analysis

This thesis is divided into three main parts:

1. The first part is designed to survey the traditional thinking about inflation targeting. We introduce the concept of inflation targeting, separate it from other monetary policy strategies and give an overview of its implementation in practice. A summary of the existing theoretical literature on inflation targeting in open economies will demonstrate that uncovered interest parity is a main building block in these models.

2. The critical analysis of the assumptions of existing models is performed in the second part. We empirically test whether uncovered interest parity holds in practice (*subject 1 of the above list*) for five inflation targeting countries (Australia, New Zealand, Canada, Sweden and the United Kingdom). Following this, we suggest that sterilised foreign exchange intervention provides a more effective tool to influence the exchange rate. We survey the existing literature on the effectiveness of sterilised foreign exchange interventions and analyse whether the respective central banks actually sterilise changes in their foreign exchange reserves (*subject 2 of the above list*).

3. The third part analyses if this tool is actually used by inflation targeting central banks. We present an empirical investigation into the intervention operations of five inflation targeting central banks using data for foreign exchange reserves (*subject 3 of the above list*). We motivate the use of reserves as an intervention proxy and present different methodologies to identify intervention activity. In a further step it will be analysed whether the intensity of intervention is reflected in the volatility of short-term interest rates (*subject 4 of the above list*) and whether the central banks incorporate the exchange rate in their interest rate setting (*subject 5 of the above list*). Finally, we compare the performance of monetary policy across countries (*subject 6 of the above list*).

In the final chapter conclusions will be drawn from the results of the analyses.

2 The Conventional View on Inflation Targeting

"Inflation targeting is the new kid on the block of monetary regimes."
(Corbo et al., 2001: 1)

Since inflation targeting is a relatively new monetary policy strategy, this first chapter will present a survey of the main features and highlight the differences to other strategies. The aim is to give a broad overview rather than to present a detailed analysis in order to motivate the later analysis of the monetary policy instruments available to an inflation targeting central bank.

2.1 Definition and Elements of Inflation Targeting

Inflation targeting as a monetary policy strategy emerged in the early 1990s and many industrial as well as emerging market countries adopted it in the course of the last years. In November 2000, 19 central banks in the world were officially classified as inflation targeters. The first countries to officially adopt this strategy were New Zealand (1990) and Canada (1991). In a survey in 1998, among 91 industrial, transitional and developing countries, 38% were found to have an explicit inflation target, 26% said they targeted a monetary aggregate and 33% had an exchange rate target in operation (Sterne, 1999).[7]

In basic terms inflation targeting can be defined as "a framework for monetary policy characterised by the public announcement of official quantitative targets (or target ranges) for the inflation rate over one or more time horizons, and by explicit acknowledgement that low, stable inflation is monetary policy's primary long-run goal" (Bernanke et al., 1999: 4). The most distinctive feature of this strategy is the lack of an explicit single intermediate target like a monetary aggregate or the exchange rate. Most countries that adopted inflation targeting abandoned either a monetary aggregate (for example Australia, New Zealand, Switzerland) or the exchange rate (Sweden, United Kingdom) as an intermediate target.[8]

---

[7] 4% of the respondents said they had no explicit target for monetary policy. These include the Bank of Japan, but not the US Federal Reserve Bank which in 1998 still published a monitoring range for broad money growth.

[8] Lars Svensson (1997a) proposes that an appropriate intermediate target for inflation targeting is an inflation forecast. We will refer to this view, which has been criticised in the literature (Bernanke and Woodford, 1997) later on.

Inflation targeting encompasses a range of elements that need to be fulfilled besides the lack of an intermediate target. While the specific design of an inflation targeting strategy may vary substantially, there are five elements that are agreed as being substantial ingredients.[9] These are:

- Lack of an explicit intermediate target;
- acknowledgement of price stability as the final target of monetary policy;
- announcement of a numerical target for the inflation rate;
- transparent communication of central bank decisions;
- increased accountability of the central bank for attaining its objectives.

This list of features emphasises that inflation targeting "entails much more than a public announcement of numerical targets for inflation for the year ahead." (Mishkin, 2000: 105).[10]

2.1.1 Lack of an Explicit Intermediate Target

Arguably the most innovative feature of inflation targeting is the lack of an explicit intermediate target. While the other elements of this new strategy like transparency and price stability are also included in former strategies, the lack of an intermediate target in inflation targeting is unique.

---

9 See e.g. Bernanke et al., 1999; Mishkin, 2000; Svensson, 2000a; Eichengreen, 2002. However, Mishkin and Schmidt-Hebbel (2001) point out, "classifying country cases into inflation targeting and other monetary regimes involves subjective choices [...]". This is because "[...] there is a lack of full agreement on the main conditions and features of inflation targeting[...]" (p. 1).

10 It is sometimes discussed whether instrument independence is a necessary feature of inflation targeting while goal independence is not required (see Bernanke et al., 1999). Goal independence refers to the final target of monetary policy and states that a central bank is able to formulate its own target. Instrument independence on the other hand means that the central bank is independent in the implementation of monetary policy, i.e. in its interest rate decisions. However, the Bank of England is a prominent example of an inflation targeter that did not have instrument independence in the first years. Only in 1997 the Bank was granted independence. However, this did not seem to have negative repercussions on the Bank's policy as will be shown later.

Table 1: Monetary policy concepts in comparison

Monetary policy concept	Operating target	Intermediate target	Final target
Monetary targeting	Short-term interest rate	Growth of money aggregate	Price stability (implicit inflation target)
Exchange rate targeting		Exchange rate	Price stability
Inflation targeting		No explicit Intermediate target	Price stability (explicit inflation target)

Note: Besides the money market rate, a central bank might also use the growth of base money as an operating target. Similarly, there also exist other final targets than price stability (i.e. a target for the nominal GDP). However, in practice most central banks use a short-term interest rate as an operating target and price stability as a final target.

Table 1 compares inflation targeting with two other prominent monetary policy concepts – namely exchange rate targeting and monetary targeting – with respect to their intermediate and final targets.[11] All three strategies have in common that their final target is price stability. While pursuing monetary targeting, the central bank needs to have at least an implicit inflation target which is used to determine the optimal growth of the monetary aggregate. Whether this target is published or not is the decision of the central bank. However, since the aim is to focus public attention on the monetary target an extensive publication of the inflation target is not necessary (or useful). Central banks that pursue exchange rate targeting do not need to have a target rate for the inflation. Rather, by pegging the exchange rate to a low-inflation foreign currency, the aim is to achieve a similar (ideally the same) inflation rate as the foreign country. Thus, there is no need to determine a quantified target for the inflation rate. This is, on the contrary, the essence of inflation targeting where the target for inflation is explicitly announced and communicated. As there is no intermediate target that can be observed by the public, the publication and intensive communication of the inflation target becomes highly important.

Neither of these three strategies differs with respect to the operating target of the central bank which is traditionally a short-term interest rate. Alternatively, the central bank could choose to target the monetary base. However, by now all major central banks in the world adjust interest rates as the weakness of monetary base targeting is higher volatility of short-term interest rates.

The major difference between the three strategies lies in the use of an explicit intermediate target. While other strategies use intermediate targets to control the final target indirectly, pure inflation targeting is characterised by the lack of an

---

11 A fourth strategy would be to target nominal GDP growth (see e.g. Hall and Mankiw, 1994). However, this is more a theoretical concept, because, as Bernanke et al. (1999) point out, no central bank "[...] has seriously considered adopting a nominal GDP target." (p. 307).

explicit intermediate target. The central bank tries to control the final target directly via its operating targets.[12] The intermediate target in other strategies also serves to focus public attention on it (whether it is a monetary aggregate or the exchange rate). Inflation targeting, on the contrary, aims at focussing public attention at the final target. A closer look at the nature of an intermediate target might serve to better understand why inflation targeting as a strategy without intermediate target emerged and what the reasons for this are.

Generally, "intermediate targets are aggregates that, in the monetary policy transmission process, occupy an intermediate position between the operating targets, which can be controlled by the central bank, and the ultimate macroeconomic objectives." (Bofinger, 2001: 246). An intermediate target has to fulfil at least the following characteristics: The central bank needs to have a good control over it and it needs to be closely correlated with the final target (see Bofinger, 2001: 247). Critics of monetary targeting argue that the lack of a stable relationship between monetary aggregates and the price level – which is a prerequisite for monetary targeting – is a major disadvantage of this strategy. Recent empirical studies find that the relation between inflation and money growth, at least for low inflation countries, "[...] is weak, if non-existing." (De Grauwe and Polan, 2001: 24).[13] The early inflation targeters New Zealand, Australia and Canada abolished monetary targeting in favour of inflation targeting because of increased instability in the relationship between monetary aggregates and prices.[14]

In a fixed exchange rate regime the exchange rate as the intermediate target is usually correlated in a stable way with the price level. By fixing the exchange rate a central bank has to give up monetary autonomy and has to follow the monetary policy of the anchor country. Fixed exchange rate regimes proved to be highly unstable in recent periods as demonstrated by several currency crises in the 1990s. The breakdown of such regimes shows that in crisis times a central bank has only imperfect control over the intermediate target exchange rate. As a consequence of these currency crises, exchange rate pegging as a monetary policy strategy lost

12 As will be seen later on, Svensson attributes the inflation forecast of a central bank as an implicit intermediate target.

13 An alternative study is that of Issing et al. (2001) who, in contrast to DeGrauwe and Polan (2001), report a high correlation between money growth and inflation in the long run. Svensson (2002b), however, points out that given the short horizons of 1-3 years that are most relevant for monetary policy, even a stable long-run relationship between money growth and inflation would be of minor importance.

14 Governor Ian MacFarlane of the Reserve Bank of Australia states that the main reason for abandoning monetary targeting in Australia has been the instability of the relationship between money supply and the objectives of monetary policy. He concludes: "we didn't abandon the monetary aggregates, they abandoned us." (Address to the 26th Conference of Economists in Hobart on 29/9/97, available at www.bis.org). See also Bernanke and Mishkin (1997) who write: "The fact that in most countries the relation between intermediate targets, such as money growth, and the central bank's goal variables has proven to be relatively unstable [...] is a major motivation for dropping formal intermediate targets and instead attempting to target the goal variable directly." (p. 101).

appeal and like monetary targeting became increasingly unpopular. Sweden and the United Kingdom introduced inflation targeting as their strategy of exchange rate targeting within the European Monetary System was forced to an end during the exchange rate crisis in 1992.

Without an intermediate target the central bank has to target inflation directly. Inflation targeting presumes that this is a superior strategy. The lack of an explicit intermediate target does not mean that the central bank should not look at certain variables that might serve to forecast inflation, including growth of monetary aggregates or the exchange rate.[15] But inflation targeting central banks do not focus on a single indicator alone. Rather, they make use of every possible variable that may signal future inflation tendencies. Thus, the rationale of inflation targeting is that inflation can be better forecast if as much information as possible is gathered and judged.

While the definition of inflation targeting as a monetary policy strategy that lacks an intermediate target is rather straightforward there also exist countries that cannot be classified this easily. For example, even though Chile and Israel define their monetary policy strategy as inflation targeting, they did have an exchange rate target as a nominal anchor for a long time.[16] The same holds true for Spain and Finland which both participated in the European Exchange Rate Mechanism (ERM) prior to adopting the euro in 1999. Peru on the other hand does issue inflation targets but uses the monetary base as an intermediate target for its monetary policy.

In the words of Svensson (2000b) inflation targeting "also implies that there is no explicit instrument rule, that is, the current instrument setting is not a prescribed explicit function of current information. Nevertheless, the procedure results in an endogenous reaction function, which expresses the instrument as a function of the relevant information." (p. 2). Unlike a simple Taylor rule, that only takes into account current inflation and the output gap, inflation targeting incorporates much more information that is necessary to forecast inflation (though the Taylor rule might be a special case of inflation targeting).

There is a long tradition in monetary policy on the question of "rules" or "discretion" that is whether the central bank has to follow strictly a predetermined rule or can make decision deliberately. Whereas Bernanke et al. (1999) argue strongly that inflation targeting should not be seen in the context of a policy rule, Svensson (2000a) advocates that inflation targeting should be implemented as a rule that comes down effectively to inflation-forecast targeting.

---

15 The European Central Bank's two pillar strategy bears some resemblance with this approach. Thus, Svensson (2000a) mentions that the Eurosystem monetary strategy to some extent "is quite similar to flexible inflation targeting" (p. 7).

16 Svensson (1997/1998: 5) mentions that a floating exchange rate is a common characteristic of inflation targeting. This follows from the fact, that besides the inflation target there are no other final or intermediate targets in such a policy. By definition this excludes any form of exchange rate targeting from inflation targeting (in the words of Debelle (1997): "[...] inflation targeting is not consistent with a fixed exchange rate regime." (p. 8)).

Bernanke et al. (1999) mention two points against the "rule"-interpretation: First, the central bank has to take into account all indicators that are necessary to pursue the aim of price-stability ("look at everything" strategy) instead of focussing on a single variable and second, inflation targeting is constructed to provide central bankers with the necessary discretion to react to different shocks. They conclude that inflation targeting means a "constrained discretion" for the central bank and thus serves as a framework rather than a strict rule. The focus on their interpretation of inflation targeting lies in two functions: "(1) improving communication between policy-makers and the public, and, not unrelatedly, (2) providing discipline and accountability in the making of monetary policy." (Bernanke et al., 1999: 23).

Svensson, on the contrary, interprets inflation targeting as a policy rule. He argues that because of the long lags of monetary policy inflation targeting in fact comes down to "inflation-forecast targeting". In this view, the inflation forecast that is calculated by the central bank functions as some kind of synthetic intermediate target. One problem with this view is that there is no 'rule' for producing an inflation forecast.

2.1.2 Price Stability as the Final Target

By explicitly taking price stability as the long run target of monetary policy, it is acknowledged that inflation is the only variable that can be controlled effectively by the central bank over the long run. Thus, one main rationale of inflation targeting is to let the central bank do what it can do best – namely keep inflation low and stable.[17] Underlying this rationale is the – by now mainstream – knowledge that there is no long-run trade-off between inflation and unemployment. This incorporates the philosophy that low and stable inflation is helping to promote other macroeconomic goals like economic growth in the long run. In this respect it is important to note that price stability does not only encompass preventing excessively large price increases but also to avoid declining prices. The Japanese economy is one prominent example for the devastating effects of deflation on the real economy. Some observers argue that Japan should adopt a target for the price level in order to generate positive inflation expectations and then switch to inflation targeting.[18]

Price stability is usually not interpreted as a zero inflation rate. Inflation targets generally lie in the range of about 2%. There are several arguments that are put forward in order to justify a non-zero inflation target.[19] One of them is that the

[17] In the words of McCallum (1996): "The pragmatic argument for inflation targeting begins with the proposition that, from a long-run (i.e. steady state) perspective, monetary policy has a dominating influence on an economy's (average) inflation rate and a negligible influence on its rate of unemployment or output relative to capacity." (p. 15).

[18] See Svensson, 2001b.

[19] See Debelle, 1997: 11-12.

measurement of inflation is biased, for example, because the traditional measurement does not account for improvements in quality and changes in the consumption bundle. Thus, a small inflation can be compatible with price stability when taking into account these measurement problems. Furthermore, it is often argued that prices and wages are downward rigid. Small inflation helps to support the necessary adjustments. A third argument relates to monetary policy: Without inflation there is no possibility of negative real interest rates due to the fact that nominal interest rates cannot fall below zero. This is exactly the kind of problem that Japan is facing since deflation started there in the late 1990s.

Price stability as the long run final target of monetary policy does, however, not mean that the inflation targeting central bank should be focussed solely on this one target and should not be concerned with other goals such as output stabilisation. Rather, it means that additional goals can be pursued as long as there is no conflict with the long run goal of price stability.[20] In the words of Marvin Goodfriend: "[...] an inflation target need not prevent a central bank from taking policy actions to stabilise financial markets and employment in the short run. It does, however, discipline a central bank to justify such actions against its commitment to protect the purchasing power of money." (Goodfriend, 1999: 9).

An inflation targeting strategy that is also concerned with output fluctuations is called "flexible" inflation targeting in the literature in contrast to "strict" inflation targeting. In a policy of strict inflation targeting the loss function of the central bank does not contain a weight on output deviations while flexible inflation targeting attributes some weight on output deviations. In practice, central bankers that follow a regime of inflation targeting are usually also concerned with output stability and mostly smooth interest rates. Thus, flexible inflation targeting seems to be predominant in reality and Svensson (2001a) argues that "there is by now widespread agreement among central bankers and academics that inflation targeting in practice is 'flexible' inflation targeting." (p. 3).

2.1.3 Publication of a Numerical Target

A crucial aspect of inflation targeting is the publication of an explicit numerical target for the inflation rate. The achievement of the target inflation rate (=final target) is the primary goal of an inflation targeting central bank. It is published either as a single figure or as a target range. The explicit numerical target distinguishes inflation targeting from other strategies like monetary targeting that have at most an implicit inflation target in mind or exchange rate targeting which does not even have an implicit inflation target. The Bundesbank, for example, had an implicit inflation target in mind to calculate the targets for money growth according to the quantity theory of money.

Three questions are of particular importance in this respect:

- Which measure of inflation is best suited for an inflation target?

---

20 Debelle (1997) writes that in an inflation targeting regime "any other goal can only be pursued to the extent that it is consistent with the inflation target." (p. 8).

- Should the target be set as a price index target or an inflation rate target?
- For which horizon should the target be set?

In choosing a measure of inflation the central bank faces a dilemma: While well-known measures like the headline consumer price inflation can be best understood and monitored by the public, they might on the other hand not be well suited to measure permanent price increases adequately. Price indices that are more suitable for monetary policy exclude temporary or first-round effects like energy prices (often called "core" or "underlying" inflation).[21] There is no consensus on which price index the inflation target should be based and central banks apply different methods. Some of them (i.e. the Bank of Canada) publish their targets in terms of headline consumer price inflation but use core inflation as an operational guide. Others, such as the Reserve Bank of New Zealand, base their inflation target on a measure of underlying inflation.

In theory, there is some discussion about whether the central bank should target a price level or an inflation rate. Targeting an inflation rate bears the risk that deviations of the target occur as one-time effects and are never offset. Price level targeting, on the other hand, implies that deviations from the target in one period need to be compensated for in other periods.[22] Svensson (2001b), for example, recently recommended that the Bank of Japan should introduce a price level target in order to fight deflation effectively. In practice, however, all inflation targeting central banks target the inflation rate rather than the price level. Except for the Bank of England, which targets a point inflation rate of 2.5%, inflation targets are also published as mid-points within a range. This demonstrates that inflation outcomes are associated with a particular amount of uncertainty.

There is also some discussion in the literature over the time horizon over which the inflation target needs to be achieved. While in Svensson's view the inflation target should be "pursued in the medium run" (Svensson, 2000a: 1), Bernanke et al. (1999) simply recommend "one or more time horizons" (p. 4). In fact, this is a crucial question since monetary policy affects price developments in a country with long (and perhaps also variable) lags. Stevens (1999) reports for Australia that the "mean lag on the effect of interest rate changes on activity is about five or six quarters. [...] The lags in the full effects on inflation are probably somewhat longer than those to activity." (p. 4). Mishkin and Schmidt-Hebbel (2001) mention the example of New Zealand where an inflation target with a one-year horizon was missed even though monetary policy seemed to be optimal.

21 Underlying inflation as a guide for inflation targeting often excludes also mortgage interest payments (such as the RPIX in the UK). This prevents that an increase in short-term interest rates by the central bank leads to a rise in consumer price inflation through higher mortgage lending rates.

22 Price level targeting does not necessarily imply a constant price level (zero inflation). Rather, it could be implemented as increasing over time.

2.1.4 Transparent Communication of Central Bank Decisions

While transparency of a central bank is certainly not a unique feature of an inflation targeting strategy it is nevertheless more important in this kind of monetary framework. Since they do not have a publicly observable intermediate target, which ideally signals future inflation tendencies, inflation targeting central banks have to rely more on the public trust in their ability to achieve the target. As inflation expectations of the public are an important determinant of actually realised inflation, it is necessary for the central bank to convince the public that its monetary policy is effective in its operation.[23] This will ideally be taken into consideration when price and wage decisions are made. To this end, the strategy needs to be communicated extensively and monetary policy decisions need to be transparent. The public needs to believe in the promise of the central bank to achieve the target. Thus, the lack of an intermediate target and the need for transparency are both interconnected features of inflation targeting.

The Bundesbank often missed its own monetary targets but nevertheless was successful in keeping inflation down.[24] Some argue that this is because of extensive communication of its decisions which made the Bundesbank highly credible. While it might be argued that the Bundesbank was not very transparent, the credibility that was given by the public surely supported its monetary policy.

Several measures are taken in order to guarantee a high degree of transparency. Bernanke et al. (1999) mention three important ones: "to provide timely information about the economy at large, the bank's monetary policy, and its policy intentions."(p. 36). In practice, transparency is enhanced by frequent speeches by central bank representatives where monetary policy is laid out and the actual situation explained to a broad public. Furthermore, most of the central banks that pursue inflation targeting regularly publish inflation reports where price developments are analysed in detail. They often also contain the inflation forecast. Another common feature is the publication of the minutes of monetary policy meetings (usually with a time lag). One issue, however, that is not consistent with the aim of transparency is the secrecy made in the field of exchange rate policy. Specifically, with the exception of the Reserve Bank of Australia, no inflation targeting central bank in industrial countries makes intervention data available for researchers.[25]

---

23 This includes giving explanations about the success or failure in achieving the inflation targets. As Bernanke et al. (1999) state: "The credibility of the central bank depends as much on the objectivity and plausibility of its communications as on its record of hitting targets." (p. 37).

24 Bernanke and Mihov (1997) find that the Bundesbank put little weight on the money growth as an information variable for future inflation.

25 While some central banks report intervention on the day they are pursued (Bank of Canada), they do not publish time series.

2.1.5 Increased Accountability of the Central Bank

Inflation targeting central banks are unusually open to accountability. While a monetary targeting central bank which misses its monetary growth target sometimes might still point to a relatively low inflation outcome (see Bundesbank), missing an inflation target leaves no excuse. Thus, by comparing the actual inflation outcome with the published target the public can judge easily whether a central bank has done a good job or not.

A special kind of accountability is set in New Zealand, where the Governor of the Reserve Bank is subject to dismissal if he fails to achieve the inflation target. In case the Bank of England misses an inflation target, the Governor of the Bank has to explain specifically the reasons for this in a letter to the government.

As Mishkin (2001) points out, increased accountability of a central bank helps to ameliorate the time-inconsistency problem which is often studied in the economic literature.[26] Thus, accountability is not a goal in itself but serves an important aim. The theory of the time-inconsistency argument assumes that the central bank has an incentive to surprise the public with higher inflation in order to try to expand output and employment in the short-run. As the public learns over time, the result of such a policy is a permanently higher inflation rate. By focussing attention on the ultimate goal of price stability and setting targets for inflation, inflation targeting central banks counter the problem of time-inconsistency. Specifically, this strategy communicates to the public what monetary policy can do (keep inflation low) and what it cannot do (expand output and employment in the long term).

Accountability is very important in order to be able to influence the inflation expectations of the public – one of the main aims of inflation targeting. As the Bank of Canada said: "The intention in setting out explicit targets [...] is to encourage Canadians to base their economic decisions on this downward path for inflation so that the lower inflation will be more readily achieved."[27]

2.1.6 Summary and Assessment

To summarise shortly: While inflation targeting includes some components of other monetary strategies it can be distinguished clearly by the lack of an intermediate target and the publication of an explicit target for the inflation rate. The renunciation of the intermediate target follows from the imperfect experiences that many countries made with earlier strategies (be it the breakdown of fixed exchange rate regimes or the missing stable relationship between the growth in monetary aggregates and inflation). As a consequence of the missing intermediate target, inflation targeting central banks need to put a high weight on communicating their operations in order to maintain a high degree of accountability. Taken to-

---

26 See e.g. Kydland and Prescott, 1977; Barro and Gordon, 1983.

27 See Bank of Canada "Press release: Targets for reducing inflation", Bank of Canada Review, March 1991, p. 5-6.

gether, inflation targeting is far from a revolutionary approach but rather combines all features that are regarded as 'best practice' of operating monetary policy. As Amato and Gerlach (2001) write: "[...] IT [inflation targeting] is best thought of as a range of strategies. The only essential elements of IT seem to be the announcement of a numerical inflation objective together with a clear desire on the part of the central bank and the government to achieve the objective, as represented, for instance, by the central bank actively adjusting its instruments whenever it comes to believe that future inflation might deviate from target." (p. 3). Thus, even if the popularity of inflation targeting increased during the last decade, critics argue that it is often used as a catch-all term.[28]

2.2 Adoption of Inflation Targeting

2.2.1 Overview

Figure 2 gives an overview of the timing of inflation targeting introduction and the inflation rates of these countries at the time of introduction. While the first countries to adopt inflation targeting were primarily industrial countries, in recent years many emerging market economies followed.

It can be seen that New Zealand has been the first country to adopt inflation targeting followed by Canada, the United Kingdom, Australia and Sweden. Though Chile and Israel have been classifying themselves as inflation targeter since 1990/91 they did not fulfil the requirements for full-fledged inflation targeting until 1997 and 1999, respectively. The same holds true for Spain and Finland.[29] In recent years a number of countries adopted the new strategy, among them emerging markets like South Korea, Mexico and Brazil as well as industrial countries like Switzerland. Regarding price developments it can be observed that the industrial countries that implemented inflation targeting in the early 1990s had already achieved low inflation rates at that time. On the other hand, emerging

[28] There is some discussion in the literature about differences in the implementation of inflation targeting frameworks in emerging markets and in industrial countries. Our focus lies on inflation targeting in industrial countries. Schaechter et al. (2000) point out that emerging market countries "tend to prefer a more formal institutional framework in support of inflation targeting" but "rely less on statistical models in the conduct of monetary policy" (p. 3). This is probably due to the fact that emerging market countries need to rely more on the trust of international investors than more advanced countries do. Furthermore, Schaechter et al. (2000) write that all emerging market countries (except for Poland and the Czech Republic), in contrast to industrial countries, include as central bank objective "stabilizing the value of the currency" (p. 6). According to Amato and Gerlach (2001: 10) this is primarily due to the financial structure of their economies.

[29] Chile and Israel operated an exchange rate band and Spain and Finland were part of the European Monetary System. All four thus did have an intermediate target (the exchange rate) in place.

market countries like Mexico introduced inflation targeting at considerably higher inflation rates.

Figure 2: Adoption of inflation targeting

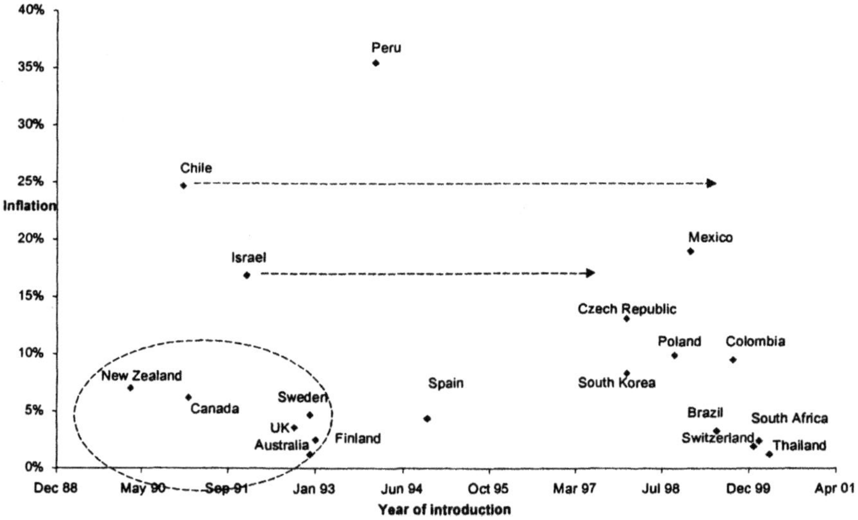

Note: Chile and Israel issued their first inflation targets in Sep. 1990 and Dec. 1991 respectively. However, according to Schaechter et al. (2000: 15) they did not adopt full-fledged inflation targeting until Sep. 1999 and June 1997. Peru is not classified as an inflation targeter by Schaechter et al. since the central bank uses the monetary base as intermediate target. Source: Schaechter et al., 2000; Mishkin and Schmidt-Hebbel, 2001; Central bank websites.

2.2.2 Country Selection

The empirical analyses undertaken in this study are based on five inflation targeting countries, namely Australia, Canada, New Zealand, Sweden and the United Kingdom. In order to qualify for our study, a country needs to be a full-fledged inflation targeter (i.e. in the sense of an absence of an intermediate target and fulfilling all the necessary characteristics mentioned above) over a sufficiently long period of time (in order to have an adequately large data sample to analyse). Because of the requirement of full-fledged inflation targeting we do not include Spain, Finland, Israel, Chile or Peru in our sample which all operated an intermediate target. The constraint of a sufficiently long time period limits our sample to the early inflation targets which have been operating under this strategy at least since 1993. As time goes by, more and more countries can be included in further studies about inflation targeting. However, right now inflation targeting is still in its infancy and presents only a limited time period to study. To motivate our selection of countries we give a short overview of their adoption of inflation targeting over time.[30]

New Zealand has been the first country to introduce inflation targeting as part of a major program of economic reform to liberalise the economy (among the measures was the decision to float the exchange rate in 1985) which started in the mid-1980s. Following the Reserve Bank of New Zealand Act of 1989 the framework was officially enacted February, 1 1990. In the so-called Policy Target Agreements the Governor of the central bank and the Minister of Finance set the numerical targets for inflation and evaluate past monetary policy performance. The first agreement included an inflation target of three to 5% and a gradual reduction of the target over the years was negotiated. Inflation targets are based on underlying inflation which excludes the first-round effects of supply shocks. The unique feature of the New Zealand framework is the potential dismissal of the Governor of the Reserve Bank if he fails to achieve the inflation target.[31]

Contrary to New Zealand, inflation targeting in Canada and Australia has not been introduced by formal legislation. On February 26, 1991 the Minister of Finance and the Governor of the Bank of Canada jointly announced a target range for inflation of 2 to 4% until the end of 1992. While the target is measured against an index of consumer prices, the Bank of Canada also relies on underlying inflation (consumer prices excluding energy and food prices) in its decision making process. The introduction of inflation targeting in Australia has been even less formal than in Canada (i.e. lacking even an official announcement). On March, 31 1993 the Governor of the Reserve Bank mentioned in a speech that achieving an inflation rate of 2 to 3% would be desirable over the next years.[32] As in New Zealand this target also refers to an index of underlying inflation.

The introduction of inflation targeting in Sweden and the UK has to be differentiated from New Zealand, Canada and Australia. The collapse of their exchange rate based monetary policy regimes during the EMS crisis in 1992 forced both countries to introduce a new regime swiftly. In the UK, the Chancellor of the Exchequer first announced an inflation target on October 8, 1992, three weeks after the Pound Sterling exited the European Exchange Rate Mechanism (ERM). Whenever inflation deviates from the target by more than 1 percentage point, the Monetary Policy Committee of the Bank of England is obliged to write a letter to the Chancellor of the Exchequer explaining the reasons for this and the strategy to

---

30 The following section draws on Bernanke et al. (1999) and Blejer et al. (1999).

31 This is one reason why the New Zealand inflation targeting framework is often characterised as the strictest and most "rule-like" of any (see e.g. Bernanke et al., 1999). McCallum (1996) writes that "the New Zealand setup [of inflation targeting] is significantly more ambitious than elsewhere." (p. 1).

32 In the view of Bernanke et al. (1999) the starting date of inflation targeting in Australia has to be dated as September 1994 since only then the Governor of the Reserve Bank described 2-3% inflation rate as a "goal". However, the Reserve Bank itself dates the starting point at March 1993 and we follow this interpretation. Nevertheless, this conflict shows that inflation targeting implementation in Australia has been more gradual and less direct as in other countries.

offset this deviation. The Swedish Riksbank announced in January 1993 that it would henceforth target an increase in the headline consumer prices of 2% with a tolerance band of plus or minus one percentage point. This announcement was made shortly after the breakdown of the fixed exchange rate regime on November 19, 1992. The era of inflation targeting with a floating exchange rate ended a period of fixed exchange rate regimes that had lasted (with short interruptions) since 1873 in Sweden.

Table 2: Operational frameworks of inflation targeting

	Adoption of inflation targeting	Target measure	Target inflation rate
New Zealand	February 1990 [2]	Underlying CPI [3]	1990: 3-5% 1991: 2,5-4,5% 1992: 1,5-3,5% 1993-96: 0-2% since Dec. 96: 0-3%
Canada	February 1991	CPI [1]	Dec. 91: 3-5% Dec. 92: 2-4% June 94: 1,5-3,5% Since Dec. 95: 1-3%
United Kingdom	October 1992	RPIX (Retail price index excluding mortgage interest payments)	1992-95: 1-4% since 1995: 2,5%
Sweden	January 1993	CPI	Since 1995: 2% (+/-1%) [4]
Australia	March 1993	Underlying CPI [5]	2-3%

Notes: [1] While the inflation-control target is expressed in terms of total CPI inflation, the Bank uses a measure of core inflation as an operational guide. [2] The inflation targeting framework is set forth in the Reserve Bank of New Zealand Act 1989. "The Act was introduced into Parliament by the government on May 4, 1989, was passed on December 15 and took effect on February 1, 1990." (Bernanke et al., 1999: 87-88). [3] Underlying CPI in New Zealand excludes interest-rate changes on the cost of living and significant changes in the terms-of-trade, changes in energy and commodity prices, changes in government charges and indirect taxes. Since 1998 the target has been the total CPI since the latter had been redefined to exclude credit services (interest rates). [4] Although inflation targeting was officially introduced in January 1993, the Riksbank declared that the target would be in effect only from 1995 on. In 1993 and 1994 monetary policy would aim at preventing inflation stemming from the depreciation of the krona in the currency crisis 1992. [5] Since 1998 the CPI has been used (redefined to exclude interest charges).

Source: Schaechter et al., 2000; Bernanke et al., 1999; Debelle, 1997; Lafrance, 1997; Central bank websites.

2.3 A Basic Model for (Closed-Economy) Inflation Targeting

For a general understanding of the mechanics of inflation targeting it seems useful to first present a basic theoretical framework that is restricted to a closed economy. Above all, despite the fact that most inflation targeting countries are small open economies, the original concept was based exclusively on closed economies.[33] Svensson (1997a) presents a simple model for inflation targeting in which the transmission channel of monetary policy runs via aggregate demand. It is based on the following set of equations:

$$\pi_{t+1} = \pi_t + \alpha_1 y_t + \alpha_2 x_t + \varepsilon_{t+1} \tag{2.1}$$

$$y_{t+1} = \beta_1 y_t - \beta_2 (i_t - \pi_t) + \beta_3 x_t + \eta_{t+1} \tag{2.2}$$

$$x_{t+1} = \gamma x_t + \theta_{t+1} . \tag{2.3}$$

$\pi_t = p_t - p_{t-1}$ denotes the yearly inflation rate, y_t is output (relative to potential output), x_t is an exogenous variable, i_t resembles the monetary policy instrument (short-term interest rate) that can be controlled directly by the central bank and $\varepsilon_t, \eta_t, \theta_t$ denote shocks that are not known in advance and are independently and identically distributed.

Equation (2.1) is a simple version of a Phillips curve that relates inflation to its own lagged value and to output. Whenever output (relative to potential output) increases, inflation reacts positively with a lag of one period. Equation (2.2) can be seen as an IS curve that relates output negatively to the real interest rate and positively to its own lagged value. Higher real interest rates will depress demand by discouraging investment. The simple model above illustrates that the interest rate influences output with a lag of one period (equation (2.2)) and output influences inflation with a lag of one period (equation (2.1)).[34] Thus, the lag between interest rate changes by the central bank and subsequent reactions of the inflation rate is two periods. Interest rate decisions in t only affect inflation in $t+2$. This is an important result for the closed-economy model and highlights the importance of forward-looking monetary policy. As will be shown later the influence of interest rates on inflation will occur with a shorter time interval when the exchange rate is taken into account (open-economy model).

These two equations form the basis of recent macroeconomic models (though they appear in different forms, for example expectations-based) which incorporates the notion of sticky-prices and thus leads to a short-run trade-off between in-

---

33 The theoretical framework was developed only years after many countries had already introduced the concept (see Bofinger, 2001: 389). See also Bofinger (2000a): "While monetary targeting had been prepared by an intensive academic discussion, inflation targeting was developed mainly as an ad-hoc solution." (p. 4).

34 This idea of the transmission channel corresponds with the right side of our stylised model of monetary policy as displayed in Figure 1 (without the exchange rate).

flation and output.[35] According to John Taylor, this way of modelling the economy "can [thus] be said to represent a modern view of macroeconomics" (Taylor, 2000a: 1) and is termed "new Keynesian economics" by Clarida et al. (1999) because of its use of sticky prices.

The loss function of the central bank in Svensson's model contains only deviations of inflation from the inflation target and no penalty for output fluctuations (strict inflation targeting):

$$L(\pi_t) = (1/2)(\pi_t - \pi^*)^2 . \tag{2.4}$$

In order to conduct monetary policy under inflation targeting today the central bank consequently needs to have a forecast of the inflation rate two periods in advance. The interest rate then has to be adjusted so that $E_t \pi_{t+2} = \pi^*$, i.e. the expected inflation rate two periods in advance needs to match the inflation target, and consequently the loss function becomes

$$L(E_t \pi_{t+2}) = (1/2)(E_t \pi_{t+2} - \pi^*)^2 . \tag{2.5}$$

The simple rule for the implementation of inflation targeting in the sense of Svensson is: "The central bank's inflation forecast [...] becomes an intermediate target, and the instrument should hence be set so as to make the inflation forecast equal to the inflation target." (Svensson, 1997a: 1120). Other than in the interpretation of Bernanke et al. (1999) inflation targeting then becomes a policy rule with the inflation forecast as the intermediate target rather than just a framework.

What is not discussed in Svensson's model, however, is how the inflation forecast is calculated. Central banks in practice use different methods for this procedure – one example is the inflation chart of the Bank of England. However, it is also indisputable that these forecasts are made under considerable uncertainty (see next Box) which make the use of these forecasts as intermediate targets difficult in reality.[36] If the inflation forecast is interpreted as an intermediate target the central bank has discretion insofar as the intermediate target itself is calculated by the authorities themselves. Thus, despite the fact that inflation targeting becomes a rule does not mean that the central bank has no discretion. On the contrary, the calculation of the inflation forecast is a discretionary feature of this monetary policy strategy. Incorporating this fact into the discussion supports the view of Bernanke et al. (1999) that inflation targeting should be seen as a framework rather than a strict rule.[37]

---

35 A higher inflation rate in (2) decreases the real interest rate which increases output in the next period.

36 Bofinger (2000c) suggests a larger role for external inflation forecasts (from analysts, households as well as derived from financial market data) to supplement the central bank's forecast.

37 Bofinger (2000b) argues similarly with respect to the difficulties of creating an inflation forecast. He mentions that "compared with a 'simple rule' like a Taylor rule or the rule of monetary targeting which both reduce the complexity of a central banker's

The Bank of England's inflation forecast

In order to demonstrate the uncertainties associated with an inflation forecast, the Bank of England publishes quarterly in its Inflation Reports probability density functions in the form of a so-called fan chart. "The published distribution illustrates the MPC's views of both the variance of likely inflation outcomes and any potential skews or asymmetric risks to inflation. The distribution quantifies these uncertainties and skews; it de-emphasises point inflation forecasts, since these are almost certain to be incorrect ex post; and it thereby allows explicitly probabilistic statements to be made about monetary policy." (Haldane, 1999: 56). The underlying assumption of the forecast is that nominal interest rates remain unchanged over the forecast period.

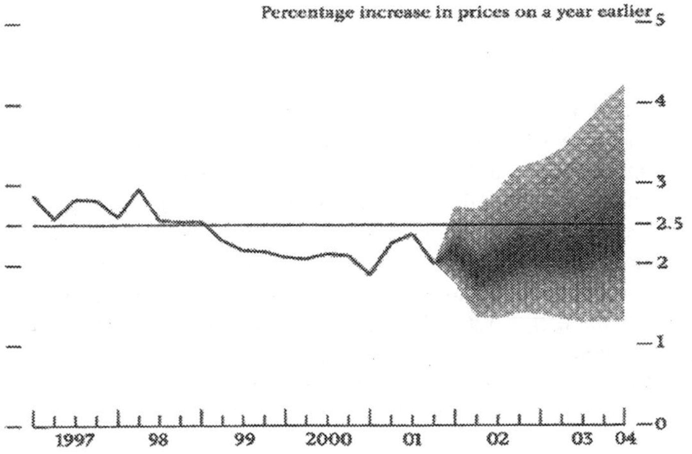

Bank of England fan chart for the retail price index in February 2002. Source: Bank of England.

2.4 Open Economy Inflation Targeting

The above summarised information about the basic concept of inflation targeting shows one basic feature of it: it is foremost a concept for a central bank in a closed economy. The role of the exchange rate is not discussed in the elements of inflation targeting. Consequently, first theoretical concepts did not take into account the exchange rate (e.g. Svensson, 1997a). This observation is somewhat puzzling, given the fact that all of the countries that first adopted inflation targeting are

decision process, 'rule' is simply a misnomer when applied to inflation targeting." (p. 37).

small open economies. Only in the last years there have been some efforts to adapt theoretical inflation targeting concepts to an open economy, i.e. to include the exchange rate and foreign variables into the models.

Table 3: GDP and degrees of openness

	GDP	0.5*(Exports+Imports) / GDP
Australia	364.9	16.0%
Canada	609.3	34.2%
New Zealand	53.4	21.3%
Sweden	237.8	32.3%
United Kingdom	1413.7	20.7%
United States	8790.2	9.1%
Japan	3808.0	10.5%

Note: All data refer to 1998. Nominal national GDP accounts are in billion US$ and are converted to US$ using yearly average nominal exchange rates. Source: IFS.

As can be seen in Table 3 the degree of openness, defined as the ratio of (exports+imports)/2 and GDP is significantly higher in the five inflation targeting countries compared with the United States. While Australia has the lowest degree of openness with 16%, Canada is the most open economy among the five countries with a ratio of 34.2%. Especially when compared with the low degree of openness of the USA or of Japan, these data suggest that the external sector is an important factor for these inflation targeting countries.[38] Taking into account the pass-through of exchange rate changes on consumer prices this dependency is relevant for monetary policy. The comparison of gross domestic products further reveals that these countries are small compared with the United States and Japan with the United Kingdom being the largest among the five inflation targeters.

2.4.1 Exchange Rate Pass-Through and Monetary Policy

Monetary policy in an open economy has to take at least two further aspects into account compared with monetary policy in a closed economy.[39] First, the exchange rate is added as a further variable that affects economic conditions and second, the economy is also affected by foreign shocks. Thus, different to the closed economy where there are only two transmission channels for monetary policy (the aggregate demand and the expectations channel), in an open economy also the exchange rate channel has to be taken into account by the central bank.

[38] "All real-world inflation targeting economies are quite open economies with free capital mobility, where shocks originating in the rest of the world are important, and where the exchange rate plays a prominent role in the transmission mechanism of monetary policy." (Svensson, 2000b: 2).

[39] See Svensson (1997b).

The exchange rate channel can be divided into a direct and an indirect one (see Figure 3). The direct channel refers to the influence of the exchange rate on import prices of an economy and further on to the consumer price level with, generally, a relatively short time lag. The indirect channel refers to the fact that an appreciation of the exchange rate makes domestic goods more expensive relative to foreign goods. This reduces foreign demand for domestic goods and leads to a fall in aggregate demand. With a longer time lag than the direct channel, this reduces domestic inflation (and vice versa for a depreciation of the exchange rate).[40]

The direct exchange rate channel differs in an important way from the other transmission channels: The lag between exchange rate changes and effects on the inflation rate is shortest. In models of monetary policy it usually takes two periods for interest rate changes to affect the inflation rate but only one period for exchange rate changes. Figure 3 summarises both channels.

A general finding of the exchange rate pass-through literature is that exchange rate changes do not translate one-to-one in changes in consumer prices, i.e. pass-through is almost always found to be incomplete. This phenomenon is even found at the import price level. Thus, the law of one price, which would demand a total adjustment of domestic prices to exchange rate changes does not hold in practice.[41] A general hypothesis, which is supported by McCarthy (2000) is that more open economies exhibit a higher pass-through of exchange rate changes.

In the following we present two models for open-economy inflation targeting to illustrate how inflation targeting has to be adjusted in such an environment and what the differences are with respect to a closed economy.[42]

---

40 See Menon (1995) for an extensive survey of theoretical and empirical studies on exchange rate pass-through and Hüfner and Schröder (2002) for a study of euro area exchange rate pass-through.

41 A popular explanation for this fact is pricing-to-market behaviour by firms: In competitive industries importing or exporting firms chose to adjust their mark-ups over prices instead of passing on exchange rate changes (see Krugman, 1987 and Dornbusch, 1987). A prominent example is the Japanese car industry: despite heavy fluctuations of the Yen versus the US dollar in the 1990s, the price of Japanese cars in the US remained relatively stable (see Goldberg and Knetter, 1997).

42 We will restrict the survey on the main features of the (complex) models in order to show how inflation targeting in an open economy differs from a closed economy and how the central bank is expected to act given the external influences.

Figure 3: Pass-through from an exchange rate depreciation to consumer prices

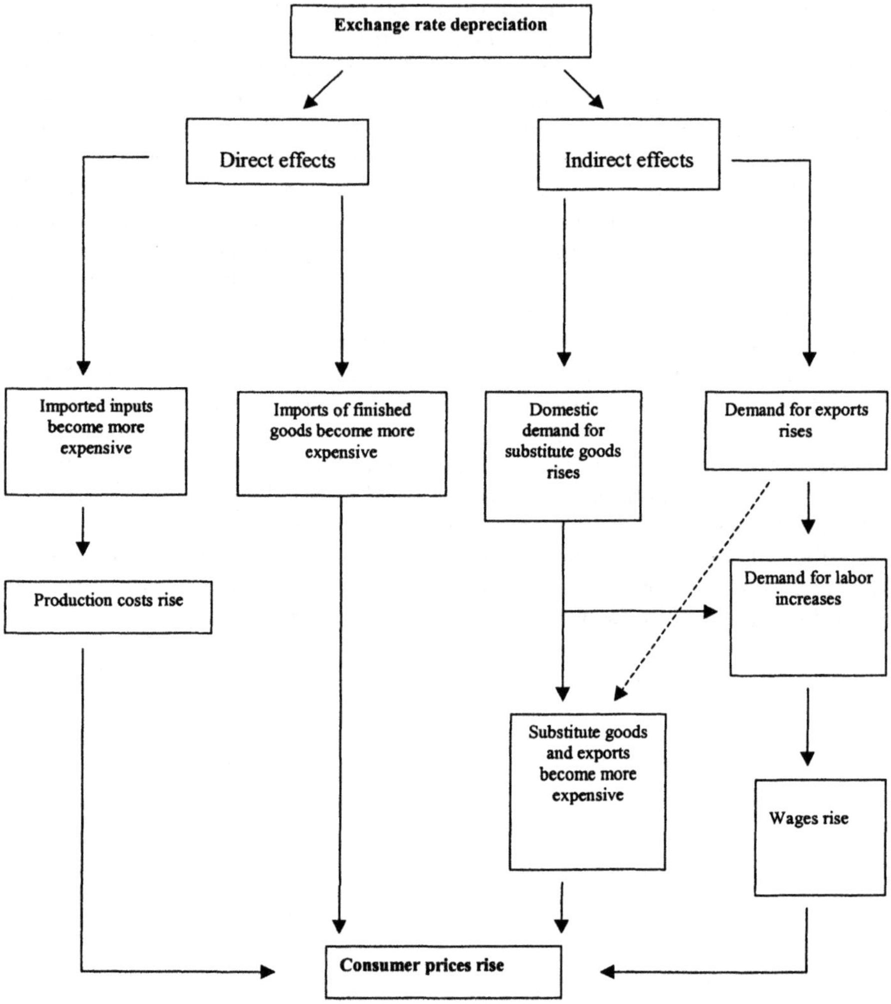

Source: Laflèche (1996).

2.4.2 The Svensson Model

In Svensson (2000b) a model is presented that extends the closed economy model to an open economy and introduces forward-looking behaviour. Again, Svensson starts with an equation for aggregate supply

$$\pi_{t+2} = \alpha_1 \pi_{t+1} + (1-\alpha_1) E_t \pi_{t+3} + \alpha_2 \left[E_t y_{t+2} + \beta (y_{t+1} - E_t y_{t+1}) \right] + \alpha_3 E_t q_{t+2} + \varepsilon_{t+2} \tag{2.6}$$

where π denotes domestic inflation (in contrast to consumer price inflation (CPI) that incorporates the direct influence of the exchange rate via import prices), y_t is the output gap and q_t is the real exchange rate.[43] ε_t denotes a supply shock with zero mean. All variables used are in logarithms. The inflation rate is predetermined two periods in advance. Hence, the expectations for the real exchange rate q in t affects inflation in $t+2$ as only the indirect exchange rate channel is modelled here. $E_t \pi_{t+3}$ denotes the inflation rate in $t+3$ that is expected by the central bank in t. As a consequence of the forward-looking modelling, inflation depends both on lagged inflation and on previous expectations of future inflation as well as on previous expectations of the output gap.

With ω as the share of imported goods, the equation for the CPI becomes

$$\pi_t^c = (1-\omega)\pi_t + \omega(q_t - q_{t-1}). \tag{2.7}$$

As is evident, no lag is assumed between actual exchange rate changes and movements in the CPI which is equivalent to the direct channel of the exchange rate.

Aggregate demand is given by the following equation

$$y_{t+1} = \beta_1 y_t - \beta_2 E_t \rho_{t+1} + \beta_1^* E_t y_{t+1}^* + \beta_3 E_t q_{t+1} - (\gamma_y^n - \beta_1) y_t^n + \eta_{t+1}^d - \eta_{t+1}^n \tag{2.8}$$

where y^n denotes the natural output level (potential output) that is achieved with perfectly flexible prices and ρ is a measure of the sum of current and expected future real interest rates. Foreign variables are marked with an asterisk. Aggregate demand is predetermined one period in advance and depends on lagged expectations of future real interest rates, foreign output y^* and the real exchange rate.

One of the central features of open economy models is the assumed behaviour of the exchange rate. In Svensson (2000b) it is modelled with an uncovered interest parity of the standard form

$$i_t - i_t^* = E_t s_{t+1} - s_t + \varphi_t \tag{2.9}$$

---

43 The real exchange rate is defined as $q_t \equiv s_t + p_t - p_t$ with p_t as the price level of domestically produced goods, p_t is the foreign price level and s_t is the nominal exchange rate (domestic currency per unit of foreign currency).

where s denotes nominal exchange rates, i and i^* are domestic and foreign nominal interest rates, respectively, and φ denotes the risk premium. Accordingly, the expected real exchange rate is given by

$$E_t q_{t+1} = q_t + i_t - E_t \pi_{t+1} - i_t^* + E_t \pi_{t+1}^* - \varphi_t \quad (2.10)$$

Given the outline of the model, what happens if the interest rate is changed by the central bank? As domestic inflation in t and t+1 is predetermined, a change in the nominal interest rate has immediate consequences for the real interest rate and the real exchange rate. According to equation (2.7) this has an immediate effect (zero lag) on CPI (direct exchange rate channel). This way, a central bank can influence CPI in period t with its interest rate setting in t. The other lags (aggregate demand channel and inflation expectations channel) remain the same as for the closed economy with the only difference that the real exchange rate also influences output and inflation in later periods. There is a one-period lag for the effect on aggregate demand and a two-period lag for the effect on domestic inflation.

Given a loss function for the central bank that incorporates variations of output, domestic and CPI inflation, Svensson calibrates the model and analyses different monetary policy response functions. Especially he looks at the difference between strict inflation targeting (no weight on output variability) and flexible inflation targeting (output deviations are also taken into account in the loss function). If the central bank focuses on strict inflation targeting it has to use the direct exchange rate channel extensively in order to achieve the lowest possible deviation of inflation from the target path at short horizons. As a result, output and the real exchange rate will fluctuate a lot since the interest rate has to be adjusted frequently. If flexible inflation targeting is pursued by the central bank then the desired inflation rate is only to be achieved in the longer run. This way, output deviations from the desired path occur less frequently and the direct exchange rate channel is not used that often which also decreases the fluctuations.

2.4.3 The Ball Model

Ball (1999) also extends the closed economy model of inflation targeting to an open economy in a similar way as Svensson. He stresses that inflation targeting in an open economy is different in an important way, namely because of "the effects of exchange rates on inflation through import prices. This is the fastest channel from monetary policy to inflation, and so inflation targeting implies that it is used aggressively. Large shifts in the exchange rate produce large fluctuations in output." (p. 128).

His model consists of three equations: aggregate demand IS curve (2.11), Phillips curve (2.12) and an equation for the exchange rate (2.13).

$$y_t = -\beta r_{t-1} - \delta e_{t-1} + \lambda y_{t-1} + \varepsilon_t \quad (2.11)$$

$$\pi_t = \pi_{t-1} + \alpha y_{t-1} - \gamma(e_{t-1} - e_{t-2}) + \eta_t \quad (2.12)$$

$$e_t = \theta r_t + \upsilon \qquad (2.13)$$

r_t denotes the real interest rate in period t, y is the logarithm of real output and e_t is the logarithm of the real exchange rate (an increase means appreciation). In contrast to Svensson's (2000b) model, Ball uses a backward-looking model, i.e. he does not incorporate expectations and consequently his model is less complex.

According to equation (2.13), the real exchange rate is linked positively and without a lag to the interest rate.[44] Expectations and other influences are captured in the shock term υ. Furthermore, the change in the real exchange rate enters the Phillips curve with a one period lag. This captures its influence on inflation via import prices (note that in Svensson's model there is no lag for the direct exchange rate channel, whereas here it is one lag). Ball interprets one period as one year which seems to be a realistic assumption for the speed of exchange rate pass-through (see Lafleche, 1996, Hüfner and Schröder, 2002).

From the three basic equations of his model Ball derives two important aspects in which his policy rule differs from a closed economy. "First, the policy variable is a combination of r and e. And second, inflation is replaced by $\pi + \gamma e_{t-1}$, a combination of inflation and the lagged exchange rate." (p. 131). While the first result is nothing else than a monetary-conditions-index which is used by some central banks as an operating target the second result determines the long-run inflation of an open economy. Ball also compares it to a measure of core or underlying inflation where temporary exchange rate fluctuations are not included.

Similar to Svensson, Ball also comes to the conclusion that strict inflation targeting in an open economy leads to high fluctuations in output and exchange rate. This is due to the fact, that next periods' inflation can only be influenced with the direct exchange rate channel which consequently means higher volatility in the exchange rate. Since the assumption is that the exchange rate is positively linked to interest rates these will also have to fluctuate more which has an adverse effect on output. The proposal by Ball to use a monetary-conditions-index and to target long-run inflation is designed to avoid excessive volatility in the economy. In practice, some inflation targeting central banks took account of the two channels through which the inflation rate can be influenced by choosing a Monetary Conditions Index (MCI) as an operating target (Canada and New Zealand for example). An MCI combines both interest rates and exchange rates and thus serves as a measure of monetary conditions in an open economy.

Bharucha and Kent (1998) suggest to target non-traded inflation in contrast to aggregate inflation in order to be able to tolerate high volatility in exchange rates. Consequently, the central bank does not have to use interest rate adjustments as

---

44 Note that $\theta = 1$ and a constant future exchange rate implies uncovered interest parity (if the current exchange rate appreciates after an increase in the interest rate and the future exchange rate is unchanged, then the exchange rate depreciates over time which is described by uncovered interest parity).

frequently to counter exchange rate movements and thus negative effects on the domestic economy are smaller.

2.4.4 Two Critical Assumptions

As has become apparent, the exchange rate is an important variable in models of open economy inflation targeting. Besides the two popular models by Ball and Svensson there exist several other theoretical models that are concerned with open economy inflation targeting such as Bharucha and Kent (1998), Batini and Haldane (1999) and Sutherland (2001). All of these models share two common features:

1. They assume a certain relationship between exchange rate changes and fundamental variables.
2. They define the short-term interest rate as the sole operating target of monetary policy.

Turning to the first point it emerges that the usual exchange rate relationship that is assumed is a variant of the uncovered interest parity.
Table 4 reviews the exchange rate equations for selected models. The assumption that the exchange rate is linked to interest rate differentials is crucial. Only if the central bank can influence the exchange rate by changing its short-term interest rate, it can take advantage of the direct exchange rate channel to inflation.

Table 4: Exchange rate equations in models of inflation targeting

Model	Exchange rate equation used
Svensson (2000b)	$i_t - i_t^* = E_t s_{t+1} - s_t + \varphi_t$ (uncovered interest parity)
Ball (1999)	$e_t = \theta r_t + \upsilon$ (with $\theta > 0$) positive link between the real interest rate (r_t) and the real exchange rate (e_t); υ denotes shocks such as expectations, investor confidence and foreign interest rates. (if $\theta = 1$ then this equation is equal to uncovered interest parity)
Bharucha and Kent (1998)	${}_t\Delta e_{t+1} = i_t - i_t^f - \rho_t$ (uncovered interest parity) ${}_t\Delta e_{t+1}$ denotes the expectation at t of the nominal depreciation between t and t+1, i_t and i_t^f represent domestic and foreign interest rates and ρ_t is a risk premium.
Batini and Haldane (1999)	$e_t = E_t e_{t+1} + i_t - i_t^f + \varepsilon_t$ (uncovered interest parity) ε_t comprises foreign interest rate shocks and other noise in the foreign exchange market, including shocks to the exchange risk premium.
McCallum and Nelson (2001)	$R_t - R_t^* = E_t \Delta s_{t+1} + \zeta_t$ (uncovered interest parity) where ζ_t denotes a time-varying risk-premium term.

The second feature we highlighted is the assumption that the short-term interest rate is the sole operating target of the inflation targeting central bank. Thus, these models do not take into account the possibility of central bank interventions in the foreign exchange market. Recent studies suggest that interventions are applied more often by central banks who operate floating exchange rates than previously thought (see e.g. Calvo and Reinhart, 2000; Reinhart, 2000; Levy-Yeyati and Sturzenegger, 2000; Hausmann et al., 2000). If sterilised interventions are used, the exchange rate can be regarded as an additional operating target which can be controlled directly by the central bank. However, this possibility does not exist so far in theoretical models.

Returning to our starting point figure about the stylised model of monetary policy we can display the traditional theoretical models in simple terms as follows:

Figure 4: The conventional view of open-economy inflation targeting

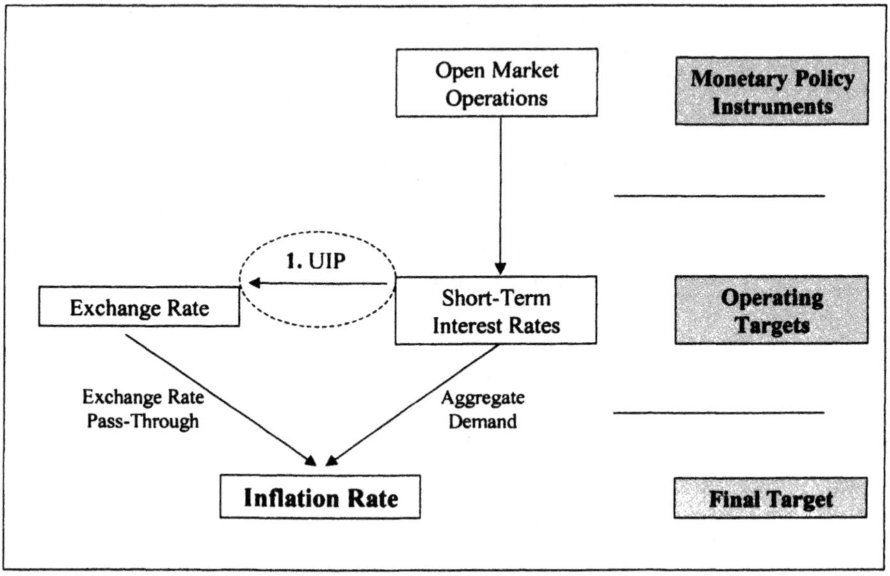

Note: UIP denotes uncovered interest parity.

Figure 4 exhibits both assumptions mentioned above: Open market operations to control domestic short-term interest rates are the only policy tool of the central bank and interest rates and exchange rates are connected through uncovered interest parity. Indeed, if this relationship holds, there is no need for a further policy tool, i.e. the central bank can conduct inflation targeting solely through interest rate policy. This relationship is crucial for the conduct of monetary policy according to the existing theoretical models.

As a starting point for our analysis whether an additional policy instrument is actually necessary, we will empirically test if uncovered interest parity holds in reality in inflation targeting countries. Thus, the next section is concerned with the question 1 from our list of issues laid out in chapter 1.

3 Uncovered Interest Parity in Practice

"[Exchange rate economics] is in crisis. It is in crisis in the sense that current macroeconomic approaches to exchange rates are empirical failures."
(Lyons, 2001b: 2)

3.1 The Rationale of Interest Parity

There are two basic approaches to exchange rate determination (both of which are often combined in models): the goods market approach and the asset market approach.[45] While in the goods market approach the idea is that exchange rates are determined basically through the trade of real assets, the asset market approach points to the importance of capital flows. The main feature of the first is purchasing power parity (PPP) and the notion of the second is uncovered interest parity (UIP). The concept of PPP states that the exchange rate equates the national price levels of two countries in the sense that the purchasing power of a unit of currency is the same in both countries.[46] On the other hand UIP states that the change in the exchange rate over time equals the interest rate differential between two countries. The following chapter is designed to outline the theoretical concept and methods for testing the hypothesis of UIP.

3.1.1 Covered Interest Parity

In order to explain the concept of *uncovered* interest parity in more detail it is useful to start with *covered* interest parity. Covered interest parity follows from the assumption of arbitrage between spot and forward foreign exchange markets. Thus, according to covered interest parity the forward discount is simply the interest rate differential, or technically with f_t as the price of the forward contract in period t and e_t as the spot exchange rate (both measured as domestic currency units per foreign currency unit),

---

45 The following draws on Isard (1995), Lewis (1995) and Meredith and Chinn (1998).

46 See Sarno and Taylor (2001b). The equalisation of two price levels is termed *absolute* PPP. In contrast, *relative* PPP holds when the change in the exchange rate is equal to the difference of the inflation rates between two countries.

$$f_t(1+i_t^*) = e_t(1+i_t) \tag{3.1}$$

Because of potential riskless arbitrage opportunities this relationship needs to hold continuously.[47] In uncovered interest parity, the forward discount is replaced by the expected depreciation of the exchange rate.

3.1.2 Uncovered Interest Parity

According to uncovered interest parity the return that investors can earn by investing in domestic and foreign deposits equals across countries through adjustments in exchange rates. Excess returns should not occur since a higher interest rate in the foreign country is compensated by a depreciation of the foreign currency. UIP is thus the result of international arbitrage considerations of risk-neutral investors. Let e_t denote the exchange rate measured as domestic currency units per foreign currency unit and let $E_t[e_{t+1}]$ denote the expected future exchange rate based on information in t and let i and i^* be the domestic and foreign interest rates, respectively. Then uncovered interest parity can be expressed as

$$e_t(1+i_t) = E_t[e_{t+1}](1+i_t^*) \tag{3.2}$$

Rearranging and taking logarithms on both sides yields[48]

$$\ln(E_t[e_{t+1}]) - \ln(e_t) = i_t - i_t^* \tag{3.3}$$

Investors will change the composition of their portfolios until the expected yield of homogenous investments is equal across countries. If UIP holds continuously it does not matter for an investor in which country he invests his money since a higher interest rate in one country is compensated with an exchange rate depreciation over the maturity of the investment. This way, interest rate returns are equalised across countries. If the interest rate difference is calculated with money market rates then there is a direct link of this theory to monetary policy. Since central banks can perfectly control short-term interest rates they can affect the in-

47 Consider e_t to be the US\$/euro exchange rate: To arbitrage, a US investor can borrow one US\$, buy one euro, invest in euro-denominated bonds paying interest of $1+i*$ and sell the return forward at rate t_t. If the forward discount is smaller than the interest rate differential, the US investor locks in a riskless profit. Thus, covered interest parity must hold. However, if transaction costs are introduced, small deviations of covered interest parity are possible.

48 An equal derivation of (3) is the following: $(1+i_t)/(1+i_t^*) = E_t[e_{t+1}]/e_t$ subtracting 1 from both sides yields

$$[(1+i_t)/(1+i_t^*)] - [(1+i_t^*)/(1+i_t^*)] = [(E_t[e_{t+1}]/e_t) - (e_t/e_t)]$$

and hence $(i_t - i_t^*)/(1+i_t^*) = (E_t[e_{t+1}] - e_t)/e_t$. For small values of i^* this is ap proximately equal to $i_t - i_t^* \approx \ln(E[e_{t+1}]) - \ln(e_t)$.

terest rate differential and thus the difference between the spot exchange rate and the expected future exchange rate. For example: If the short-term lending rate of the European Central Bank is higher than the US Federal Funds Rate then the euro will tend to depreciate according to UIP in order to equalise the positive interest rate differential investors can earn by investing in euro denominated money market papers. If the euro area short-term interest rate increases relatively to the US rates then either the euro spot exchange rate appreciates and the expected exchange rate change remains constant or the spot exchange rate remains constant and the euro is expected to depreciate in the future.

An important underlying assumption for UIP to hold is, however, that investments in different countries are equivalent (homogenous) and that there are no obstacles to capital mobility (such as capital controls, etc). Furthermore, this relation holds only for risk-neutral investors for whom home and foreign investments are perfect substitutes. Risk-averse investors instead require a risk-premium for the risk of holding the foreign currency (for example to compensate for default risk). Home and foreign investments are no longer perfect substitutes for risk-averse investors. In this case the expected exchange rate depreciation differs from the interest rate difference. This is illustrated in the following equation with $p_{t,t+1}$ as the required risk premium from period t to t+1:

$$\ln(e_{t+1}) - \ln(e_t) = \Delta e_{t,t+1} = (i_t - i_t^*) - p_{t,t+1} \tag{3.4}$$

In covered interest rate parity the existence of a risk premium is reflected in a deviation of the forward discount from the pure interest rate differential. However, it is difficult to test whether deviations from UIP reflect a risk premium or simply expectational errors since one would need a measure of expectations.[49]

As a first stylised fact consider the following table which contains interest rate parity calculations for the five inflation targeting countries we focus on: Australia, New Zealand, Canada, Sweden and United Kingdom. We calculated changes in exchange rates over a time horizon of three months and compared the absolute average value with the interest rate differential to the US using three-month money market rates (measured in % per quarter). The sample contains the period 1993/1 to 2001/8 since during this time all of the countries pursued inflation targeting. It becomes evident that the change predicted by uncovered interest parity explains only a small fraction of the actual exchange rate movements. Obviously, exchange rates fluctuate a lot more than postulated by uncovered interest parity. Thus, a first doubt about the validity of UIP can be cast. However, the issue is worth inspecting in more detail.

[49] One way to analyse this is by using survey data. Studies using such data (see Froot and Frankel, 1989) find that risk premiums only account for a small proportion of the bias in the interest differential. Expectational errors seem to be much more important.

Table 5: Predicted and actual exchange rate changes

	Absolute average value of exchange rate changes	Absolute average predicted changes according to UIP
Australia (US$/A$)	3.70	0.27
Canada (US$/C$)	1.78	0.25
New Zealand (US$/NZ$)	3.66	0.58
Sweden (US$/SEK)	3.73	0.52
United Kingdom (US$/GBP)	2.29	0.30

Note: Data is monthly and the time period considered is 1993/1-2001/8. Exchange rate changes are the average absolute percentage values over a time horizon of three months. Predicted change according to UIP was calculated as the average absolute value of the difference between domestic and US 3-month interest rates (measured in % per quarter). We follow Isard (1995) with this illustration and calculation. Source of data: IFS.

3.2 An Empirical Test for Inflation Targeting Countries

For the purpose of testing whether uncovered interest parity holds in practice, the following equation, which regresses the realised exchange rate depreciation on the interest rate differential, is used[50]

$$\ln(e_{t+1}) - \ln(e_t) = \alpha + \beta(i_t - i_t^*) + \varepsilon_t \tag{3.5}$$

The hypotheses of foreign exchange market efficiency is $H_0 : \beta = 1$ and $\alpha = 0$. Note, that this implies the joint hypotheses of testing (1) that the interest rate differential is the best predictor of the actual depreciation of the exchange rate (risk-neutrality) and (2) rational expectations. Many studies indeed test only for $\beta = 1$. This reflects that a non-zero value for the constant term α might mirror a constant exchange risk premium demanded by risk-averse investors. If β is not found to be significantly different from 0 then the exchange rate change would simply follow a random walk (with a drift if the constant is non-zero). The error term ε_t consists of both expectational errors and a possible risk premium.

For the estimation of the test equation we use the ordinary least squares (OLS) method which is the standard choice in the UIP literature (see Froot and Frankel, 1989, Flood and Rose, 1996, 2001). We do not pool our data across countries since we are interested in the individual results for each country. To obtain a sufficiently large number of observations we use daily data on bilateral exchange rates versus the US$ and daily data for the 3-month Treasury Bill interest rates.[51] Inter-

[50] This corresponds with the procedure used among others by Flood and Rose (1996, 2001).

[51] All data are obtained from Thomson Financial Datastream (Mnemonics: BBAUDSP, BBNZDSP, BBGBPSP, BBCADSP, BBSEKSP, AUST90D, NZTBL3M,

est rate differentials were calculated with respect to US interest rates and are expressed as three-month rates. We also estimate the equation and report results with weekly and monthly data to check for the robustness of our results. The period analysed is 1993:1 to 2001:1 – a period where all five countries pursued inflation targeting.

Figure 5 displays scatter diagrams of exchange rate changes versus interest rate differentials. If UIP holds continuously, then all points should lie on a slope with an angle of +1 (positive interest rate differentials, i.e. a higher interest rate in the non-US country, should be associated with a positive exchange rate change, i.e. a depreciation of the domestic currency vis-a-vis the US$). Instead, there does not seem to be a clear tendency in neither of the countries, rather there seems to be clustering of observations in the middle of the diagrams.

Table 6 presents the results of our empirical estimation. All our estimated coefficients $\hat{\beta}$ for the interest rate differential are negative thus proving a common result of related studies. Instead of equalising returns from investment between countries, movements in exchange rates rather seem to reinforce the difference. This way, excess returns can be earned regularly by investing in a country with higher interest rates as the exchange rate will tend to appreciate. However, significance of the coefficient varies across countries and depends on the data frequency. For daily and weekly data, $\hat{\beta}$ is highly significant with the exception of the UK. In the monthly data only the coefficient for Australia is significant at the 1% level and the coefficient for Sweden is significant at the 10% level. The constant is highly significant for all countries only for daily frequency. In order to test hypotheses based on the uncovered interest parity we performed coefficient tests for $\hat{\beta}$, $\hat{\alpha}$ and for both coefficients simultaneously.

LDNTB3M, CNTBL3M, SDTB90D, FRTBS3M). Exchange rates are measured as domestic currency per US dollar– thus an increase corresponds to a depreciation. Most of the studies that analyse UIP and usually reject it use interest rates with a maturity of up to 12 months. There is evidence that UIP finds more support if long-term interest rates are used. Meredith and Chinn (1998), for example, estimate a positive slope parameter β (which is evidence in favour of UIP) using the yield of 10-year government bonds. While this shows that the hypothesis of UIP cannot be dismissed completely, it is the short run that matters most for monetary policy. Macro models such as the ones presented in the second chapter assume that the central bank can influence exchange rates through changes in interest rates that affect the exchange rate via UIP. Since central banks have direct control only over short-term money market rates it is important in this respect to test the UIP with these maturities. Long-term interest rates are also affected by central bank behaviour but only very indirectly and imperfectly.

Figure 5: Exchange rate changes versus interest rate differentials

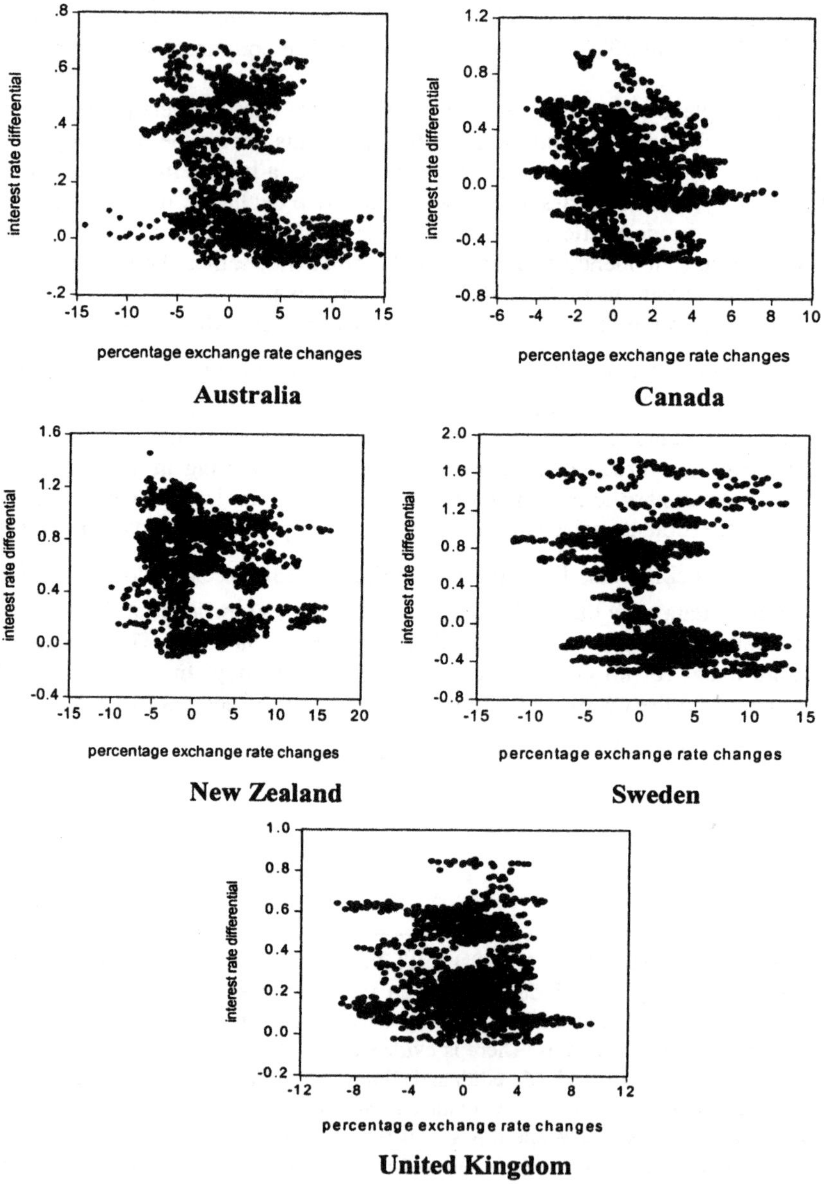

Note: Daily data, 1993:1 – 2001:1. Exchange rate changes are computed over a time horizon of three months – interest rate differentials are computed as three-month yields.

The result points strikingly against the validity of the strong form of UIP. The hypothesis, that $\hat{\beta}=1$ could be rejected in all cases except for the UK using monthly and weekly data and the joint hypothesis that $\hat{\beta}=1$ and the constant is 0 could be strongly rejected in all cases except for New Zealand and the UK. In the case of the UK, however, the hypothesis of $\hat{\beta}=0$ could also not be rejected for monthly data. Thus, while there are differences in the results across countries, there is little evidence that the actual exchange rate depreciation leads to the equalisation of investment returns across countries. On the contrary, there are obviously enormous excess returns to be earned in the foreign exchange markets analysed in our study. This is the result of the majority of related studies that look at the efficient market hypothesis in the foreign exchange market for various countries.[52] Mark and Wu (1998) conclude: "While the forward premium is found to help in prediction, it does so with the wrong sign." (p. 1689). Our results support Flood and Rose (2001) who state that "uncovered interest parity (UIP) is a classic topic of international finance; a critical building block of most theoretical models and a dismal empirical failure." (p. 1).[53]

52 Surveys are provided among others by Hodrick (1987), Froot and Thaler (1990), Lewis (1995), Flood and Rose (1996, 2001).

53 An interesting result has been detected by Flood and Rose (1996). They find that the forward discount puzzle might depend upon the choice of exchange rate regime. Using data from the European Monetary System they show that UIP performs much better in this system of fixed but adjustable exchange rates than under floating arrangements. However, since our focus is solely on countries that have no official exchange rate target and are classified as independent floaters their result has no relevance for our case.

Table 6: Regression results

Country	Frequency[a]	No of obs.	$\hat{\alpha}$	$\hat{\beta}$	Wald test $H_0: \hat{\beta} = 0$	Wald test $H_0: \hat{\beta} = 1$	Wald test $\hat{\alpha} = 0, \hat{\beta} = 1$
Australia	D	2022	0.025*** (0.004)	-6.548*** (1.117)	34.32***	45.61***	23.23***
Canada	D	2022	0.007*** (0.001)	-1.272*** (0.335)	14.42***	46.0***	35.89***
New Zealand	D	2022	0.025*** (0.005)	-2.929*** (0.681)	18.51***	33.30***	16.69***
Sweden	D	2022	0.014*** (0.003)	-2.063*** (0.502)	16.88***	37.21***	24.52***
United Kingdom	D	2022	-0.003 (0.003)	-0.695 (0.928)	0.56	3.33*	2.93*
Australia	W	406	0.027*** (0.007)	-6.131***(1.929)	10.1***	13.66***	6.93***
Canada	W	406	0.006** (0.002)	-1.215**(0.567)	4.59**	15.24***	11.33***
New Zealand	W	406	0.022** (0.009)	-2.614*** (1.214)	4.64**	8.86***	4.46**
Sweden	W	406	0.013*** (0.005)	-1.859**(0.863)	4.64**	10.97***	7.27***
United Kingdom	W	406	0.002 (0.006)	-0.568 (1.506)	0.14	1.08	1.03
Australia	M	101	0.025*** (0.009)	-6.545***(2.438)	7.21***	9.58***	5.03***
Canada	M	101	0.006* (0.003)	-1.219 (0.783)	2.42	8.03***	6.76***
New Zealand	M	101	0.020 (0.013)	-2.345 (1.828)	1.65	3.35*	1.68
Sweden	M	101	0.015**(0.006)	-1.818 (1.184)	2.36	5.67**	5.24***
United Kingdom	M	101	0.003 (0.008)	-0.775 (1.861)	0.17	0.91	0.79

Notes: Reported standard errors (in parentheses) are estimated using the Newey and West (1987) heteroskedasticity and autocorrelation consistent covariant estimator. The statistic of the Wald test beta=0 corresponds with the t-statistic of the beta-coefficient. [a] Frequency D, W and M refers to daily, weekly and monthly data. Sample range: 1993:1 – 2001:1. ***, **, * denotes significance at the 1, 5 and 10% level. Estimation method: OLS.

The partial exploitation of these excess returns can be observed in financial markets. Consider, for example, the popularity of carry trades that have been conducted with high volume in the Yen-US$ market in the 1990s. Investors borrowed money in Yen because of the relatively low interest rates and invested the funds in US government bonds that offered a higher yield than Japanese bonds. According to uncovered interest parity this strategy would not have been profitable since the interest rate differential would have been offset by a depreciation of the US$ versus the Yen. The significantly negative coefficient, however, suggests that such strategies actually are profitable in foreign exchange markets. Indeed, the Yen depreciated against the US$ in the mid-1990s, thereby rendering such carry trades very profitable. A further prominent example of the failure of UIP is the British pound that appreciated significantly versus the German mark in the second half of the 1990s despite a higher interest rate level in the UK. Lyons (2001b: 206) offers an explanation for the persistence of the forward bias puzzle. He argues that the Sharpe ratio for the currency trade that would arbitrage the difference between the future spot rate and the forward rate calculated by the interest rate differential is too small for institutional investors.[54] Bofinger (2001) argues that the failure of uncovered interest parity can be explained with the short-term orientation of many foreign exchange traders. As they usually hold their foreign exchange positions only intra-day the interest rate differential does not matter for their trading decisions and therefore on the exchange rate behaviour.

The failure of uncovered interest parity is not only important from an investor's point of view. It does have serious consequences for monetary policy since the relationships assumed in theoretical models do not hold in practice. "In particular, the rejection of the simple efficiency hypothesis as applied to the foreign exchange market and the stylised empirical fact of a negative covariation between the rate of depreciation and the forward premium challenges conventional macro-based approaches to the foreign exchange market since it suggests that one cannot take for granted many of the efficiency conditions that are typically subsumed in macro-based exchange rate models." (Flood and Taylor, 1996: 286).

Moreover, the efficiency of the interest rate policy of the central bank with regard to the exchange rate has to be questioned. Apparently, the UIP assumption in the models summarised before (Ball, 1999; Svensson, 2000b) is not supported by the empirical reality. Given this fact it seems surprising that so many macroeconomic models still use exchange-rate equations like purchasing power parity or uncovered interest parity (UIP). This assumption is seldom criticised even though modern literature on exchange rate economics tends to move away from macroeconomic models given their poor performance in explaining actual exchange rate behaviour. Instead recent studies refer to the so-called microstructure approach of

[54] From interviews with proprietary traders he reports that they require a Sharpe ratio (i.e. risk-adjusted returns) that is larger than 0,4 (which is the Sharpe ratio of a buy-and-hold strategy in U.S. equities). For the major floating exchange rates this would require that β in equation (5) would need to be either smaller than -1 or larger than $+3$ – well outside a standard deviation band of $\pm 2\sigma$ around 1 that a statistician would require to accept the null hypothesis of uncovered interest parity.

the foreign exchange market since as Flood and Taylor (1996) conclude: "[...]our understanding of the short-run behaviour of exchange rates is unlikely to be further enhanced by further examination of the macro fundamentals." (p. 286). This is especially relevant for the analysis of monetary policy for which the short term perspective is more important than the long run behaviour of exchange rates.

An interesting question is why UIP is still such an important building block of theoretical models despite the lack of empirical support. Sutherland (2001) acknowledges the dilemma and says that the results of his model might change if exchange rate shocks are included. However, he admits that it is "[...] technically difficult to include such shocks while preserving a tractable and consistent structure." (p. 27). Lars Svensson was confronted with the problem when he had to comment on a paper by Robert Flood and Mark Taylor on a conference about the microstructure of the foreign exchange market. Flood and Taylor's paper (1996) was named "Exchange rate economics: what's wrong with the conventional macro approach" and they concluded that the failure of the simple speculative efficiency hypothesis (uncovered interest parity) challenges many conditions that are taken for granted in macro-models. In his discussion of their paper Svensson (1996) acknowledges the fact that the existing exchange rate theories do not outperform a random walk. However, he points out that this only holds true for floating exchange rates and presents evidence that within fixed exchange rate regimes with bands these theories perform much better.[55] Since pure inflation targeting countries usually operate a floating exchange rate regime, Svensson thus seems to be aware that his assumption of UIP in open-economy models do lack some empirical relevance.[56]

3.3 Consequences of the Failure of UIP

A straightforward conclusion of the UIP tests is that central banks in reality cannot rely on the theoretical models of Svensson and Ball with regard to their exchange rate approach, i.e. it seems difficult to influence the exchange rate with a single instrument (open market operations to control short-term interest rates. The exchange rate seems to behave fundamentally different to what these models assume. Consequently, link 1 in Figure 6, i.e. perfect control of the exchange rate via short-term interest rates is essentially missing in reality. In order to have influence over the exchange rate it would be desirable for a central bank to have a sec-

55 This result is also found by Flood and Rose (1996) who study the performance of uncovered interest parity within fixed exchange rate regimes and conclude that the "[...] deviation from uncovered interest parity, known as the 'forward discount puzzle' does not appear to characterise our fixed exchange rate data set." (p. 751).

56 Interestingly, Svensson also refers to foreign exchange intervention in his comment (though he does not interpret them as an additional policy tool for central banks). He asks: "Most macro studies find little or no effect of sterilised intervention. If they are correct, why do central banks keep doing it?" (Svensson, 1996: 300). He suggests that the micro approach to the exchange rate might help to answer this question.

ond instrument with which the exchange rate can be influences more effectively. Such an instrument provide foreign exchange interventions through which a central bank directly influences the exchange rate by purchasing and selling foreign currency against domestic currency.

Consider again our figure of a stylised model of monetary policy, this time including the additional instrument of interventions:

Figure 6: Introducing interventions in the conventional view of monetary policy

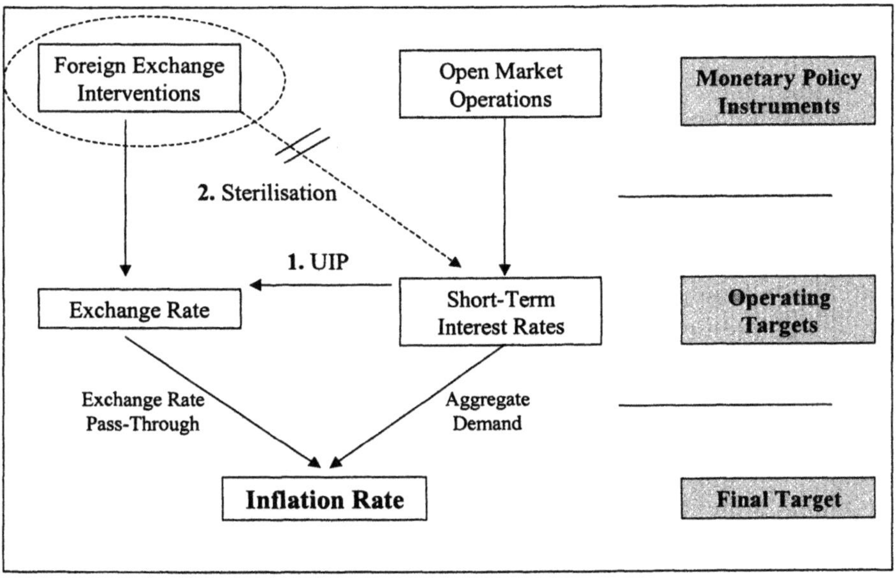

Note: UIP denotes uncovered interest parity.

In order to be an independent instrument besides open market operations, these interventions need to be sterilised. Regarding Figure 6 this means that link 2 between interventions and short-term interest rates need to be cut off. By sterilising foreign exchange interventions a central bank undertakes operations that cancel the change in the domestic money supply caused by the initial intervention and thus leave interest rates unchanged. In the following we will elaborate more on the rationale and the mechanics of sterilised foreign exchange interventions and will analyse whether inflation targeting central banks routinely sterilise their foreign exchange operations (= question 2 on our list of issues mentioned in chapter 1).

4 Sterilised Interventions as an Additional Policy Instrument

"Would concerns about the level of the exchange rate in the context of foreign exchange market crisis better be dealt with by an interest rate response than by direct intervention using reserves? The answer is probably yes [...]",
(Archer and Halliday (Reserve Bank of New Zealand Financial Markets Department), 1998: 351)

4.1 Explaining and Interpreting Sterilised Interventions

4.1.1 Channels for Influencing Exchange Rates

Theoretically, there are two possible ways for a central bank to influence the exchange rate:

1. indirectly via interest rates
2. directly through foreign exchange market interventions.

The first channel works through the uncovered interest parity as shown in the last chapter. It is indirect in that it relies on investors to effect the necessary transactions which cause the exchange rate to move. These transactions, however, can be effected by the central bank, too. By intervening in the foreign exchange market, i.e. by directly buying or selling the domestic currency the monetary authorities can influence exchange rates. The statement above of the Reserve Bank of New Zealand points to these two possibilities – and argues that the interest rate response is more adequate. This answer is in line with the theoretical models of Svensson and Ball who do not take interventions into account. As our test of UIP showed, however, the indirect channel, i.e. a close link between exchange rate changes and interest rate differentials according to UIP is not existent in practice. Comparing both interest rate policy and interventions, Kim (2002) finds that "foreign exchange intervention shocks have a larger effect on the exchange rate than conventional monetary policy shocks." (p. 11).[57] Consequently, we propose a

[57] As a consequence, Kim (2002) suggests that "it is important to consider foreign exchange intervention in the studies on monetary policy and the exchange rate." (p. 17).

closer look at the second channel as an alternative monetary policy tool which is so far rather neglected in theories of inflation targeting.

It is important to note at this point, that the use of foreign exchange interventions does not mean that the exchange rate is kept fixed or controlled all the time.[58] Rather, it is a tool that, under floating exchange rates, should be used only when the exchange rate is threatening the objectives of monetary policy, i.e. the achievement of the inflation target. Consider, for example, this statement of the Swedish Riksbank: "[...] because the target for monetary policy is to stabilise inflation in the medium-term perspective, there is normally no motivation to intervene in the foreign exchange market [...]. However, the issue is complicated by the fact that substantial deviations from the expected exchange rate path on which monetary policy is based can increase uncertainty as to whether the monetary policy target will be achieved. Interventions in the foreign exchange market could from this point of view be regarded as a means of contributing to a future development of the exchange rate that aided the inflation rate to develop in line with the Riksbank's target [...]." (Riksbank, 2002: 5).

Such an exchange rate regime can be defined as managed floating in the terms of the IMF nomenclature (see next box). The idea of managed floating, i.e. irregular interventions to move the exchange rate in the desired direction (in the case of inflation targeting to help achieve the inflation target) without publicly announcing an official exchange rate target, is not to control the exchange rate on an ongoing basis. Rather the idea is that the central bank acts like mentioned by Dominguez and Frankel (1993a): "The foreign exchange market is a herd of steers and central banks are herd dogs." (p. 2). That means the central bank steps into the market whenever exchange rates have moved in a direction that is not compatible with underlying fundamentals and provides a threat to the objectives of the central bank.

58 Thus, foreign exchange intervention as a policy tool in the context of inflation targeting differs fundamentally from strategies such as fixed exchange rates.

IMF Classification of exchange rate regimes

Exchange rate with no separate legal tender: The currency of another country circulates as the sole legal tender, or the member belongs to a monetary or currency union in which the same legal tender is shared by the members of the union.

Currency board arrangements: A monetary regime based on an implicit legislative commitment to exchange domestic currency for a specified foreign currency at a fixed exchange rate, combined with restrictions on the issuing authority to ensure the fulfilment of its legal obligation.

Conventional pegged arrangements: The country pegs its currency (formally or de facto) at a fixed rate to a major currency or a basket of currencies, where the exchange rate fluctuates within a narrow margin of at most +/- 1% around the central rate.

Pegged exchange rate with horizontal bands: The value of the currency is maintained within margins of fluctuation around a formal or de facto fixed peg that are wider than +/- 1% around the central rate.

Crawling peg: The currency is adjusted periodically in small amounts at a fixed, preannounced rate or in response to changes in selective quantitative indicators.

Crawling band: The currency is maintained within certain fluctuation margins around a central rate that is adjusted periodically at a fixed preannounced rate or in response to changes in selective quantitative indicators.

Managed floating: The monetary authority influences the movements of the exchange rate through active intervention in the foreign exchange market without specifying, or precommitting to, a preannounced path for the exchange rate.

Independently floating: The exchange rate is market determined, with any foreign exchange intervention aimed at moderating the rate of change and preventing undue fluctuations in the exchange rate, rather than at establishing a level for it.

Source: IMF Annual Report on exchange arrangements and exchange restrictions 1999.

Although there have been several discussions of the monetary policy of inflation targeting countries (see Bernanke et al., 1999; Mishkin and Schmidt-Hebbel, 2001; Debelle, 1997) none of them explicitly addresses the issue of foreign exchange rate occurs frequently but solely with respect to the setting of interest rates. This is insofar problematic as interest rates also affect the domestic economy and thus a reaction of interest rates to exchange rate fluctuations might actually worsen the performance of monetary policy with respect to output and inflation. Mishkin and Schmidt-Hebbel (2001) conclude for inflation targeting: "The discussion above therefore suggests that targeting on an exchange rate is likely to worsen the performance of monetary policy." (p. 24). This is explained by the fact that changing the interest rate in response to exchange rate fluctuations that are not caused by underlying fundamentals has adverse effects on the domestic economy. Thus, it is important that in trying to influence exchange rates the central bank needs a tool that leaves interest rates unchanged but nevertheless is effective in influencing the exchange rate. When using foreign exchange interventions the central bank therefore has to make sure that these are always sterilised.

4.1.2 Sterilised Interventions as a Monetary Policy Instrument

A common argument in international finance discussions is that foreign exchange interventions do affect interest rates and thus are not an independent tool for the central bank. Indeed, if the central bank buys or sells domestic currency, the monetary base is changed and thus has an effect on interest rates similar to a domestic open market operation.

Consider the following stylised central bank balance sheet:

Figure 7: Stylised central bank balance sheet

Assets	**Liabilities**
Foreign Assets	Monetary Base
Domestic Assets	

Any sale or purchase of central bank assets (domestic or foreign) results in an equivalent change in the supply of monetary base (central bank liabilities):

$$\Delta MB = \Delta FA + \Delta DA \tag{4.1}$$

with MB as monetary base (which comprises deposits held by private banks and currency in circulation), FA as foreign assets and DA as domestic assets. Any increase or decrease in FA or DA simultaneously affects MB and therefore interest rates. Consider, for example, an intervention in support of the home currency (aimed at appreciating the home currency). This transaction involves a purchase of own currency against a sale of foreign currency. The central bank thus sells part of its foreign assets and receives home currency. Taken together this transaction leads to a decline in the foreign assets and a decline in the monetary base of the central bank (since the commercial banks' account with the central bank is debited with the equivalent amount of home currency that the central bank bought with its foreign exchange). Such an operation is called unsterilised intervention since the operation by the central bank involves a change in the monetary base that is not offset (sterilised). However, a central bank might also chose to equalise the change in FA (DA) resulting from a foreign exchange intervention through a subsequent change in DA (FA) in order to leave MB unchanged. This is the central idea of sterilisation:

$$\Delta FA = -\Delta DA \tag{4.2}$$

It implies "that in the case of an increase (decrease) in the monetary base induced by interventions, the central bank reduces (increases) its credits to the domestic banking system" (Bofinger, 2001: 388). To this end the central bank buys or sells domestic assets from the public and thereby increases or decreases its monetary liabilities to the level that existed prior to the intervention operation. This operation is usually conducted simultaneously or with a very short time lag. Thus, a sterilised intervention simply includes a change from net foreign assets in net domestic assets.

$$\Delta NFA + \Delta NDA = \Delta MB = 0 \tag{4.3}$$

An unsterilised intervention on the other hand is equivalent to domestic monetary policy since it changes the monetary base.[59] This explains why many critics argue that sterilised interventions cannot be effective from a theoretical point of view: As monetary theory explains exchange rate movements with changes in the money supply (via interest rates and expectations) between countries there should be no effect on exchange rates if the monetary base is left unchanged (or put differently: If the exchange rate is viewed as the relative price of monies then sterilised interventions do not have an effect).[60]

When the European Central Bank, for example, intervenes in support of the euro, i.e. buys euro against US dollar, the monetary base decreases and money market interest rates will tend to rise. In order to sterilise the liquidity effect (i.e. supply the banking system with the liquidity it took out of the market by buying euros), the ECB has several options (see Bofinger, 2001).

1. It can use outright open-market operations to buy short-term bonds from private banks.

---

59 While in a domestic market operation domestic assets of the central bank are used, foreign assets are used in a foreign exchange intervention. The resulting effect on the monetary base, however, is equal in both cases which is why unsterilised interventions are equivalent to domestic open market operations regarding their effects on the monetary base.

60 The question whether sterilised interventions can still be effective is analysed in detail in chapter 4.2.

2. It can extent the amount of liquidity supplied in the main refinancing operation.
3. Through its marginal refinancing facility the ECB has an upper limit for the short-term interest rate in place. Should money market rates increase following intervention operations, banks can always borrow money at this rate and thus satisfy their additional liquidity demand.

Dominguez and Frankel (1993a) describe how sterilisation works in practice at the US Federal Reserve Bank: "The Federal Reserve Bank of New York is reported to fully and automatically sterilise its intervention operations on a daily basis. In practice, the foreign exchange trading room immediately reports its dollar sales to the open market trading room, which then buys that many fewer bonds so that the daily money supply is unaffected." (p. 87).[61]

The distinction between sterilised and unsterilised intervention is very important in our context. Since unsterilised intervention is nothing else than a domestic monetary operation that changes the monetary base it has a direct effect on interest rates. Thus, unsterilised intervention is a complement or an alternative to changing the domestic interest rate. Sterilised intervention on the other hand is independent from domestic open market operations since it solely affects exchange rates and leaves interest rates unchanged. Sterilised intervention and domestic interest rate policy are therefore two independent instruments that the central bank has available.

[61] Any US foreign exchange interventions are undertaken by the Federal Reserve Bank of New York on behalf of the Federal Reserve System and the US Treasury (see www.ny.frb.org).

Sterilisation: A practical example

To illustrate a practical sterilisation procedure consider the following case of the European Central Bank (ECB) intervening in support of the US dollar, i.e. US dollars are bought, euros are sold (see Bofinger and Wollmershäuser, 2001: 25-26). The following parties are involved: A European investor initially holds 100 € as deposits and a euro area commercial bank holds 100 € as reserves with the ECB. These reserves were obtained through a security repurchase agreement (repo credit) that are conducted on a weekly basis and have a maturity of up to two weeks. The monetary base in the euro area initially amounts to 100 € (equal to the commercial bank's reserves held with the ECB).

1. Intervention

In a first step the investor sells his 100 $ deposit to the euro area commercial bank in exchange for euro deposits (a US$/€ exchange rate of 1.00 is assumed – the commercial bank thus credits the investor's account with 100 €). The euro area commercial bank in turn sells the 100 $ in the foreign exchange market. To prevent an effect of this sale on the US$/€ exchange rate, the ECB then chooses to intervene and buys the 100 $ from the euro area commercial bank. Consequently, the ECB foreign exchange reserve holdings (asset side) increase by 100 $. As the ECB credits the commercial bank's account with 100 € the monetary base (liability side of the ECB) increase by 100 €. Thus, after the intervention operation of the ECB the monetary base is 200 € in contrast to the initial level of 100 €.

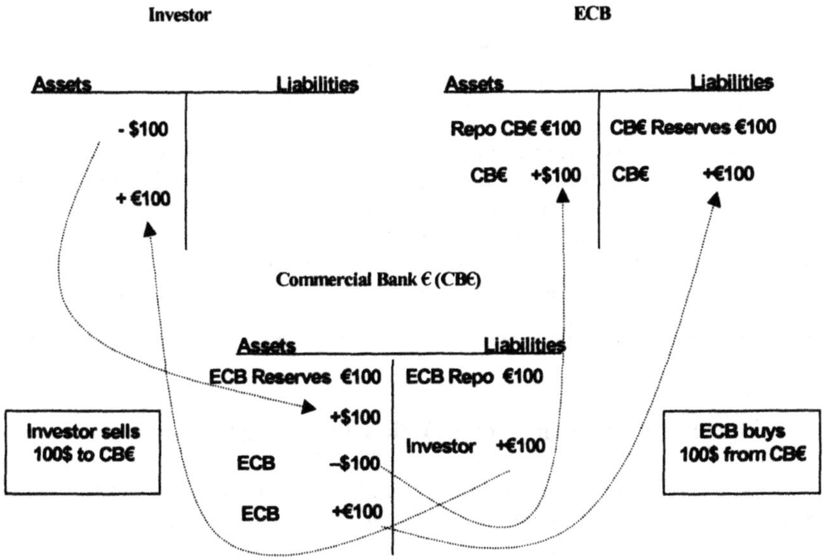

2. Sterilisation

In order to sterilise the increase in the monetary base caused by the initial intervention the ECB does not revolve the repurchase agreement (repo). This reduces the credit to the banking system and thus the reserves of the commercial bank at the ECB decline by 100 €. Hence, the increase in the monetary base due to the intervention is offset and the monetary base amounts to 100 € just as before the intervention.

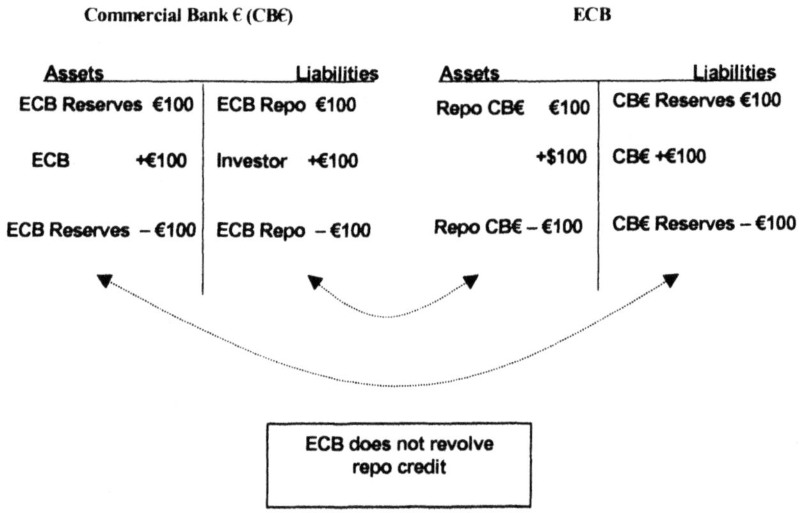

At the end of the intervention and the sterilisation process, the ECB – instead of the investor – holds the 100 $. The amount of € that is held by non-banks (the investor) has increased by 100 €. However, the ECB compensated this by reducing its € repurchase agreement with the commercial bank by 100 €. Taken together, the ECB simply swapped a domestic asset (in the form of the repo credit to the commercial bank) for a foreign asset (the $ amount which increases its foreign exchange reserve level).

4.1.3 Sterilisation Evidence for Inflation Targeting Countries

In order to analyse whether sterilised interventions are used as an additional policy instrument in inflation targeting countries it is necessary to look if foreign exchange operations are indeed sterilised. Table 7 provides an overview of statements about official sterilisation policies in the five inflation targeting countries of our sample. As can be seen, all of them state that they do sterilise any intervention operations. This suggests that should these countries use foreign exchange interventions, they would use them as an *additional* policy tool by leaving short-term interest rates unchanged.

Table 7: Official sterilisation policies

Central bank	Statement about sterilisation
Bank of England	"If the Government so instructs, the Bank, acting as its agent, will intervene in the foreign exchange markets by buying or selling the Government's foreign exchange reserves. All such intervention will be automatically sterilised." (HM Treasury, 1997)
Sveriges Riksbank	"The Riksbank stated publicly that its interventions are all sterilised." (Sjöö and Sweeney, 2001: 223)
Bank of Canada	"If the Bank wants to moderate a decline in the price of the Canadian dollar, it will buy dollars in foreign exchange markets in exchange for other currencies, mainly U.S. dollars. [...] To make sure that the Bank's purchases do not take money out of circulation and create a shortage of Canadian dollars, the Bank "sterilizes" its purchases by redepositing the same amount of Canadian dollar balances in the financial system." (Backgrounders: Intervention in the exchange market, available at www.bankofcanada.ca)
Reserve Bank of Australia	"This is called sterilised intervention and it is the form in which the Reserve Bank has always undertaken its intervention." (Rankin, 2000: 10)
Reserve Bank of New Zealand	"The default option would be that any intervention would be sterilised. Any decision not to sterilise would require a separate decision – a decision to engage in a quantitative easing of monetary policy." (Michael Reddell, Head of RBNZ Financial Markets Department)[1]

Note: [1]This quote was provided upon Email request.

However, to see if policymakers actually back up their words with actions regarding the sterilisation of interventions we analyse the actual sterilisation behaviour of the inflation targeting countries by estimating a simple sterilisation equation for all countries. This is done by using the following test equation (see Bofinger and Wollmershäuser, 2001)[62]

$$\Delta NDA_t = \alpha_1 + \beta_1 \Delta NFA_t + \beta_2 \Delta NDA_{t-1} + \varepsilon_t \tag{4.4}$$

with NDA as net domestic assets and NFA as net foreign assets. Under complete sterilisation we would expect $\beta_1 = -1$, i.e. changes in foreign reserves would be completely offset in order to leave the monetary base unchanged. For example, an increase in NFA resulting from a purchase of foreign currency would be countered with a decrease in NDA (e.g. outright sales of short-term bonds to the banking system). Our estimation is by OLS and monthly frequency data are taken from the

62 The lagged dependent variable is included to capture other influences on NDA than sterilisation.

IMF's International Financial Statistics. The sample range is 1990:01 to 2001:11 and for each country only the period of inflation targeting was included.

Table 8: Regression results

Country	α_1	β_1	β_2	adj.R^2	P value of fourth-order LM-test
Australia	90.64 (154.02)	-0.73*** (0.10)	0.02 (0.08)	0.33	0.42
Canada	0.13*** (0.03)	-1.03*** (0.07)	-0.02 (0.06)	0.73	0.26
New Zealand	10.94*** (3.34)	-1.03*** (0.04)	-0.07* (0.04)	0.87	0.88
Sweden	0.06 (0.99)	-0.76*** (0.12)	0.02 (0.08)	0.26	0.12
United Kingdom	-0.02 (0.10)	-1.33*** (0.19)	0.04 (0.10)	0.48	0.09

Note: ***,**,* denotes significance at the 10, 5 and 1% level, respectively. An MA(1)-term was added in the equations for Canada, New Zealand and United Kingdom to correct for serial correlation.

As can be seen from Table 8 the coefficient β_1 is highly significant in all countries and close to one. Wald coefficient tests indicated that the hypothesis of $\beta_1 = -1$ could not be rejected for New Zealand, Canada and the UK (on the 5% significance level). This supports the view that inflation targeting countries usually offset most of the changes in the monetary base that result from a change in their foreign assets, i.e. sterilise any foreign exchange interventions. Consequently, foreign exchange interventions of these central banks should not affect their level of short-term interest rates and thus can be regarded as an additional independent policy instrument. Accordingly, the question whether inflation targeting central banks regularly sterilise their interventions (question 2 of our list of issues in the first chapter) can be approved.

4.1.4 Managed Floating in Theory

Prior to analysing whether sterilised interventions are actually effective in influencing exchange rates, we shortly give an overview of the concept of managed floating as presented by Bofinger and Wollmershäuser (2001) in order to give some more theoretical background for the use of sterilised interventions.[63]

Bofinger and Wollmershäuser (2001) interpret managed floating "as a comprehensive monetary policy strategy within the two extreme cases of absolutely fixed and independently floating exchange rates." (p. 22). A central bank that conducts a policy of temporarily intervening in the foreign exchange market can be classified as a regime of "managed floating". It can be distinguished from other regime

[63] See also Goldstein (2002) as another proponent of the concept of managed floating.

forms by the fact that the central bank intervenes without publicly announcing an exchange rate target (see Box IMF Classification). Bofinger and Wollmershäuser (2001), Calvo and Reinhart (2000), Reinhart (2000) and Levy-Yeyati and Sturzenegger (1999) show that managed floating is indeed performed by an increasingly large number of countries. A common finding of these studies is also that countries actually often conduct a different exchange rate regime than officially declared especially those with an officially independent floating regime. As Calvo and Reinhart (2000) state: "Countries that say they allow their exchange rate to float mostly do not – there seems to be an epidemic case of 'fear of floating'." (p. 2).

With the background of the empirical failure of the uncovered interest parity it seems natural for central banks to use the tool of foreign exchange intervention and manage their exchange rates. Bofinger and Wollmershäuser (2001) show how central banks can use the tool of sterilised interventions in their monetary policy strategy. Their approach is based on the assumption that both interest rates and exchange rates can simultaneously serve as operating targets as they can some extent be controlled perfectly by the central bank (interest rates through domestic open market operations and exchange rates through foreign exchange interventions).[64] To see how both operating targets should be set they distinguish between *internal* and *external* equilibrium (which above all is important for small open economies).

Internal equilibrium requires that the loss function of the central bank is minimised. Both operating targets are combined in a so-called monetary conditions index – a measure that incorporates interest and exchange rates with individual, country-specific weights.[65] Such an MCI has also been used in the model of Ball (1999). However, Ball assumes that this MCI can only be influenced by interest rate policy. Bofinger and Wollmershäuser (2001) deviate from this assumption by introducing sterilised foreign exchange interventions with which the exchange rate can be controlled independently from the interest rate.

The *external* equilibrium in their approach requires that the exchange rate follows a path that is consistent with uncovered interest parity. Since in reality floating exchange rates do not follow such a path (see our analysis above) the central bank has to use sterilised interventions in order to fulfil UIP continuously.

64 The exchange rate is only perfectly controllable in a situation of appreciation. In a situation of continuous depreciation the level of central bank foreign exchange reserves limits the ability to control exchange rate movements (see Bofinger and Wollmershäuser, 2001: 21).

65 In their model, the MCI consists of the real interest rate and the real exchange rate. However, since they assume sticky prices in the short run, both variables can be controlled directly with their nominal counterparts.

Figure 8: Managed floating in small open economies

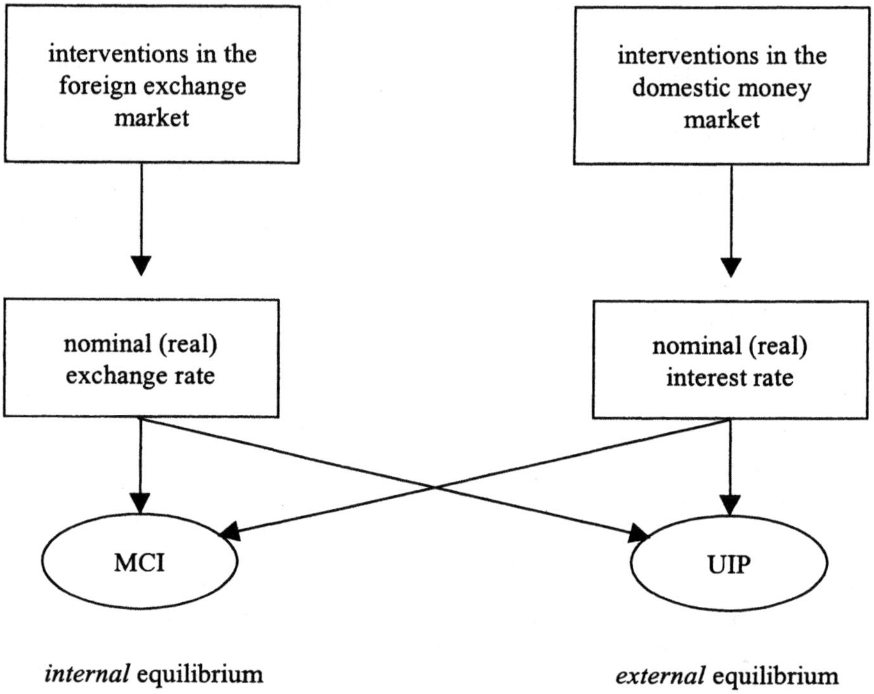

Note: As sticky prices are assumed in the short run, both nominal and real exchange and interest rates can be controlled by the central bank. Source: Bofinger and Wollmershäuser, 2001: 30.

Note the major difference between the Bofinger and Wollmershäuser (2001) model and earlier work on Monetary Conditions Indices (e.g. Ball, 1999): The central bank has two independent instruments – short-term interest rates and sterilised interventions. Although MCIs have been implemented in practice it was always assumed that it could be controlled with short-term interest rates only. The Bank of Canada was the first central bank who used an MCI and it was followed by the Reserve Bank of New Zealand in 1996.[66] However, in both central banks only short-term interest rates are declared as policy instruments.

The analysis of Bofinger and Wollmershäuser (2001) shows that there is indeed a systematic scope for foreign exchange intervention in monetary policy. The fact that achieving the inflation targets is the only aim of monetary policy does not

66 For the Canadian MCI the weights of interest rates to exchange rates are 3:1 and for the New Zealand MCI the weight of interest rates to exchange rates is 2:1. For the New Zealand MCI this means that a 2% rise in the exchange rate has the same effect on future inflation as a 100 basis point (one percentage point) increase in short-term interest rates (accordingly, the relative influence of the exchange rate versus the interest rate is smaller in Canada with its 3:1 weighting). See Bernanke et al., 1999.

mean that the exchange rate needs to be floated purely (above all given the experience that floating exchange rates do mostly tend to follow a random walk that is not predictable by the central bank). On the contrary, as long as exchange rate policy helps to achieve the inflation target there is no argument against measures to influence the exchange rate. This is also one of the results of the open economy models of inflation targeting presented earlier that stressed the importance of the exchange rate channel. However, they focus solely on the interest rate channel to influence exchange rates and thereby neglect the possibility of using foreign exchange intervention.

The role of sterilised intervention is also highlighted by Dominguez and Frankel (1993a) who write: "If sterilised interventions [...] can influence the exchange rate, authorities have a second instrument with which to achieve internal and external targets simultaneously." (p. 58). As Isard (1995: 77) mentions, sterilised interventions and UIP are connected in the following way: If UIP holds all the time, then sterilised interventions would not be effective since they do not change the current interest rates (as any effects on the monetary base are offset). Only if sterilised interventions signalled a future change in interest rate policy, the exchange rate today would be affected. Furthermore, if the interest rate channel provides an effective tool for influencing the exchange rate then interventions would not be necessary at all.

Mishkin and Schmidt-Hebbel (2001) acknowledge that "[...] interventions might be necessary at times because of the possibility that such interventions can prevent dynamics in the micro structure of this market that may lead to exchange rate fluctuations that are divorced from fundamentals. However, continuing exchange market interventions, particularly unsterilised ones, are likely to be counterproductive because they are not transparent." (p. 24). The last point of the lack of transparency of interventions might be the answer to the question why central banks mostly keep their intervention operations secret. This does not necessarily have to be a superior strategy. Imagine that central banks could communicate the rationale of sterilised interventions, namely to address exchange rate fluctuations that have negative effects on the economy, without affecting domestic monetary policy. This procedure might instead serve to understand the central banks' operations better and thus would enhance transparency. A major negative side effect of using interest rates to influence exchange rates in the desired direction is that "the change in interest rates necessary to induce the appropriate movement in the exchange rate in the short term, may cause an undesired movement in domestic demand and inflation in the medium term." (Debelle, 1997: 15). Accordingly, interest rate setting tends to be very volatile. By using sterilised foreign exchange interventions the exchange rate channel could be used without the adverse effects on interest rates.

These statements show that sterilised interventions are indeed a topic, albeit a small one, in the current economic literature. However, to incorporate them into a strategy of monetary policy is still unusual – the Bofinger and Wollmershäuser (2001) model is a first step in this direction.

4.1.5 Limitations of Sterilised Interventions

When interpreting sterilised interventions as an additional instrument of a central bank and comparing them to open-market operations to control short-term interest rates one also has to note important differences between these two instruments. One of the differences is the limitation of the central bank to prevent a depreciation of the domestic currency. This is a direct consequence of the limited foreign currency reserves that the monetary authorities have available. While an appreciation of the own currency can always be prevented (due to the unlimited ability of a central bank to print domestic currency that can be sold against foreign currency), a depreciation can only be countered as long as the central bank has enough foreign exchange reserves.[67] This asymmetry is a fundamental difference between the intervention instrument and open-market operations in the domestic money market: Since the central bank is a monopolist in the supply of domestic currency it can control the domestic price for it (=short-term interest rates) perfectly. Whenever interest rates are above target, the central bank supplies additional liquidity to the market and vice versa. This procedure works symmetrically for increasing and decreasing short-term interest rates.

A further issue in the discussion of interventions are the costs that are associated with the sterilisation process.[68] These consist of a valuation component and an interest rate component. A central bank purchase of foreign currency, for example, bears the risk of exchange rate changes. If the domestic currency appreciates against the foreign currency following the intervention, then the central bank incurs a loss (as its purchased foreign currency units decline in value). However, as pointed out in Friedman (1953), the central bank only incurs a valuation loss if the intervention is unsuccessful. Consider the following example: The Swedish Riksbank purchases US dollars and sells Swedish krona in order to depreciate its domestic currency. If the depreciation materialises, the Riksbank makes a profit since its purchased US dollar holding increase in value. Thus, a successful intervention is always associated with a valuation profit for the central bank.

In addition to valuation losses or profits a central bank also has to consider profits (or losses) that stem from interest earnings. Put simply, these profits depend on the interest rate level of the currencies that are purchased or sold by the central bank. Consider the again the case of the Swedish Riksbank purchasing US dollars: If interest rates for US dollar assets are higher than those for Swedish krona assets then the Riksbank makes a profit by swapping its domestic currency for foreign currency. If, however, interest rates in Sweden are higher than in the US then the sale of higher-yielding kronas for lower-yielding US dollars would result in a loss (i.e. opportunity costs for investing in a lower yielding currency) for the Riksbank. Bofinger and Wollmershäuser (2001) show that sterilisation costs are zero if the central bank intervention leads to a change in exchange rates that is

[67] This inability of central bank to stop sudden and massive capital outflows is exemplified in the event of currency crises: a fixed exchange rate can only be defended as long as the central bank has enough foreign currency reserves.

[68] See for the following Bofinger and Wollmershäuser (2001).

equal to the interest rate differential between the two currencies, i.e. if uncovered interest parity holds.

4.2 Effectiveness of Sterilised Interventions: A Review of the Literature

"Interventions represent a more potent policy instrument than most officials and especially most outside analysts have in recent years imagined it to be. Hence, it can make a more significant contribution both to policy now and to the ongoing debate over how best to organise the international monetary system."
(Dominguez and Frankel, 1993a: 140)

4.2.1 The Intervention Debate

One factor that is responsible for the neglect of sterilised interventions in the theory of monetary policy so far is the scepticism of many economists regarding their efficiency. In order to be an additional policy instrument for a central bank, sterilised interventions need to be able to have an influence on the exchange rate just like open market operations in the domestic money market influence short-term interest rates.

The debate over the effectiveness of sterilised foreign exchange interventions has been going on in the literature over the past decade. Although many academics are still deeply sceptic about interventions there have been numerous studies that found a significant effect of such operations on the exchange rate. However, there is currently no consensus in the literature. Interestingly, the case of sterilised interventions seems to be treated fundamentally different in theory and in practice. Notwithstanding the fact that academics are sceptic about interventions there have been intensive intervention operations by central banks in the past years. As Lewis (1995) writes: "Whether these [sterilised] interventions affect the exchange rate or not remains an issue of active empirical research. Nevertheless, it is clear that central bankers continue to intervene. This obvious fact has led researchers to search for reasons why intervention may be effective in changing the exchange rate." (p. 1935).

While there exist many insightful studies on interventions, a common characteristic of them is that they overwhelmingly focus on interventions in the DM/US$-market. However, this is one of the markets where the fewest interventions have taken place, i.e. the number of intervention events is limited. As illustrated in Table 9 the frequency of US interventions in the period 1990-97 has been significantly smaller than Australian intervention. These numbers refer to the official data that is released by both central banks which means they only include transactions that are officially characterised as interventions. During the period 1990 to 1997 the number of intervention days of the Reserve Bank of Australia has been nearly eight times higher than the number of US intervention days. While the probability of an US intervention on a trading day is only 4% it is over 30% for the Australian foreign exchange market. The figures also illustrate that the majority of Australian interventions was aimed at a depreciation of the Australian dollar. This is different for the US interventions. However, the average volume of interventions is significantly smaller in the Australian case. This is surely due to the fact that the market for Australian dollars is small in relation to the market for US dollars. A look at the statistics of the BIS survey of foreign exchange activity of 2001 reveals that daily market volume in US$/EUR is about 352 billion US$ and volume in US$/Yen is about 230 billion US$. In contrast, the volume in US$/A$ only amounts to 47 billion US$.[69] The relation between market size and intervention size, however, has not been studied in detail yet due to the lack of official intervention data from central banks.[70]

Table 9: US and Australian official intervention compared

	US Federal Reserve	Reserve Bank of Australia
Number of intervention days between 1.1.1990 – 31.12.1997	82	647
Probability of intervention	3.93%	31.81%
Probability of a purchase of domestic currency	2.73%	6.59%
Probability of a sale of domestic currency	1.20%	25.22%
Average intervention volume in US$	262.96	30.86

Note: The statistics are calculated using daily intervention data for the period 1.1.1990-31.12.1997. The Australian intervention volume was converted from A$ into US$ using the exchange rate at end-March 2001 (0.489 US$ per A$). Source: US Federal Reserve, Reserve Bank of Australia, own calculations.

The objective of this chapter is to review the existing literature on the effectiveness of sterilised interventions with a focus on new approaches that take a look at the market microstructure and with a focus on the empirical relevance of these models. We do not perform own empirical tests of the effectiveness as this is not our aim: We are interested in studying actual intervention behaviour and try to explain the motivation of their use. Years of sceptical analysis of economists regarding interventions have not lead to central banks refraining from this tool.

[69] See BIS, 2001, Table 4.

[70] There are only a number of central banks which provide official intervention data as a time series for researchers (to our knowledge these are the Bundesbank, the Swiss National Bank, the US Federal Reserve, the Reserve Bank of Australia and a number of smaller emerging market countries). Some central banks provide on their websites information about interventions on the day they occur but do not publish them in time series format (like the Bank of Canada or the Sveriges Rikbank). Usually, also the volume of intervention is kept secret.

4.2.2 The Inefficiency of Sterilised Interventions in Monetary Models

Monetary models were predominantly used for exchange rate determination in the early 1970s after the breakdown of the Bretton Woods system.[71] The main assumption in these models is that the exchange rate is the relative price of two monies and is thus determined by the relative domestic and foreign supply and demand for money.

There exist two variants of models: The first assumes perfectly flexible prices and therefore concludes that purchasing power parity holds continuously whereas in the second variant sticky prices are assumed which consequently leads to the conclusion that purchasing power parity is achieved only gradually. We will present a simple model of the flexible price monetary theory (taken from Taylor (1995)) and show why sterilised interventions do not lead to exchange rate effects in this model.

The demand m_t for money in both the domestic and foreign country (denoted with an asterisk) is presumed to depend positively on real income y_t and the price level p_t and negatively on the nominal interest rate i_t (all variables except interest rates are in logarithms):

$$m_t = p_t + \kappa y_t - \theta i_t \tag{4.5}$$

$$m_t^* = p_t^* + \kappa^* y_t^* - \theta^* i_t^* \tag{4.6}$$

where κ and θ are the income elasticity and interest rate semielasticity of the demand for money which are assumed to be identical across countries. With flexible prices purchasing power parity holds all the time:

$$s_t = p_t - p_t^* \tag{4.7}$$

where s_t is measured in domestic currency per unit of foreign currency (an increase in foreign prices relative to domestic prices leads to an appreciation of the domestic currency). Solving the system for the exchange rate yields

$$s_t = m_t - m_t^* - \kappa y_t + \kappa^* y_t^* + \theta i_t - \theta^* i_t^* \tag{4.8}$$

Now an increase in the domestic money supply relative to foreign money supply leads to an increase in s_t (=depreciation) since the money supply increase leads to an instantaneous increase in the price level which via purchasing power parity results in a depreciation of the exchange rate.

The assumption of continuously purchasing power parity proved to be rather unrealistic in the 1970s as real exchange rates were highly volatile.[72] As a consequence, sticky prices were introduced into the monetary model by Dornbusch (1976) which led to the creation of the so-called overshooting model. He showed

71 This paragraph draws on Taylor (1995) and Spolander (1999).

72 If purchasing power parity holds continuously, the real exchange rate is a constant.

that exchange rates tend to overshoot their equilibrium values and purchasing power parity is only achieved in the medium to longer term as variations in interest and exchange rates compensate for the sticky prices of goods. The adjustment mechanism is thus slightly different: A rise in domestic money supply leads to a rise in real money supply M / P since prices are sticky. This in turn results in a decrease in nominal interest rates and consequently capital outflows lead to a depreciation of the exchange rate until the expected exchange rate appreciation just equals the interest differential between the home and foreign country (uncovered interest parity holds). However, in the medium run prices will increase because of the rise in domestic money supply and interest rates will increase again since the real money supply decreases. As a consequence the exchange rate adjusts gradually to its long-run equilibrium (purchasing power parity).

The role of interventions in both variants of the monetary model is simple. Since the exchange rate adjusts to changes in the relative money supply it is straightforward that only unsterilised interventions (that have an effect on the monetary base) can influence exchange rates. Sterilised interventions, on the other hand, are not effective according to monetary models. Unsurprisingly, the general attitude of academics in the 1970s was against sterilised interventions even though central banks during this period were rather active in foreign exchange markets. However, the monetary model posits assumptions that researchers relaxed more and more since the empirical evidence on monetary models was very weak (see Taylor, 1995: 28-30; Meese and Rogoff, 1983). One of these assumptions is that domestic and foreign assets are perfect substitutes which means that investors are indifferent between both.

4.2.3 The Portfolio Balance Channel of Interventions

Unlike monetary models of exchange rate determination portfolio balance models assume that domestic and foreign currency bonds are imperfect substitutes. This corresponds to the idea that investors are risk-averse which in this context means that they are not indifferent to the currency composition of their portfolios. "The imperfect substitutability of domestic and foreign assets [...] is equivalent to assuming that there is a risk premium separating expected depreciation and the domestic-foreign interest differential, and in the portfolio balance model this risk premium will be a function of relative domestic and foreign debt outstanding." (Taylor, 1995: 30).[73] Since in monetary models individuals were indifferent as to the currency composition of their bond portfolios there is no role for a bond market. Also the wealth distribution effects of current account imbalances are taken into account in portfolio balance models. The exchange rate brings the asset market in equilibrium.

---

73 Consequently, the uncovered interest parity condition does not prevail in portfolio balance models (see Isard, 1995: 107). It does, however, prevail in monetary models since perfect substitutability in these models does not require that investors be given a risk premium for holding a particular currency.

The wealth of the domestic agents consists of money M, domestic bonds B and foreign bonds B^* (multiplied with the exchange rate S, which is measured as domestic currency per unit of foreign currency)

$$W \equiv M + B + SB^* \tag{4.9}$$

$$M^D = M^D(i, i^* + E[\Delta S]) \text{ with } M_1^D < 0, M_2^D < 0 \tag{4.10}$$

$$B^D = B^D(i, i^* + E[\Delta S]) \text{ with } B_1^D > 0, B_2^D < 0 \tag{4.11}$$

$$SB^{D*} = B^{D*}(i, i^* + E[\Delta S]) \text{ with } B_1^{D*} < 0, B_2^{D*} > 0 \tag{4.12}$$

According to (4.9), foreign agents hold foreign money and domestic and foreign bonds. Equations (4.10) to (4.12) represent demand functions for money, domestic bonds and foreign bonds. The term $E[\Delta S]$ denotes the expected depreciation of the nominal exchange rate and X_k denotes the partial derivative of X with respect to the k-th argument. While the demand for money is negatively dependent on both home and foreign interest rates, the demand for home (foreign) bonds depends positively (negatively) on domestic interest rates and negatively (positively) on foreign interest rates plus expected exchange rate depreciation. The supply of foreign bonds held by domestic residents changes with the current account, which comprises the trade balance T and interest income

$$\Delta B^* = T(S/P) + i^* B^* \tag{4.13}$$

The trade balance depends positively on the real exchange rate S/P (a real depreciation improves the trade balance). Now consider an open market purchase of domestic bonds that is financed with an increase in money supply. In order to give the agents an incentive to hold more money and fewer bonds, domestic interest rates must fall. This in turn increases the demand for foreign bonds and the exchange rate will depreciate since agents purchase B^*. The new portfolio thus consists of more foreign bonds and less domestic bonds.

Now the trade balance is positively affected since the depreciated real exchange rate boosts exports. Since a current account surplus must be matched by a capital account deficit, domestic agents purchase foreign bonds (according to (4.12)). However, in order to rebalance their portfolios these foreign bonds are sold and the exchange rate subsequently appreciates. This holds on until the trade balance is in its original level.

Other than in the monetary models of the exchange rate the portfolio balance model also uses non-monetary assets and current account developments (goods market) to determine exchange rates. However, the most important difference from the point of sterilised interventions is the assumption that domestic and foreign assets are imperfect substitutes which requires that investors are risk-averse. Since a sterilised intervention of the central bank involves a change in the relative supply of domestic and foreign bonds, there are resulting effects on the exchange rate if the private sector is not indifferent to changes in the composition of its portfolio.

Consider a sterilised intervention by the European central bank (ECB) in support of the euro. Initially, the money supply in the Euro area decreases since home currency is bought against foreign currency (US$). The sterilisation operation then includes a purchase of domestic bonds by the ECB from the public, thus decreasing the supply of bonds held by the public but restoring the original money supply. Because of this operation the relative stock of foreign bonds (US-Treasuries) to domestic bonds has increased. Investors therefore demand a higher expected return on US$-denominated bonds in order to hold the relatively larger outstanding stock. As long as the interest rate of foreign bonds and the exchange rate are unchanged compared with the situation before the intervention investors will thus sell foreign bonds and buy domestic bonds. Consequently, the US$ depreciates and interest rates on foreign bonds increase. Since the depreciation of the US$ and the appreciation of the euro was intended by the intervention of the ECB the portfolio balance channel is leading to the correct result.

Note, however, that the portfolio balance channel presupposes that sterilised interventions alter the relative stock of outstanding bonds. As has been demonstrated in the example in chapter 4.1.2, this is not necessarily the case in reality (if sterilisation is pursued by not revolving security repurchase agreements). This might be just one reason why the empirical evidence on the portfolio balance channel remains scarce. As Edison (1993) notes: "In most of the studies reviewed, the researchers do not find a statistically, and/or quantitatively, significant role for sterilised intervention." (p. 14).[74] Even sterilisation changed the outstanding stock of bonds, intervention operations are generally too small relative to the total outstanding stock of domestic and foreign bonds to exert a marked influence on relative asset supplies. Lewis (1995) mentions: "The plausibility of this [the portfolio balance] channel clearly depends upon how much the exchange rate must respond in order to maintain portfolio balance." (p. 1937).

4.2.4 Interventions as a Signal of Future Monetary Policy

Apart from the portfolio balance channel conventional wisdom mentions the signalling channel as the second model with which effects from sterilised interventions on exchange rates can be explained. In contrast to the monetary and portfolio balance approach the signalling channel interprets intervention as new information to the market rather than as a change in the money supply or the relative supply of bonds. First introduced by Mussa (1981), the signalling channel interprets interventions as a signal from the central bank that is intended to influence the expectations of market participants concerning future monetary policy and thus also exchange rate expectations. If exchange rate expectations are revised the spot exchange rate will also adjust, thus making interventions effective.

---

[74] One study that finds significant effects for the portfolio balance channel in interventions of the early 1980s is Dominguez and Frankel (1993b).

For example, if the central bank plans a more expansionary monetary policy in the future it might intervene to weaken the domestic currency (buy foreign exchange) today and thus signal to the market its future strategy. According to Mussa such a policy would be more credible to the market participants than simply announcing the objectives since by buying or selling foreign exchange "[...] the authorities 'put their money where their mouth is' [...]" (Isard, 1995: 144). Thereby, the central bank engages in an open position in a foreign currency and risks to loose money if the intended exchange rate reaction (and the following change in monetary policy) does not materialise.

While the signalling channel is rather intuitive, there are basically two drawbacks of this theory in our view.

First, the signalling channel implicitly assumes that central banks regularly make their interventions public (since the public needs to learn of the signal). What can be observed in the foreign exchange markets, however, is that most interventions are kept secret. Even if central banks publish intervention data they usually do so with a considerably time lag of about six months. Table 10 compares actual intervention data published by the Federal Reserve after six months with newspaper reports of intervention for the day they actually occurred. As can be seen, reported interventions in the press by far underestimate the true extent of actual intervention. Only 56% of US interventions were correctly reported in the newspapers.[75,76] According to the signalling channel this should not be in the interest of the central bank.[77] If the monetary authorities want to signal their intentions then it would be reasonable for them to publish their operations.[78] It should be noted that this statistic refers to the DM/US$ market which is arguably the foreign exchange market most closely watched by the public. Thus, it can be expected that in smaller markets like Sweden, intervention can be hidden more easily by the central bank. The fact that intervention is so often conducted secretly suggests that it is not the authorities' objective to send a signal to the market.

---

75 The discrepancy between actual and correctly reported intervention might also stem from the fact that the Fed conducted customer transactions in the markets that it not published as official interventions (see the discussion in the chapter on foreign exchange reserves).

76 A Bloomberg news report cites a Bank of Canada money trader as saying "The Bank of Canada won't announce when it's buying or selling currencies to help the dollar [...]. 'There will not be an official statement' about sales or purchases, said Christian Dupont, a currency trader at the central bank. ‚We will not publish anything and will not go ahead without the market asking'." (Bloomberg News, March 25, 1999, 4.14 PM, Bank of Canada to confirm currency market activities).

77 The portfolio balance channel also gives no justification for secret intervention operations.

78 Dominguez and Frankel (1993a) argue similarly: "How can intervention signal future monetary policy intentions if the market does not hear the signal?" (p. 71).

Table 10: Actual versus reported US intervention

Period	Days of actual intervention	Days of reported intervention	Days of correctly reported intervention
Jan. – Aug. 1985	8	13	3
Sept. – Dec. 1985	22	20	15
Jan. – Dec. 1986	0	3	0
Jan. – Dec. 1987	53	35	22
Jan. – Dec. 1988	50	45	37
Jan. – Dec. 1989	99	69	53
Jan. 1985 – Dec. 1989	232	185	130

Source: Hung (1997). Days of actual intervention are based on published data of the US Federal Reserve. Data on reported intervention are based on the list of newspaper reports related to foreign exchange intervention provided in Dominguez and Frankel (1993a).

Second, it is not clear why interventions should be sterilised after all in the signalling channel. If the central bank, for example, plans an expansionary monetary policy it simply needs to pursue unsterilised intervention to weaken the exchange rate (which in turn expands the monetary base and reduces interest rates). This would be even more credible than sterilised interventions and far less complicated: Why sterilise the effects on domestic money supply and interest rates first when interest rates are adjusted later on nonetheless? Since most interventions are sterilised (see chapter 4.1.3), this leaves a puzzle in the signalling channel.

Empirical evidence for the hypotheses that interventions signal future monetary policy remains scarce. While Kaminsky and Lewis (1996) do find a significant relation between interventions and monetary policy, the coefficient has a different sign than would be expected from the signalling channel. According to their study, interventions to weaken the US$ were frequently followed by a contractionary interest rate policy in the late 1980s. Using a different time period, Fatum and Hutchinson (1999) do not find any significant relationship between interventions and subsequent interest rate changes. Thus, empirical literature supports the shortcomings of the signalling approach we mentioned above.

It is interesting to note that despite the lack of solid empirical evidence both the portfolio balance and the signalling channel are frequently mentioned as the two models through which sterilised interventions can be effective. However, in recent years two further approaches have emerged which are not only concerned with explaining interventions but who take a different look at the foreign exchange market as a whole.

Secrecy and foreign exchange intervention

"Most monetary authorities usually chose to intervene secretly, releasing actual intervention data with a lag, if at all." (Neely, 2001: 7). How does a central bank operate such "unannounced" interventions? Lyons (2001b) mentions two different ways:

First, the intervention order can be placed with a private bank dealer without an accompanying official news release. This way, the market will learn from the intervention operation (through rumours among the bank dealers) and subsequently newswire reports will speculate about the central bank actions (see Appendix I for examples of such reports).

Second, the central bank can place the order through an agent who does not reveal the source of the order. By operating this way, there will be no reports of interventions. "One reason a central bank want to do this is to mimic the trades of private players." (Lyons, 2001b: 227).

The existence of secret interventions is puzzling to many economists and provides evidence against the signalling channel. How can this secrecy be explained? Dominguez and Frankel (1993a) mention practical reasons grouped into three categories why central banks may want to hide their foreign exchange transactions:

Doubts about the efficacy of interventions at a point in time

Central banks may choose to keep interventions secret when they do not seem to conform with their monetary policy stance at the time. Such an event may occur when the instruction to intervene comes from outside the central bank. It is usual practice that the government decides over foreign exchange policy and the central bank has to implement it. Occasionally, if the government instructions do not conform with its monetary policy objectives, the central bank might prefer to keep the intervention transactions secret.

Furthermore, interventions might be kept secret if the central bank has doubts about the public perception of such an event. An example would be the participation in co-ordinated intervention operations in support of a foreign exchange target.

Doubts about the depth or volatility of the foreign exchange market at a point in time

Secret interventions might be used in order to "provide a sense of two-way-risk" (Dominguez and Frankel, 1993a: 61), i.e. to prevent foreign exchange market participants from betting against the central bank. This is especially important if the aim of the intervention is to break an existing trend in the exchange rate. Moreover, since the intervention volumes are limited it is in the interest of the central bank to enter thin and disorderly markets in order to achieve the desired effect. This holds particularly for a central banks without a strong reputation.

Reasons based on portfolio adjustment

Finally, a central bank may chose to keep interventions secret if their aim is simply to adjust the foreign exchange reserve portfolio.

The Swedish Riksbank mentions among its reasons for secrecy that transparency might decrease the efficiency of its interventions: "Interventions are more complicated to implement with the intended effects than are repo rate decisions, as the Riksbank can normally determine the short market rate through its position in the daily lending market, while in currency interventions the bank is merely one operator among many in the market. Interventions can thereby have a greater effect if the Riksbank does not show complete openness with regard to its readiness to intervene, the length of its operations, the time the decision was made, and the scope, currencies or counterparties involved in the intervention." (Riksbank, 2002: 8).

Source: Dominguez and Frankel, 1993a: 61-62.

4.2.5 Noise-Traders and the Role of Sterilised Interventions

The deficits of both the portfolio balance and the signalling channel have led to the emergence of a further model that seems to better capture the reality of foreign exchange trading: the noise-trading channel. Especially it can explain why central banks usually intervene secretly – a fact which the former models were unable to make sense of. The novelty of the noise trading approach to the foreign exchange market is the assumption that investors are heterogeneous with respect to their trading style. As Rosenberg (1996) states: "The noise trading channel provides central banks with a means of exploiting the behaviour of short-run technical-oriented traders who now dominate trading activity in the world currency markets." (p. 311). Besides fundamental investors which base their trading decisions on macroeconomic fundamentals there exists a group of noise traders. According to Hung (1997) noise traders can de defined as "[...] investors whose demand for currencies is influenced by beliefs or sentiments that are not fully consistent with economic fundamentals." (p. 781). Since models that tried to forecast exchange rates with fundamental variables proved not to be very useful (see e.g. Meese and Rogoff, 1983) the assumption that there exist market participants that base their decisions on other facts seems to be rather obvious. Many of them use chart analysis for the short term prediction of exchange rate movements.

Since there is mounting evidence that technical trading rules can generate excess profits in the foreign exchange market (see e.g. Neely et al., 1997) it seems likely that the share of noise traders is not negligible. Furthermore, surveys among professional foreign exchange dealers routinely show that a significant share of them uses technical analysis for exchange rate determination (while Cheung and Chinn (2001) report that technical trading describes about 30% of trading behaviour, Taylor and Allen (1992) find that about 90% of London traders use technical analysis).[79]

Whereas fundamental traders will always tend to stabilising speculation which brings exchange rates back to their fundamental value, noise traders might take exchange rates away from their equilibrium values as they usually follow trend lines. "As a rule, they [noise traders] are more comfortable trading with the trend, buying when the price is rising and selling when the price is falling." (Rosenberg, 1996: 311).[80] According to Hung (1997) risk-averse fundamentalists may not always exploit the difference between the actual and the equilibrium value of the exchange rate for two reasons. First, they might not be sure if their valuation of the equilibrium is correct and second, the existence of noise traders presents a risk that the exchange rate might not return to its fair value over a certain time horizon. Thus, in such an environment there can be persistent deviations of the exchange rate from its fundamental correct value.

The noise trading approach recognises a conventional view of financial market practitioners, namely that "[...] the key to investment success is not just predicting future fundamentals, but also predicting the movement of other active investors." (Shleifer and Summers, 1990: 26). The popularity of trend following models like technical analysis stems from the desire to forecast the behaviour of other market participants.

The role of sterilised interventions in the noise trading approach is straightforward.

First, the noise trading approach of exchange rate determination offers an explanation for the fact that exchange rates may deviate from their fundamental

---

79 Djoudad et al. (2000) provide evidence of the existence of chartist traders in the foreign exchange markets of Australia, Canada and New Zealand. Allen and Taylor (1990) find that the importance of chart analysis declines over the forecast horizon. While 90% of their survey respondents use chart analysis for short horizon currency forecasting (intraday up to one week), fundamental analysis becomes more important at forecast horizons of one year or longer.

80 Frankel and Froot (1990) state: "It has long been remarked that if there exist traders who tend to forecast by extrapolating recent trends (i.e., who have 'bandwagon expectations'), then their actions can exacerbate swings in the exchange rate." (p. 183).

value for a prolonged period of time. As this possibility does not exist in models of the asset approach (though the signalling channel also justifies central bank intervention) as they assumed efficient markets there was no need for the central bank to intervene in the market.[81] Thus, the existence of noise traders does provide a rationale for foreign exchange intervention, namely to prevent that trading which is driven by investor sentiment and trend-following techniques leads to exchange rates that are not justified by underlying fundamentals and thus are a potential threat to price stability.

Secondly, within the noise trading approach the effectiveness of interventions can be explained. The aim of the central bank in this view is to break an existing appreciation or depreciation trend of the exchange rate.[82] Chartists (noise traders) may then decide to change their positions in favour of the new trend that has been initiated by the interventions. In other words, noise traders may support a bandwagon effect that began with the central bank intervention. This way, the effects of a sterilised intervention might be lasting longer than the initial price impact of the central bank purchase/sale of foreign exchange. If these interventions are conducted secretly the chartists will judge them simply as a new source of demand and include the price movement in their trend analysis.[83]

Consider the following graph which displays the interventions of the Bank of Japan against the development of the Yen/US$ exchange rate. The movement of the exchange rate can be characterised by a clear pattern of trend lines. It appears that the breaking of a trend line and the establishment of a new trend is associated with the occurrence of foreign exchange intervention (for example in July 1995 or in July 1998).[84] This suggests that the noise trading channel has a role in intervention behaviour and effectiveness.

---

81 Nonetheless, the central bank itself might be tempted to move the exchange away from its fundamental value which, however, is not an issue in the literature.

82 Saacke (2002) provides further insight into the relationship between the role of interventions in breaking existing exchange rate trends. He finds that exchange rates tend to move counter to central bank's intentions shortly after interventions but that this effect reverses in the long run. This might be an explanation for the finding of many studies that cast doubt on the effectiveness of interventions by analysing only a short period around intervention operations. As is illustrated in Figure 9 it can take some time before the trend is reversed; all interventions before the actual trend reversal would be interpreted as ineffective in the short run. In the long run, however, the operations proved to be rather successful. Neely (2002) finds evidence for some countries that high returns from trading rules (technical trading) precede intervention operations which supports the hypothesis that interventions are intended to break existing trend lines.

83 This serves also as an explanation for the observation that central banks often decide to enter markets when volume is low, for example late in the Asian trading session or before weekends, as the price impact of the intervention is larger and the likelihood of breaking an existing trendline is higher.

84 This view is supported by the empirical analysis of Ramaswamy and Samiei (2000) who find that "interventions have succeeded on a number of occasions during 1995-99 in changing the path of the yen-dollar rate in the desired direction." (p. 23).

Figure 9: Japanese interventions and the Yen/US$ exchange rate

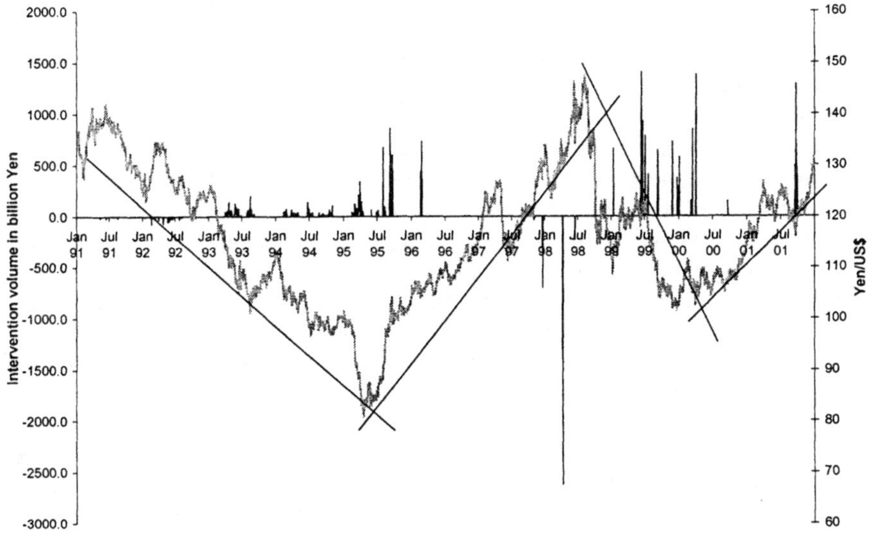

Note: Bars indicate intervention operations. Positive (negative) intervention volume denotes a purchase (sale) of US$ and a sale (purchase) of Yen. Source: Bank of Japan, Thomson Financial Datastream.

Unlike in the signalling channel, the central bank according to the noise-trading channel is not using intervention to signal its policy intentions but rather to force investors to bet on a trend reversal. According to Rosenberg (1996), this might be one justification for the fact that empirical researchers have found only scarce evidence for the signalling channel.

However, in order to effectively influence the exchange rate in this model the central bank needs to have information about the reaction function of noise traders. This might be one reason why central banks regularly engage in foreign exchange markets without the purpose of intervention but rather to learn more about the behaviour of market participants. The Reserve Bank of New Zealand in its Annual Report 1996/97, for example, states: "Our presence in the market is now limited to small positions we initiate. This trading helps our understanding of market dynamics, maintains links with market participants, and ensures that systems and procedures are in place should the Bank need to intervene in the foreign exchange market." (p. 12).

4.2.6 The Microstructure Approach and Sterilised Interventions

The microstructure approach is distinct from the noise trading approach and all earlier approaches in that the focus is put on the transmission mechanism from information to price formation – thus focussing more on the micro- than the macro-issues of exchange rate determination. Lyons (2001b: 3) describes it as "an in-the-trenches, trading-room perspective." Whereas in all other models the actual foreign exchange trading plays no role the microstructure approach regards trading as the main driving force for exchange rate determination. It thus looks at the level where the prices are determined and does not presuppose an Walrasian auctioneer who looks at the fundamentals first, then determines a price and afterwards allows trading in this price only.

To depart from the macro approach of exchange rate determination seems appropriate for a single reason: As mentioned by Flood and Taylor (1996): "[...] there seems to be little professional disagreement with the view that, as a guide to the short-run behaviour of the major exchange rates, exchange rate models based on macro fundamentals have largely failed." (p. 285).[85] This is illustrated by the fact that none of the macro variables that have been used to explain exchange rates such as money supplies, inflation rates or interest rates have exhibited volatility that comes anywhere close to the variation observed in exchange rates. This is not to say that macro variables should not be used at all. According to Flood and Taylor (1996), "the macro fundamentals in an important sense 'set the parameters' within which exchange rates move but [...] these parameters are very broad indeed over the short run." (p. 287). Since monetary policy operates over the short run (which can be defined as up to one year) there is a need for better models of exchange rate determination.

Probably the main differences of the microstructure approach to the conventional macro-models is that it relaxes two assumptions of the latter models (see Lyons, 2001b: 17):

- Traders do share the same amount of information
- All market participants use the same information to form their beliefs about the exchange rate.

In contrast, microstructure assumes that information is spread unevenly and is used in different ways to influence exchange rates. One example for unevenly spread information is foreign exchange intervention: The dealer who receives the initial order from the central bank has an information advantage over other market participants.[86] Another example is that fundamentals underlying exchange rate determination such as capital flows resulting from the trade of goods and services generate foreign exchange trades that are observable via order flow long before they appear in official statistics (about the trade balance for example).

---

85 This result is common knowledge since the early 1980s following the seminal paper by Meese and Rogoff (1983).

86 Peiers (1997), for example, finds evidence that intervention is associated with asymmetric information flows among foreign exchange traders and that "certain commercial bank dealers have privileged information regarding central bank activities." (p. 1607). Her results suggest that Deutsche Bank has been a price leader up to 60 minutes prior to Reuters news reports of Bundesbank intervention activity. Dominguez (1999) reports similar results: she finds significant exchange rate returns up to one hour prior to Reuters news reports of intervention operations by the US Fed, the Bank of Japan and the Bundesbank.

Furthermore, even if all participants share the same amount of information it is not clear if all of them interpret the implications of this information for exchange rates in the same manner. This means practically that the underlying model of price determination is not publicly known. For example, it is not obvious if an interest rate cut by the European Central Bank leads to an appreciation or depreciation of the currency. While one trader could opt for appreciation since an interest rate cut might help to foster economic growth and thus makes investments in the Euro area more attractive, another trader might argue that the Euro has to depreciate as a consequence of uncovered interest parity (given that US interest rates remain constant). One implication of this uncertainty about the mapping of information into prices is that traders try to uncover the behaviour of other traders in order to get a feeling in which way the majority of market participants interprets the news.

One way of uncovering information about price formation in the market is by looking at order flow. Indeed, order flow analysis is the centerstage of the microstructure approach. Surveys among foreign exchange dealers indicate that large market participants who observe a lot of order flow have an informative advantage.[87] Since the foreign exchange market is organised as a dealer market rather than an auction market with an open order book it matters how much of the order flow can be monitored.

If order flow is an important factor in the foreign exchange market then the role of intervention is relatively straightforward. As mentioned by Lyons (2001a), the price impact of foreign exchange orders by financial institutions is significantly higher than from non-financial institutions. That illustrates that the source of order flow matters. Research on interventions in the microstructure approach focuses on portfolio-balance effects, similar to the approach mentioned above. Risk-averse market participants need to be compensated for holding a currency (taking the other side of the order) they would otherwise choose not to hold. However, different to the conventional macro approach portfolio-balance effects now are studied at the level of foreign exchange dealers. This is illustrated in a recent paper by Evans and Lyons (2001) who are taking a trading-theoretic approach to portfolio balance. They distinguish between two types of effects: While at the level of the single dealer, consequences of inventory management lead to only a temporary portfolio balance effect, on the market-wide level portfolio balance effects can be persistent.

Take a model of a typical day in the foreign exchange market as example. At the beginning, the public (customers like companies or individuals) place their orders. Foreign exchange dealers take the other side of these orders. However, since they are risk-averse they need to be compensated for the risk of holding the currency. This compensation is reflected in prices and thus leads to a temporary port-

87 In the survey by Cheung and Wong (2000) 56% of respondents state that large market players have a competitive advantage that stems from a larger customer base as well as better information about the market as a whole. The former gives them better knowledge about customer order while the latter is due to a better market network that allows large traders to gain knowledge about the order flow of other banks.

folio balance effect. The effect is only temporary because the trader shares the position with the market ("hot-potato trading") in order to manage his inventory of foreign exchange accordingly. It is common knowledge that dealers end the day with a net zero position which requires that they pass on their positions to the public. Since the demand of the public is not perfectly elastic, these transactions can also lead to effects on exchange rates. Contrary to the inventory effect of the single dealer this effect is persistent since the whole market requires a compensation for holding a position it would otherwise not hold. This second, persistent effect is the same as in the conventional macro approach of portfolio balance. What is important in this regard is that if the second effect exists then the initial customer order at the beginning of the day leads to price changes that endure.

Evans and Lyons (2001) set up an empirical model to test for the existence of portfolio balance effects using intraday data on order flow. They find that both the temporary and the persistent effect are significant. Their results indicate that a US$ 1 billion customer order leads to an effect of 0,44% on the exchange rate. 80% of this effect can be attributed to the second, persistent portfolio-balance effect. This can be viewed as a guideline for the consequences of central bank intervention. However, intervention needs to be sterilised, conducted secretly and convey no information about future monetary policy in order to be classified as a normal customer order and compared with these results. This might be an explanation for the fact that central banks try to hide their intervention operations.

Trading volume and market microstructure

The microstructure approach is also able to explain some of the exchange rate puzzles. Take, for example, the high volume of daily foreign exchange trading. In 2001, as the most recent BIS survey shows, volume amounted to 1,21 trillion US$ per day (of which 390 billion US$ are spot transactions and 820 billion US$ are outright forwards and fx swaps; see BIS, 2001).[88] This number leads many economists and non-academics to the assumption that central bank interventions are ineffective as the average daily intervention volume seldom reaches more than 1 billion US$.[89] The microstructure approach explains the high volume with the trading mechanism, specifically with risk management of traders, which is known under the name "hot potato trading" (see Lyons, 2001b: 129). Hot potato trading means that dealers pass on unwanted positions from an initial customer order to other dealers in order to control their inventory of foreign exchange. As foreign exchange traders usually end their day with a net zero position, they control their inventory throughout the day in order to keep their open positions as small as possible (since the major dealers trade up to 10 million US$ on one transaction, exchange rate exposure can be very significant). Thus, if a customer sells 10 million US$ to a risk-averse dealer he is likely to pass on 9 million US$ to another dealer who will act similar. In the end the initial 10 million US$ customer order can generate volume of up to 90 million US$ (assuming each dealer passes on 90% of his position). By recognising this volume-enhancing hot potato trading it is not difficult to imagine that even relatively small interventions of a central bank, which represent the initial customer order, can easily multiply to a larger volume and thus effect significant exchange rate changes.[90]

88 In 2001 the US$/Euro currency pair was by far the most traded with a share of 30%, followed by US$/Yen (20%) and US$/GBP (11%) (BIS, 2001).

89 Dominguez and Frankel (1993a) report for the 1980s an average intervention volume of 200 million US$ per day. However, volume can be assumed to have increased since then. Official intervention data of the Bank of Japan, for example, show an average volume of 1.2 billion US$ per day for the period 1991-2001 with the largest intervention occurring on April 10, 1998 when the Bank of Japan sold an equivalent of 20 billion US$ in support of the Yen.

90 Proponents of the microstructure approach also use this argument against the idea of Tobin taxes on foreign exchange transactions. Since according to inventory control the high volume simply represents risk management of foreign exchange dealers rather than excessive speculation, such a tax would seriously impede this risk management (see Lyons, 2001b: 13).

4.2.7 Assessment of Intervention Models

The above surveyed approaches yielded different results concerning the effectiveness of interventions. In order to assess which model is capable of explaining the most phenomena that are associated with interventions we look at how central banks operate interventions in practice and then ask which of the existing theories are able to explain this behaviour.[91]

Intervention operations can be classified into nine different types (see Lyons, 2001b: 228). They can either be sterilised or unsterilised and in the case of sterilisation the central bank might use the intervention as a signal of future monetary policy.[92] On the other hand, interventions differ in the extent of their publication: they can either be publicly announced, kept secret or be unannounced but partially revealed through market perceptions (if the central bank operates the intervention with a private bank dealer instead of an agent). Typically, intervention operations in practice are sterilised and unannounced. However, it does not make sense for a central bank to keep its intervention operations secret if it wants to take advantage of the signalling channel. Therefore, the shaded area in Table 11, i.e. interventions are sterilised and kept secret and thus do not serve as a signal for future monetary policy, seems to be an appropriate description of intervention in reality.

Concerning the fact that interventions are mostly undertaken secretly, only the noise trader and the microstructure approach offer reasonable explanations. While in the former the aim of the central bank is to break an existing trend (which does not require the revelation of the customer identity), the latter justifies secret operations as the central bank may try to mimic a conventional customer order. Secrecy makes no sense at all in the signalling channel since in this model the central bank has an interest that the public knows about their operations.[93] In addition, a model that captures the reality should make sense of the fact that central banks usually sterilise their interventions. Apart from the monetary models all other approaches explain the effectiveness of sterilised interventions. Regarding empirical evidence for the different models no clear conclusions can be made. Rather undisputed, however, is the fact that monetary and portfolio-balance models perform

[91] Surely, one could take a different approach and argue that the existing practice of central banks lacks a theoretical fundament and therefore is doomed to failure. However, central bank intervention occurred frequently over the past three decades. We doubt that agents in central banks would use this tool without proper theoretical justification and thus proceed to try to understand the reasoning behind these operations.

[92] As mentioned above, it might be asked why the central bank sterilises the intervention at all if the intention is to signal future monetary policy. This question, however, does not occur in discussions of the signalling channel.

[93] A further argument for secret interventions can be derived from a statement in Mishkin (2000): "Responding too heavily and too frequently to movements in a 'flexible' exchange rate runs the risk of transforming the exchange rate into a nominal anchor for monetary policy that takes precedence over the inflation target, at least in the eyes of the public." (p. 109). In order to let the public believe that the inflation target is the primary goal, central banks may chose to keep interventions secret.

poorly in empirical tests. On the other hand, evidence for the signalling channel is mixed while the noise trader and the microstructure approach yield relatively positive results in recent empirical studies. However, it must be admitted that the latter two approaches are relatively new and thus have not been tested as extensively as the older models. Thus, it must be seen in the future if the success of these approaches continues.

Table 11: Classification of intervention models

	Sterilised: no signal	Sterilised: signal	Unsterilised
Announced	Portfolio balance channel	Portfolio balance channel Signalling channel	Monetary models
Unannounced, but partially revealed	Portfolio balance channel Noise trading channel Microstructure approach	Portfolio balance channel (Signalling channel)	
Secret	Portfolio balance channel Noise trading channel Microstructure approach	Portfolio balance channel	

Note: The classification of intervention types is taken from Lyons, 2001b: 228. The shaded area characterises the typical type of intervention that is used in practice.

Taken together, it can be seen that the noise trader and the microstructure approach perform best in explaining the issues connected with the typical type of intervention.[94] It can be assumed that central banks rely on some version of the models when they discuss interventions.[95] While the portfolio balance channel also describes the effects of typical intervention behaviour its lack of empirical relevance suggests that interventions functions in a different way. The fact, that

94 A different but important question is if these theoretical models do justify interventions at all. In order to make sense of interventions the underlying exchange rate model has to allow for the possibility of exchange rates deviating from their fundamentally justified range. This is not the case in monetary and portfolio-balance models, but is an essential part of the noise trader approach. In the signalling channel interventions are necessary for signalling future monetary policy. Since the microstructure approach is no pure exchange rate model it does not tackle the issue whether interventions are necessary at all (though Lyons (2001b: 230) argues that the central bank knows that the current exchange rate is inconsistent with fundamentals whenever there are significant imbalances between buyer- and seller-initiated orders).

95 Indeed, the minutes of a recent monetary policy meeting of the Swedish Riksbank include a discussion of the noise-trader and microstructure approach with regard to their relevance for central bank interventions (see Riksbank, 2001b). Riksbank (2002), however, attributes an important role for the signal channel.

sterilised intervention is regularly used as a monetary policy tool makes clear that most central banks today do not think in terms of monetary models.

Which conclusions about the effectiveness of sterilised interventions can be drawn from the above survey? While there is still no final consensus emerging in the economic literature, Portes (2001) mentions: "[...] the scepticism about sterilised intervention that took root in the 1980s has been challenged in recent years [...] New research [...] suggests that the impact [of sterilised interventions] could be substantial and sustained." (pp. 7-8). Already in 1993 Dominguez and Frankel (1993a) concluded: "Intervention represent a more potent policy instrument than most officials and especially most outside analysts have in recent years imagined it to be. Hence, it can make a more significant contribution both to policy now and to the ongoing debate over how best to organise the international monetary system." (p. 140).

5 Sterilised Foreign Exchange Intervention in Practice

We now turn to the evidence for the use of foreign exchange intervention in inflation targeting countries. So far, we have seen, that UIP does not hold in practice and that central banks regularly sterilise their foreign exchange operations (thus, they can be regarded as an additional policy tool). In this final chapter we aim to fulfil two tasks: to determine to what extent interventions are used *at all* and, secondly, to analyse if they are *used as an additional policy instrument.* Our indicator for the first issue are changes in foreign exchange reserves. As an indication for the use of interventions as additional policy tool we look at each central bank's policy reaction function and at the volatility of its short-term interest rate.

Figure 10: Interventions as an additional policy tool

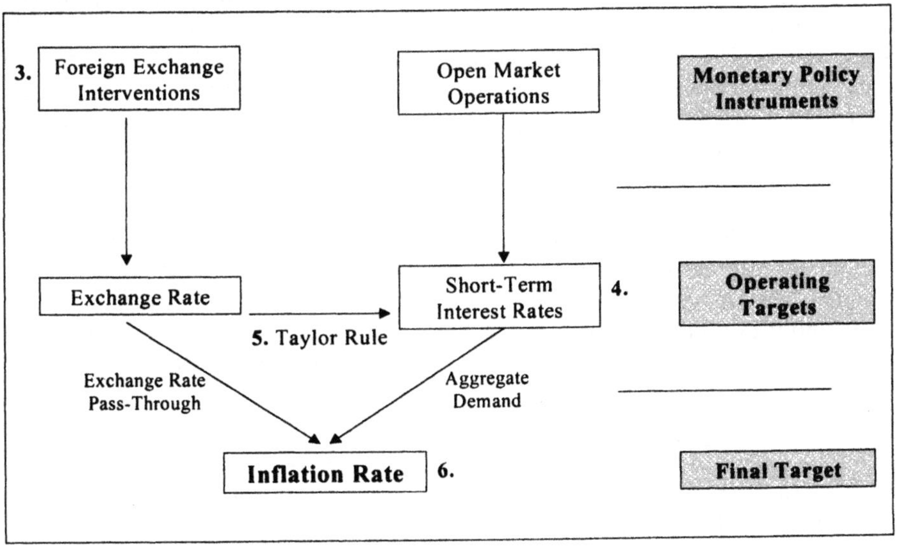

Note: UIP denotes uncovered interest parity.

Firstly, we compare the extent of interventions across our five countries (issue 3), secondly we analyse whether a higher intervention intensity is associated with a lower interest rate volatility (issue 4) and thirdly we ask whether a higher intervention intensity results in a different focus of interest rate policy (issue 5).

Finally, loss functions are computed and compared across countries (issue 6) to see whether the use of interventions has any positive impact on the performance.

In a first step to analyse issue 3 we briefly describe and motivate the use of foreign exchange reserves to proxy intervention activity of central banks.

5.1 Foreign Exchange Reserves as an Intervention Proxy

"[...] the whole activity of central bank intervention appears to have a certain mystique."
(Baillie, 2000: 226)

The study of intervention activity of central banks faces an important restriction: Most central banks do not publish their intervention operations.[96] This also holds true for the case of the five inflation targeting countries that we focus on. The notable exception is the Reserve Bank of Australia which provides a daily time series of intervention from 1983 on. Sweden, Canada and the UK mention on their websites that they will inform the public whenever they enter the foreign exchange market to conduct interventions but neither of them provides intervention volumes or time series for economic analysis. New Zealand is a special case since they denied to have intervened in the foreign exchange market since March 1985 (see Archer and Halliday, 1998: 346). For the five countries we focus on there exist some studies from the respective central banks that use confidential intervention data (see Sjöö and Sweeney, 2001; Aguilar and Nydahl, 2000, for Sweden and Murray et al., 1996; Beattie and Fillion, 1999, for Canada).[97] However, these confidential data are not available for researchers outside the central banks.

As is the usual procedure in the literature given the lack of official intervention data we examine changes in the foreign exchange reserves of these central banks to proxy their intervention activities.[98] We will argue later in the chapter that these data might provide an even more accurate picture of actual central bank intervention than official intervention data, since changes in reserves also include passive interventions or other transactions that are not classified as official intervention by the central bank.[99] Data on central bank reserves are provided by the IMF in its

96 The only exceptions for industrial countries, to our knowledge, are the US Federal Reserve Bank, the Bank of Japan, the Reserve Bank of Australia and to some extent the Bundesbank. However, all data is published with a time lag of usually six months.

97 There are also some papers that use actual daily intervention data from the US Federal Reserve or the Bundesbank to study the effects of interventions (see e.g. Dominguez and Frankel, 1993a).

98 See for example Szakmary and Mathur, 1997; Kearney and MacDonald, 1986; Takagi, 1991; Taylor, 1982; Ghosh, 1992.

99 Publications of reserve data are also interpreted as an intervention proxy by foreign exchange market participants. For example, Agence France Press news states in their news release of Bank of England reserve data: "The level of reserves is watched as an indication of the extent of intervention by the Bank of England on foreign exchange

International Financial Statistics on a monthly basis. Under the headline "official foreign exchange reserves" the following items are subsumed:[100]

(1) Foreign currency reserves (in convertible foreign currencies)
  (a) Securities
  (b) Total deposits with
    - other central banks and Bank for International Settlements (BIS)
    - banks headquartered in the reporting country
    - banks headquartered outside the reporting country
(2) IMF reserve position
(3) Special Drawing Rights (SDRs)[101]
(4) Gold.

For the purpose of studying intervention activity the item (1) foreign currency reserves is the most interesting since it is the most liquid of all. Furthermore, IMF reserves and SDRs usually represent only a small fraction of total reserves (see Figure 13 further down).

Critics sometimes argue that reserve changes are an insufficient proxy as not all reserve changes need to be associated with an intervention by the central bank. To be sure, the availability of actual intervention data would without doubt be desirable for researchers. However, since these are seldom available, foreign exchange reserves are the only proxy since by definition every transaction of the central bank using foreign currency has an effect on its reserve holdings. Furthermore, we will present a methodology with which the intervention volume can be estimated more precisely. Taken together, this chapter will justify our procedure of referring to changes in foreign exchange reserves to identify intervention operations of central banks.

Our main points are:

– Since official intervention data is seldom published by the central banks, foreign exchange reserves are the only proxy that researchers can use. Using the data published by the Reserve Bank of Australia we will also study to what extent these data are correlated with reserve changes and thus extent the study by Neely (2000) who analyses German, Swiss and US data.
– There are external factors other than intervention that may lead to changes in the level of foreign exchange reserves such as valuation effects and interest earnings gained on the reserve portfolio. These effects will be estimated for each country and the reserve data adjusted accordingly.

---

markets." (Agence France Press (AFX) news, August 3, 1993, "British M0 money supply rises 1.5% in July").

100 See BIS, 1998.

101 Special Drawing Rights (SDR) are an international reserve asset created by the IMF in 1969. Its value is determined from a basket of four currencies (Euro, Japanese yen, pound sterling, and U.S. dollar). Today's role of SDRs is relatively limited. They serve as a unit of account of the IMF as a potential claim on the freely usable currencies of IMF members (holders of SDRs can exchange their SDRs for these currencies)(See www.imf.org).

- Since there exists no universal definition for intervention activity it is not obvious that official intervention data that is published by central banks really contains every transaction that might influence the exchange rate. Thus, we argue that changes in foreign exchange reserves present a much more objective measure of intervention activity. Indeed, the major reason for central banks to hold foreign exchange reserves is to intervene in the market.

5.1.1 Reasons for Holding Foreign Exchange Reserves

Economic theory suggests that the level and variability of foreign exchange reserves is closely related to the underlying exchange rate regime.[102] According to this view countries with a more fixed exchange rate system need to intervene in the market more often in order to keep their exchange rate within the desired path. As a consequence its foreign exchange reserves will fluctuate more and also the level of reserves will be higher for reasons of credibility (market participants need to be confident that the central bank is able to uphold the regime on a sustained basis).

However, according to this theoretical view countries with a flexible exchange rate regime do not intervene in the foreign exchange market and thus do not need to hold reserves. Given this background it is astonishing that world-wide reserve holdings by central banks have been increasing immensely since the breakdown of the Bretton Woods system of fixed but adjustable exchange rates (see Figure 11) and the subsequent rise in the number of floating exchange rates.

The reason for holding reserves under a floating regime is thus not explicitly explained by economic theory. So are there other reasons for countries to maintain sometimes significant amounts of foreign currency or is economic theory misleading? The justification for holding reserves is especially important given the fact that there are costs associated with the maintenance of reserves.[103] Roger (1993) distinguishes between three groups of motives:

- Transaction needs;
- Intervention needs; and
- Wealth diversification.

---

102 See e.g. Krugman and Obstfeld, 1991.

103 According to Roger (1993) "[...] the most appropriate definition of the cost of holding reserves is the net social opportunity cost – that is, the best alternative social yield on the resources tied up in reserves minus the actual yield on reserves." (p. 32). In New Zealand the costs for maintaining a reserve level of 4 to 5 billion NZ$ are about 5 million NZ$ per year (this includes financing of the reserves, personnel, systems and overhead expenses) (see Archer and Halliday, 1998).

Figure 11: Worldwide foreign exchange reserve holdings

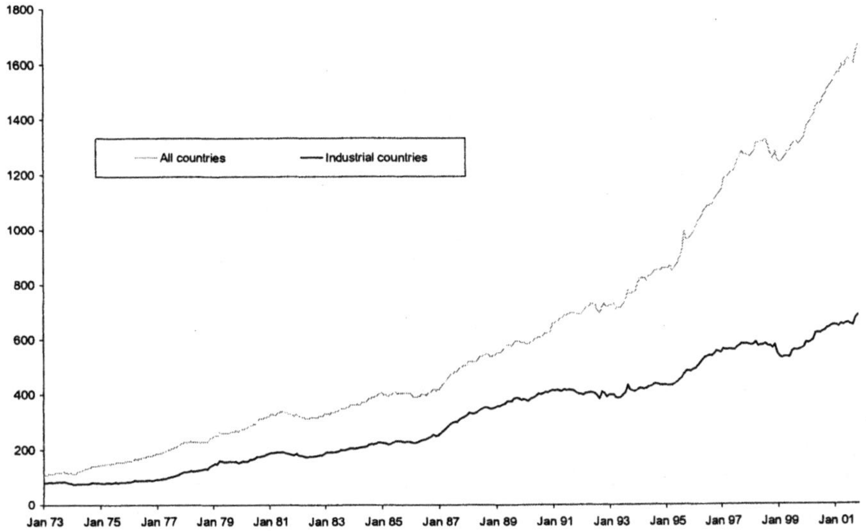

Source: IMF Annual Report, various issues. Numbers are total reserves minus gold holdings.

Hereby, transaction needs means that countries hold reserves to meet foreign exchange demand of the public or private sector. The IMF (2001) gives more detailed arguments for why countries usually hold foreign exchange reserves:

1. To support and maintain confidence in the policies for monetary and exchange rate management including the capacity to intervene in support of the national currency;
2. To maintain foreign currency liquidity that can be used to allow time to absorb shocks in situations when access to borrowing is curtailed or very costly;
3. To provide a level of confidence to markets that a country can meet its external obligations, particularly during times of crisis or external shock;[104]
4. To demonstrate the backing of domestic currency by external assets;
5. To assist the government in meeting its foreign exchange needs and external debt obligations;
6. To maintain a reserve for national disasters or emergencies;
7. To generate fiscal income for the country; and
8. To set aside national savings for future generations, for example, from the sale of non-renewable natural resources.

---

104 The importance of reserves as signalling confidence to financial markets has been highlighted during the Asian crisis. One of the triggers of the crisis in Thailand was the fact that financial markets were in doubt about the true level of foreign exchange reserves at the Bank of Thailand (see Blustein, 2001, for a detailed account of the Asian crisis).

Archer and Halliday (1998) from the Reserve Bank of New Zealand present a more practical view of the rationale for holding foreign exchange reserves and they add two further points that are important: Credit rating agencies often look at a country's level of foreign exchange reserves in their judgement of the capability to service debt. A positive rating might reduce real interest rates and consequently enhances overall welfare. Secondly, foreign exchange reserves enable a central bank to gain knowledge about the foreign exchange market and the management of reserves.

Among the various reasons for holding reserves the ability to intervene in the foreign exchange markets is the most important one. This view is shared by the Reserve Bank of New Zealand, as Archer and Halliday (1998) write: "[...] we know that much damage could be caused by foreign exchange markets in serious trouble, and it would be dangerous to rule out in advance the potential for successful intervention – the stakes are just too high. At heart, this is the fundamental reason justifying our foreign currency intervention capacity." (Archer and Halliday, 1998: 354). Similarly the Reserve Bank of Australia remarks: "[Australia's international reserves] are held primarily for the purpose of permitting intervention in the foreign exchange market." (Reserve Bank of Australia, 1999: 17). This view is also supported by Roger (1993) who states that "[...] the intervention motive is considered to be the most important source of demand for reserves [...]" (p. 11). Wealth diversification determines the composition of reserves rather than its level and thus is also a less relevant factor. Transaction needs are also of minor importance especially for industrialised countries which have access to international capital markets.

A further aspect that so far has not been tackled in the relevant literature is that reserve holdings are the result of a regime of managed floating: Reserve levels may increase because the central bank is trying to depreciate its own currency. Rather than *actively* accumulating reserves for future intervention needs (as mentioned above), an increase in reserves in a regime of managed floating simply (*passively*) results from central bank activities to achieve a certain exchange rate target. Examples are Japan or Korea, whose reserve levels have risen by over 100 and 400%, respectively, over the time period 01/1998 – 07/2002 (reflecting attempts to depreciate their currencies).

To summarise: The fact that even countries that operate under a floating exchange rate regime hold considerable amounts of foreign reserves supports the view that the ability to intervene in the currency market is very important for these countries. In some ways this contradicts with the pure theory of floating exchange rates that does not hold a role for foreign exchange intervention.

5.1.2 Mechanics of Foreign Exchange Intervention

The mechanics of an intervention operation will now be illustrated with the central bank balance sheet, since "Intervention operations and other financial policy actions can be represented by changes in the stylised balance sheet." (Adams and Henderson, 1983: 2). This way it will also become clear why changes in foreign exchange reserves present a proxy for intervention activity. Consider the balance sheet of a central bank in Figure 12.[105]

The monetary base comprises total currency in circulation and deposit liabilities to commercial banks. The net worth changes whenever the central bank runs a current spending surplus, receives interest earnings or makes a capital gain on its assets. Net foreign assets comprise the foreign exchange holdings of the central bank. These holdings can de divided into Gold, Special Drawing Rights (SDR), the reserve holdings at the IMF and the actual foreign exchange. Of these, foreign exchange presents the largest part of all as can be seen from Figure 13 which shows the composition of world-wide reserve holdings. Thus, in the following we will refer to foreign exchange holdings when we speak of a central banks' reserve.

Figure 12: Stylised central bank balance sheet

Assets	Liabilities
Net domestic assets (NDA) -Gold -SDR -Reserve at IMF -Foreign exchange	Monetary base (MB) -Total currency in circulation -Reserve liabilities to commercial banks
Net foreign assets (NFA) -Government securities -Loans on commercial banks -other	Net worth (NW) -Spending surpluses -Net interests and capital gains from assets

Source: Adams and Henderson, 1983: 1; Sarno and Taylor, 2001a: 5.

A look at the central bank balance sheet shows why "an intervention operation occurs if and only if the authorities' net foreign assets change." However, "isolating the effects of intervention is no trivial task, even when intervention is defined in this apparently clear-cut way." (Adams and Henderson, 1983: 29).

105 Strictly speaking this represents the balance sheet of a country's monetary authorities (the central bank and exchange-stabilisation authorities) as in many countries the foreign exchange reserves belong to a special fund that is owned by the government (e.g. the US Exchange Stabilisation Fund or the Exchange Equalisation Account in the United Kingdom).

Figure 13: Components of world-wide foreign exchange reserves

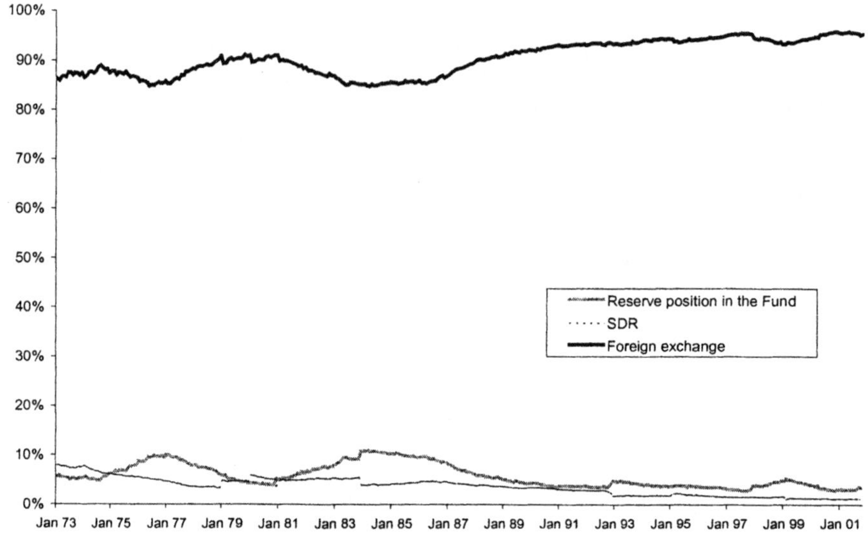

Source: IMF Annual Report, various issues.

For example, intervention might be intentionally kept secret by the central bank by using its reserve holdings at the Bank for International Settlement (BIS). According to the Deutsche Bundesbank (1997: 189) one of the purposes of the BIS is to perform interventions on behalf of their members (which are the central banks)[106]. Details of these transactions are not published. However, as mentioned above, deposits of the central bank with the BIS are still part of the foreign exchange reserves that are published in the International Financial Statistics. Thus, even if the BIS intervenes on behalf of a central bank, this transaction should be reflected in the reserve holdings of the central bank. A case in which interventions are undertaken without changes in the foreign exchange reserves is found in Dominguez and Frankel (1993a). They state as example "the Japanese so-called hidden reserves, which are changes in official deposits of foreign exchange with Japanese commercial banks." (p. 69). They are used for intervention purposes and do not affect official reserves as reported by the IMF. In these cases it is not possible for researchers to investigate intervention operations in-depth. However, given the fact that the reserve holdings of the countries analysed in this study fluctuated significantly this indicates that there have been regular transactions performed. Furthermore, as mentioned above, the concept of inflation targeting is above all designed to improve the transparency of the central bank. A systematic

---

106 In 1996 the BIS held US$ 91 billion of foreign exchange reserves (about 7% of world-wide foreign exchange reserves) for around 120 central banks (see Deutsche Bundesbank, 1997: 189).

misleading of the public by hiding transactions would surely not be in the best interest of the central banks.

A further problem arises if the central bank intervenes in the forward market or uses foreign exchange options to influence the exchange rate. However, we will not follow this aspect further for two reasons: First, every transaction in the forward market is followed by an transaction in the spot market some time later. Therefore, only the timing is different to spot transactions. The second reason is that "official exchange market intervention takes place mainly in the spot exchange market." (Dominguez and Frankel, 1993a: 66). The recent survey of Neely (2001) among 22 monetary authorities supports this view: 95% of the survey respondents said their intervention transactions always include spot transactions.

5.1.3 External Influences on Foreign Exchange Reserves and Their Adjustment

Besides intervention activities from central banks reserve holdings might also change due to external influences. Since the reserve portfolio is invested in different currencies and financial instruments, its value changes over time. The two most obvious reasons for reserve fluctuations are changes in the exchange rates of the currencies that are held in the portfolio (valuation effect) and interest earnings that are received on the bond holdings of the portfolio (interest earnings effect).[107] While the valuation effect might lead to both increases and decreases of the reserve holdings, interest earnings should in principle lead only to increases. In order to assess whether fluctuations in reserves reflect intervention operations or not the reserve data need to be adjusted for both effects.

5.1.3.1 Identification and Correction of Valuation Effects

The reserve data that are published by the IMF are denominated in US$. Since the reserve portfolios are invested in several currencies, the value of the reserve portfolio fluctuates with the exchange rates of the respective currencies vis-a-vis the US$. Thus, the valuation effect depends on the composition of the portfolio. Generally, the larger the share of the portfolio that is invested in US$ the smaller the valuation effect. Many studies (see e.g. Calvo and Reinhart, 2000) neglect the valuation effect on reserves and argue that the majority of reserves is held in US$. While this might hold for many emerging market countries that peg their exchange rates to the US$ this holds not true for European countries. In these countries the share of the DM (Euro) is larger as a consequence of earlier membership in the

---

107 A further reason for fluctuations stems from losses on the bond holdings if bond prices decline. However, since reserves are due to liquidity concerns primarily invested in short-term bonds, fluctuations in bond prices should not have an important effect. Nevertheless, this point might gain in importance since the investment performance of the reserve portfolios become more and more important for central banks.

European Monetary System. Figure 14 displays the currency composition of world-wide reserve holdings in 1999 and it becomes clear from this view that a significant proportion is invested in non-US$ currencies.

The share of the US$ has risen from 50% in 1990 to over 65% in 1999 while the amount invested in European currencies has remained fairly stable at about 12%. The Euro is by now the second most important reserve currency. The share of the Japanese Yen has fallen slightly over the past decade from 7 to 5% whereas the share of unspecified currencies rose from just over 3% to 12%.[108]

Figure 14: Currency composition of world-wide reserve holdings in 1999

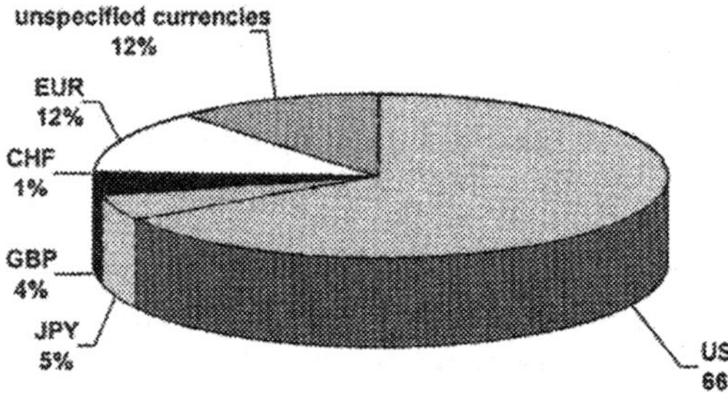

Source: IMF Annual Report 1999.

Usually, the accurate composition of a country's reserve portfolio is not published (the IMF data are highly aggregated).[109] However, many central banks report guidelines for the management of their reserves which often include the desired long-term currency distribution. From these data the valuation effect can be calculated and adjusted. The data that the IMF publishes call for the conversion of the currencies into US$ with end-of-month exchange rates.[110] Thus, different accounting practices are not reflected in the IMF data – which is why these data are comparable across countries.[111]

5.1.3.2 Estimation of Interest Earnings

Central banks' reserve holdings are invested in the capital markets. Although here again little is known about the portfolio composition of each central banks' reserves there are some guidelines for the management of a reserve portfolio. The IMF (2001) mentions as such guidelines that

- first, reserves need to readily available to meet the objectives of the central bank

[108] The IMF does not give further details about this phenomenon. The increase might be due to an increasing number of emerging market currencies that are held in the reserve portfolios of developing countries.

[109] See Dal Bosco, 1998: 295.

[110] See IMF International Financial Statistics Yearbook, various issues.

[111] See also Hüfner (2000) for an analysis of the relationship between the Bank of England's' reserve data and IFS data.

- second, risks need to be controlled efficiently
- third, reasonable earnings need to be generated.

The highest priority in the management of reserves is the liquidity of the assets that ensures that the reserves are available on short notice, for example to intervene in foreign exchange markets. To this end it is often assumed that reserve holdings are primarily invested in short-term money market assets.[112] Risk management seems also to receive considerable attention in reserve management. The reserve portfolio of central banks incorporates both market and credit risk. Since the latter is dependent on the solvency of the debtor, it can be assumed that reserve holdings are primarily invested in government bonds that have the highest possible rating in order to minimise the risk of credit defaults. Besides the need for liquidity and security it is also in the interest of the central bank to generate reasonable earnings with their reserve holdings. This desire is not least because of the costs that are associated with the maintenance of a reserve portfolio.

5.1.4 The Correlation Between Official Interventions and Reserves

A natural way to analyse whether foreign exchange reserves are a good proxy for intervention is to study the correlation between officially published data from single central banks and the development of their reserve holdings. However, since many central banks do not publish intervention data such studies are restricted to only a few countries that do so. Neely (2000) is one of the first studies that undertakes this analysis. Analysing data from Germany, Switzerland and the USA he finds correlation coefficients between 0,42 (USA) and 0,12 (Switzerland). He also finds that these coefficients improve only slightly when they are adjusted for valuation changes[113] and interest earnings but he does not study more deeply why interventions and reserve changes differ in these cases.[114]

A further central bank which publishes official intervention data is the Reserve Bank of Australia. This presents an opportunity for our case to study the correlation for this country.[115] Figure 15 displays the level of foreign exchange reserves in Australia against official interventions from 1983 to 2000.

---

112 However, there also exist more sophisticated strategies. The Swedish central bank, for example, holds an investment and a liquidity portfolio of reserves with different maturities (see Ragnartz, 1999).

113 Neely (2000) assumes that all reserves are held in US$ (p. 28) – a rather unrealistic assumption. This might also contribute to the results he obtains for the correlation coefficients after the adjustment for external factors.

114 Furthermore, his results for Germany might be biased since his German data only include interventions undertaken in the US market and not interventions in European currencies. Unless all interventions in the EMS were undertaken in the US$-market this measure might be biased.

115 For an investigation of the Bank of England's' foreign exchange reserve changes and the GBP/US$ exchange rate see Hüfner (2000).

Figure 15: Foreign exchange reserves and official interventions in Australia

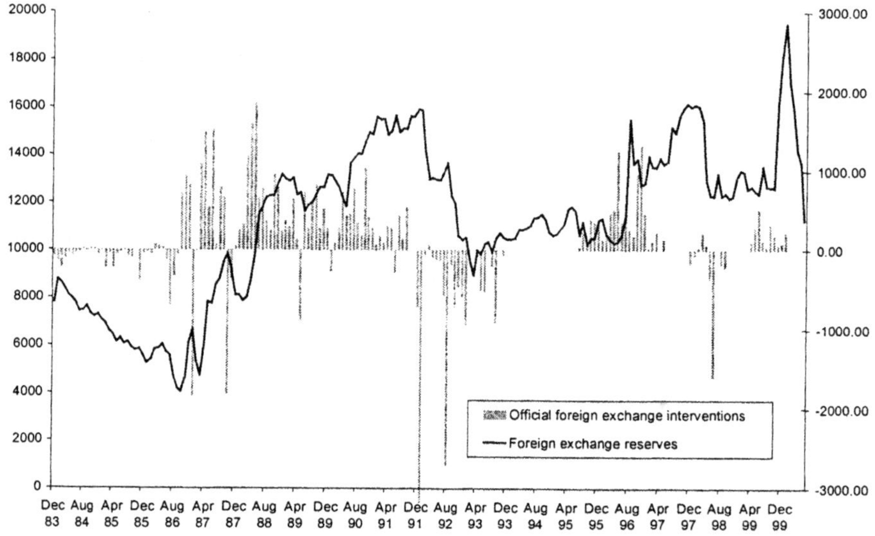

Notes: Data are in million US$. Daily intervention data are aggregated to monthly data. Foreign exchange reserves are measured by the left-hand scale while interventions are measured by the right-hand scale. A negative intervention volume indicates the sale of foreign currency and the purchase of domestic currency. It should thus be associated with a decrease in the reserve volume. Source: Reserve Bank of Australia, IMF.

It can be seen that in periods of foreign exchange purchases (1986 to 1991 or 1995 to 1997) the level of reserves tends to increase whereas in selling periods (1991 to 1993 or 1998) the level of reserves decreases. This simple graphical illustration thus seems to support the hypothesis that foreign exchange reserves are a good proxy for intervention operations. The correlation coefficient computed over the time period 1983 to 2000 is 0,408. Rolling correlations over a one-year time window reveal that the correlation varies significantly over time with the highest correlation in times of heavy intervention activity. During periods where there have been few intervention operations the correlation decreases.

One reason for the rather low correlation lies in the neglect of external factors like valuation and interest earning effects. But these do account only for a small proportion. One of the main reasons for the low correlation might instead lie in the definition of foreign exchange intervention. Since the official data of the central banks depend crucially upon which transactions the central bank considers as interventions or more concretely wants to be seen as intervention. Since there is no universal definition of interventions the compilation of the data is to some extent subjective. However, as mentioned before, all foreign exchange operations of a central bank can be traced in the balance sheets – thus, there seem to be other operations than the official interventions released.[116]

5.1.5 Active versus Passive Interventions

A narrow definition is given in Adams and Henderson (1983): "This definition [of intervention] embraces purchases and sales by central banks of foreign exchange against domestic currency." (p. 3). This is the case that is usually referred to as intervention. More broadly foreign exchange intervention can be defined as "...any transaction or announcement by an official agent of a government that is intended to influence the value of an exchange rate or the country's stock of foreign exchange reserves." (Dominguez and Frankel, 1993a: 55).[117]

The literature on the subject of intervention distinguishes between active and passive interventions. Active intervention refers to a transaction where the central bank directly buys or sells foreign assets to influence the exchange rate. These interventions can either be public or secret. Appendix I gives an overview of active intervention reports of inflation targeting countries.

Whereas active interventions are characterised by the fact that the central bank initiates the trade, passive interventions are initiated by another authority (though they are usually performed by the central bank) and are often labelled as "customer transactions". Customers of central banks might be the own or foreign government as well as other central banks (see Dominguez and Frankel, 1993a: 64). Since the central bank usually decides over the timing of these transactions they can be used to signal information to the market. It has thus often been argued in the literature that these passive interventions should be taken as potential intervention activity.

In the words of Adams and Henderson (1983): "Such direct dealings of central banks, sometimes called 'passive' intervention, are actually as active an effort to affect the ultimate relative supplies of securities denominated in different currencies as conventional operations are; they should therefore be included in a comprehensive intervention measure." (p. 3). All transactions whether they are active or passive transactions require a change in the reserve holdings of a central bank (given that they are performed in the spot market). Thus, we argue that changes in the reserve data provide an adequate measure of intervention activity – it might even be a more comprehensive measure than official intervention data provided by the central bank. For example, when the European Central Bank (ECB) announced in August/September 2000 that it would henceforth sell the interest income from its foreign exchange holdings, the US$/Euro exchange rate appreciated signifi-

---

116 In his study of the effects of US intervention, Kim (2002) uses both official data and reserves and finds that "many similar results can be obtained by using foreign exchange reserves [instead of official intervention data]." (p. 25).

117 See also the similar definition of Dominguez (1999): "Foreign exchange market intervention is a transaction or announcement by an official agent of a government that is intended to influence the value of an exchange rate." (p. 5).

cantly. However, the ECB stressed that this has not been an intervention operation and thus would not have been included in official intervention data.

A classical example of passive intervention is reported for the Czech Republic: The continued appreciation of the krona throughout 2001 was undesirable for policy-makers as it undermined the competitiveness of the export sector. The government feared that foreign exchange receipts from privatisation transactions could further strengthen the domestic currency if these receipts were converted into kronas. Thus, it was decided to keep these receipts out of the market through the following mechanism:

"One of the elements of this mechanism, however, must be direct conversion of the State's foreign exchange revenues into CNB [Czech National Bank] foreign exchange reserves. This is the only way to ensure that the State's foreign exchange revenues will be available to cover its current koruna needs without entering the foreign exchange market." (Czech National Bank, 2002).[118]

This transaction is passive, since it is initiated by the government rather than the central bank. It is designed to influence the exchange rate and changes the level of foreign exchange reserves. However, this transaction would not be classified as official intervention in the narrow sense – incorporating such operations in a comprehensive analysis of foreign exchange intervention is thus only possible by studying changes in foreign exchange reserves.

The Reserve Bank of Australia states very clearly the purpose and the procedure of passive interventions: "Normally, these transactions with the Government are passed more or less directly through to the market, so that they do not act as a drain on (or a source of augmentation for) foreign reserves. However, at times when the exchange rate is under downward pressure and well below its long-run average, such as in 1998, the Bank usually refrains from passing the transactions through to the market, to avoid exacerbating market pressures. These transactions are initially met from the Bank's holdings of foreign exchange and put through the market at a later time, when the exchange rate is more favourable." (Reserve Bank of Australia, 1999: 16).

That the central bank indeed has a variety of tools available besides direct public interventions is also supported by statements of Bank of England associate director Ian Plenderleith. According to a Bloomberg report he pointed out "[...] that even when the Bank of England does operate directly to try to influence the pound's movements, there is a wide variety of ways that it could choose to operate. The run from 'limited and occasional' undisclosed operations, 'essentially of a tactical nature,' to outright, visible intervention."[119]

The above mentioned examples demonstrate the usefulness of studying foreign exchange reserves instead of officially declared intervention operations (which are, as stated above, mostly not published anyway). Relying simply on officially

---

[118] The costs of the central bank for the sterilisation of these additional foreign exchange reserves were covered by the State.

[119] Bloomberg News, February 14, 1994, 1:01 pm, "Bank of England emphasises pound's role in monetary policy".

declared intervention operations for analysis thus seems to understate the true extent of interventions

5.2 Intervention Activity in Inflation Targeting Countries

"Interventions play a role in a central bank's range of instruments."
(Riksbank, 2001b: 19)

In order to see whether inflation targeting central banks in practice actually apply foreign exchange intervention we now turn to the case studies of New Zealand, Australia, Canada, Sweden and the United Kingdom. The goal of this chapter is to identify differences in intervention behaviour by creating a ranking of intervention activity. Since there is no universal method for this procedure we perform several different analysis and will summarise the results at the end. Referring again to our stylised model of monetary policy, we now tackle question 3 of our subjects of inquiry.

5.2.1 Comparison of Intervention Capacities

As a first stylised fact we compare the average level of reserves – which corresponds to the intervention capacity of a country. To see whether this level is 'large' compared with other countries we also calculate the ratios of the reserve level and a measure of the openness of a country and the size of its foreign exchange market. The United States, which is often defined as a country with a purely floating exchange rate, is taken as a comparison country. While the size of the reserve holdings does not reveal anything about the intervention transactions of a country it is nevertheless a first hint at how much weight a country puts on exchange rate policy. It is often mentioned in the literature that the reserve level serves as a kind of credibility function in that it signals to the market that a central bank has the power to influence the exchange rate when necessary. As Spolander (1999) remarks: "The question of the optimal amount of reserves is related to the credible conduct of exchange rate policy. In other words, if the central bank wants to manage the exchange rate by intervening in the foreign exchange market, it must have enough reserves to do so in a credible way." (p. 94).

Table 12: Level of reserves compared

	Average abs. level of reserves (in mln.US$)	Reserves/ ((1/2)(Imports+ Exports))	Re-serves/ GDP	Global daily FX spot market turnover involving the cur-rency (in bln US$)	Reserves/Share of currency on global spot markets
New Zealand	3879	34%	8%	2.32	167%
Australia	13249	24%	4%	16.25	82%
Canada	14919	8%	2%	17.42	86%
Sweden	16801	27%	8%	10.06	167%
United Kingdom	33682	14%	3%	51.08	66%
USA	41074	7%	0.6%	349.85	12%

Note: Ratios are calculated as the average of yearly data from 1990-1998 for USA and for the other countries from the year of introduction of inflation targeting until 1998. Nominal GDP, imports and exports in national currency were converted into US$ using yearly average nominal exchange rates. FX spot market turnover is taken from the BIS survey published in 2001. Source: IFS, BIS.

Judging from the absolute average level of foreign exchange reserves among inflation targeting countries, the UK is clearly ordered first with a reserve level more than twice as large as in any other country except the United States. New Zealand, on the other hand, has a low absolute level which is only a tenth of the UK numbers. However, a different picture emerges when the absolute numbers are compared with the openness of the countries (measured as the average of imports and exports), with the gross domestic product (GDP) of a country and with the size of the foreign exchange markets. While the New Zealand reserve level amounts to 34% of the size of the openness, this ratio is only 14% for the UK. An equal ranking emerges if reserves are measured against local GDP. Similarly, when measured against the size of the spot market that involves the currency the reserve holdings of New Zealand seem to be quite large. Comparable results are found for Sweden, while Australia is placed in the middle. The reserve holdings of Canada appear small in relation to the size of the economy. But as a ratio of the currency market size this number is larger than the UK ratio. Canada has indeed been concerned about the level of their reserve holdings and thus in the last years has more than tripled its holdings in absolute terms.

To summarise, New Zealand and Sweden maintain relatively large holdings of foreign currency reserves, while the UK holds relatively few reserves. Australia and Canada are ranked in the middle. The capacity to intervene effectively is therefore highest in Sweden and New Zealand and is lowest in the UK.

5.2.2 Comparison of Reserve Changes

In order to measure actual intervention operations, changes in the foreign exchange holdings have to be compared. This follows from the fact that foreign exchange interventions should be reflected in a change of a central banks foreign assets. However, as mentioned in the previous chapter, foreign exchange reserve may also fluctuate due to valuation and interest earning effects. Before comparing reserve changes, these have to be adjusted for these two effects.[120]

5.2.2.1 Correction for Valuation Changes

In order to correct for the valuation effect the asset allocation of a reserve portfolio with respect to the currency composition has to be known. This information, which we collected from various central bank sources, is presented in the following table. Again, the United States are mentioned for comparison.

Table 13: Asset allocation of reserve portfolios

	Currency composition			
	USD	DEM	JPY	GBP
Australia	40%	30%	30%	-
Canada	80%	10%	10%	-
New Zealand	50%	20%	30%	-
Sweden	35%	35%	15%	15%
United Kingdom	45%	50%	5%	-
United States	-	50%	50%	-

Note: The currency composition for Australia is the benchmark portfolio that can be found in the Reserve Bank of Australia Annual Report 2000, p. 16. For Sweden it is taken from Ragnartz (1999), p. 33 and relates to the allocation in 1999. According to Ragnartz, "the relative distribution between the different currencies is fixed and is therefore not actively managed." (p. 33). The allocation for Canada is taken from De León (2000-2001), p. 17 and is the estimated average for the period 1991-2000. The currency allocation for the UK reserves refers to the benchmark portfolio mentioned in HM Treasury (1998), p. 4. New Zealand figures are taken from the currency composition as published in the Reserve Bank of New Zealand Annual Report 2000. The US allocation is taken from Federal Reserve Bank of New York (2001).

Some central banks, such as the Reserve Bank of Australia or the Bank of England, publish benchmark portfolios for their reserve holdings. For the other central banks the composition for one year can be calculated from balance sheets in Annual Reports. While the composition may fluctuate over time, it is often stressed that the relative distribution is roughly the same over time since it is determined by various fixed factors like the composition of trade partners and so on. As can

[120] If these effects are not corrected then an increase in reserves that is simply due to an appreciation of the reserve currencies in the portfolio, for example, might be wrongly interpreted as a purchase of foreign exchange by the central bank (in order to weaken the domestic currency).

be seen the share of currencies is rather diverse: the US$-share, for example, fluctuates between 80% (Canada) and 35% (Sweden).

The monthly valuation change is calculated using the following equation:

$$VC_t = ((Res_t + Res_{t-1})/2)(\sum_{i=1}^{n} \alpha_i \Delta e_i) \quad (5.1)$$

with Res_t and Res_{t-1} as the level of reserves in period t and t-1, respectively, α_i as the weight of the (non-US Dollar) currency i and Δe_i as the monthly percentage change of the exchange rates $DEM/USD, GBP/USD$ and JPY/USD from t-1 to t. Thus, the valuation change is calculated with regard to the average monthly reserve level and is expressed in millions of US$. If $VC_t > 0$, the central bank has incurred a valuation loss (when measured in US$), i.e. the reserve currencies depreciated in period t. Consequently, when adjusting for valuation changes, VC_t has to be added to the reserve level each month.

5.2.2.2 Correction for Interest Earnings

The monthly interest earnings on the reserves are calculated as follows:

$$IE_t = \sum_{i=1}^{n} \alpha_i (r_{i,t-1}/12) Res_{t-1} \quad (5.2)$$

with α_i as the weight of the (non-US Dollar) currency i in the reserve portfolio, $r_{i,t-1}$ as the three-month money market rate of currency i in period t-1 and Res_{t-1} as the level of reserves in period t-1 in millions of US$.[121] For simplicity, we assume that all foreign exchange reserves are invested in short-term money market instruments. Since liquidity is an important factor in the investment process of foreign exchange reserves this assumption can be regarded as reasonable.

With VC as valuation change and IE as interest earnings the adjusted time series for each country is calculated as

$$AdjRes_t = Res_t + VC_t - IE_t \quad (5.3)$$

Note that $VC_t > 0$ means that in period t the reserve currencies have depreciated against the US$ (since e_i is measured as foreign currency per US$). Consequently, VC_t has to be added to the reserve holding in t to compensate for the depreciation. IE is always positive and has to be subtracted in order to correct for an increase in reserves that is only due to interest earnings. AdjRes thus displays the level of foreign exchange reserves that results after external effects have been corrected.

Figure 16 displays the relative development of foreign exchange reserves for each country, individually adjusted for valuation effects and interest earnings.

---

121 See also Takagi (1991) for the estimation of foreign exchange reserves interest earnings.

Figure 16: Foreign exchange reserves compared to the US

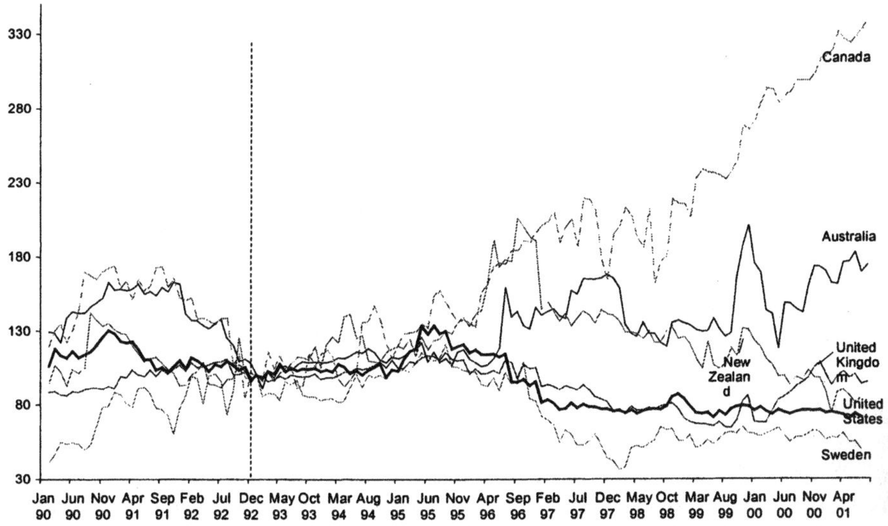

Source: IFS, own calculations. 01/1993=100.

As can be seen from the graph the development of reserve levels across inflation targeting countries has been diverse. The reserve series of the United States is included for comparison since the US is often characterised as one of the purest floaters in the world. While the reserves of the United Kingdom move rather closely with the US, the other four countries exhibit more volatility. The reserves of the Swedish Riksbank were decreasing in the past years. Australia, New Zealand and Canada on the other side had seen their reserve levels increasing. The sharp and continuous increase in the foreign exchange holdings of the Bank of Canada of more than 300% is especially striking. The reasons for this development are given by the Bank as follows: "In the early 1990s, the level of reserves declined, reflecting official efforts to dampen the volatility of a declining Canadian dollar. The mid-1990s was a period of relative stability. Then, reserves began to rise again in the late 1990s, particularly after 1998, reflecting increased flows and volatility in foreign exchange markets as well as government's commitment to maintain a prudent level of liquid reserves more in line with that of comparable countries." (De León, 2000-2001: 14). Indeed, as if evident from Table 12 Canada had during the past years on average a relatively low level of reserves compared with the other inflation targeting countries.

5.2.3 Identification of Intervention Activity

For the following analysis we will always refer to the time series that are adjusted for valuation changes and interest earnings. Figure 16 suggests that intervention activity differs among inflation targeting countries. However, the reserve level alone does not say much about whether intervention activity is relatively high or low. In order to assess this question it is more important to study the monthly fluctuations and to see whether these are large relative to other countries. We apply several different methods to identify these changes and put them into perspective.

5.2.3.1 Absolute Reserve Changes

First, we look at absolute average monthly changes in foreign exchange reserves.

Table 14: Absolute reserve changes compared

	Average absolute monthly change in fx reserves in mln US$
New Zealand	205.24
Sweden	978.71
Australia	649.02
Canada	826.06
United Kingdom	1157.20

Note: The numbers for each country are calculated as the average during the period in which inflation targeting was pursued. Source: IFS, own calculations.

As can be seen from Table 14 the UK had on average the largest monthly change in reserves with 1,16 billion US$ compared with only 0,2 billion US$ in New Zealand. While this is a first evidence for intervention activity we do not know whether these amounts are actually 'large' relative to country size, size of foreign exchange markets or else. Thus, in order to build a ranking of intervention activity across countries these changes need to be normalised.

5.2.3.2 Normalisation with the Degree of Openness

Bofinger and Wollmershäuser (2001) suggest in their study of managed floating to normalise reserve changes with a measure of the openness of the country. They calculate a so-called "sum of absolute changes" S^{abs} which they define as:

$$S^{abs}(n)_t = \sum_{i=0}^{n} \left| \frac{Res_{t-i}}{\frac{Ex_{t-i} + Im_{t-i}}{2}} - \frac{Res_{t-i-1}}{\frac{Ex_{t-i-1} + Im_{t-i-1}}{2}} \right| \qquad (5.4)$$

with n as the number of months to be included in the sum. The interpretation is: The larger the degree of openness of a country the smaller the weight that is attached to the level of reserves. According to this concept, a country with high values of S^{abs} can be said to intervene more intensely. Table 15 displays the results for n=12 as probability values, i.e. the probability that S^{abs} lies under or above values from 0,5 to 2.

Table 15: "Sum of absolute changes" across countries

	<0,5	<1,0	<1,5	<2
New Zealand	0.51%	2.78%	10.38%	27.45%
Sweden	1.54%	6.96%	20.71%	45.30%
Australia	10.03%	25.28%	47.93%	71.33%
Canada	23.84%	85.66%	99.78%	100.00%
United Kingdom	26.93%	97.07%	100.00%	100.00%

Note: The percentage values indicate the probability that S^{abs} is smaller than 0,5 (1,0; 1,5; 2) within the period of inflation targeting.

The higher S^{abs} the larger the weighted intervention volume. As can be seen the probability of large changes is rather small in the UK while it is relatively larger in New Zealand, Sweden and Australia. One potential disadvantage of this method is that the degree of openness varies over time. In our concrete example of the five inflation targeting countries it turns out that Canada's degree of openness has increased significantly over the past decade and thus S^{abs} remains relatively small despite significant reserve changes (see Figure 16). Thus, we introduce a further measure by using the size of the foreign exchange market as normalisation.

5.2.3.3 Normalisation with the Size of Foreign Exchange Markets

Another possible normalisation method is to put the absolute reserve changes in perspective to the size of the foreign exchange markets for the different currencies. From the point of each individual intervention policy it matters if the intervention volume is small or large with regard to the size of the foreign exchange market involving the respective currency.

Table 16: Average monthly reserve changes as a ratio of daily fx market turnover

	1995	1998	2001	Average ratio 1995-2001
Sweden	14.1%	16.8%	3.1%	6.7%
New Zealand	9.0%	4.8%	2.9%	4.5%
Canada	2.1%	1.6%	1.6%	1.7%
Australia	2.1%	1.5%	1.3%	1.6%
United Kingdom	1.1%	0.8%	0.8%	0.8%

Note: The market volume for each country is taken from BIS (2001), table 3: Currency distribution of reported global foreign exchange market turnover. This includes turnover in spot, forward and swap markets.

The fact that the ratios are declining over time reflects the growing share that each currency had on the turnover on international foreign exchange markets and thus is not due to a decline in the absolute reserve changes over time. Compared with the results in Table 15 there is no significant qualitative change. As expected, Canada moves up in the order of intervention activity as a result of its increasing degree of openness. Furthermore, Sweden is leading the ranking in this measure with New Zealand being second. The position of the United Kingdom is unchanged – suggesting that the Bank of England indeed pursued relatively less interventions than all other inflation targeting countries.

5.2.3.4 Response to Shocks

The performance of inflation targeting countries, above all their record of low inflation rates has been favourable throughout the 1990s. However, lower inflation rates were generally observed in industrial countries over the last decade. Thus, some economists argue that there is no proof that the presence of inflation targeting regimes has indeed been responsible for this positive inflation environment but rather that there were no large shocks during this time that could have challenged monetary policy. Conversely, as pointed out by Mishkin and Schmidt-Hebbel (2001) there have actually been crisis times during the 1990s, for example the Asian financial crisis in 1997/98 or the oil price shock in 2000. Especially the Asian and Russian financial crises present good cases to study the behaviour of the central banks.

Table 17: Reserve development during Asian and Russian financial crises

	Australia	Canada	New Zealand	Sweden	United Kingdom	United States
Development of FX reserves in the period 10/97 - 08/98	-22.3%	-23.6%	-9.7%	-7.5%	-9.9%	-1.6%

Source: IFS, own calculations.

Table 17 shows the development of foreign exchange reserves over the whole crisis period. October 1997 marks the spread of the Asian crisis with the sharp declines in the Hong Kong and US stock markets. The Russian crisis took place in the summer of 1998 when the Russian government defaulted on its debt. Both crises had consequences in the financial markets world-wide. As can be seen all inflation targeting countries record a decrease in reserves over this period with the sharpest drop occurring in Australia and Canada with –22.3 and –23.6%, respectively. This corresponds with several news reports about Australian and Canadian interventions during this time (see appendix I). The reserves of Sweden, New Zealand and the UK declined by just under 10%. For comparison we also report the development of the US reserves which dropped by only 1.6%. This is in line with the observation that the US presents an example of a relatively pure floater. The declines in the other countries support the assumption that foreign exchange was sold during this period in order to strengthen the domestic currency and prevent a depreciation. The table also illustrates that these operations are conducted by each country to a different extent.

Australia and New Zealand were more directly affected by the large devaluation of the Asian currencies as a large proportion of their trade is conducted with these countries. However, while Australia intervened heavily in the markets, the New Zealand interventions appears to be smaller. Nevertheless, despite the official declaration of the Reserve Bank of New Zealand that it does not intervene in foreign exchange markets, the development of its reserves suggests that there have been some operations (which might not be called foreign exchange intervention in the definition of the central bank, for example ‚passive' interventions).

5.2.4 Ranking of Intervention Activity

After assessing different methods to identify intervention activity there emerges a ranking which points out which countries have intervened more in the market and which countries let their exchange rates float more freely. As there are different methods for identifying intervention activity such a ranking surely includes some subjectivity. However, there are some points that appear fairly clearly:

Although at first sight the UK exhibits the largest absolute average reserve change among the five countries, this change appears relatively small when normalised with the degree of openness or the size of the fx market.

In New Zealand and Sweden, on the contrary, the reserve changes are relatively large when measured against the openness and market size.

Canada and Australia were found to intervene less than Sweden and New Zealand, albeit considerably more than the UK.

From this evidence we construct a rough ranking as illustrated in Figure 17.

Figure 17: Intervention ranking of inflation targeting countries

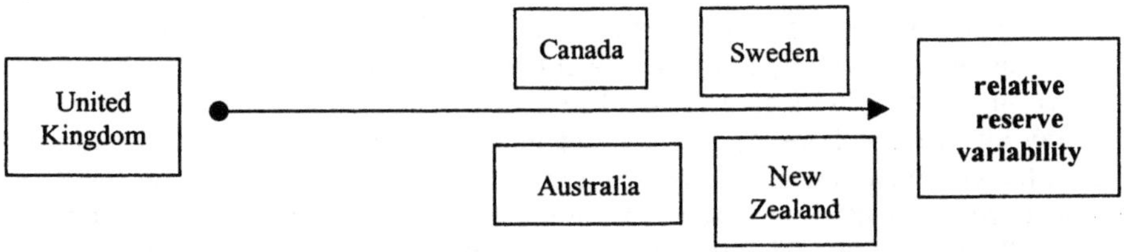

As mentioned in chapter 5.1.5 there is a distinction between active and passive interventions. Both kinds of intervention are reflected in reserve changes. To get a feeling for the extent of active interventions we provide a list of news reports about interventions in the Appendix. These reports from major newswire agencies give a rough proxy for the frequency of direct interventions in the foreign exchange markets (except for secret interventions, rumours of direct purchases or sales of foreign exchange by a central bank spread fast among market participants). The most intervention reports in the past ten years were found for Australia (40 reports), followed by Canada (24 reports) and Sweden (18 reports). For the UK and New Zealand only 10 and 2 reports were found, respectively. Most strikingly is the divergence between New Zealand reserve changes and official statements and news reports. One potential explanation might be that these reserve changes reflect secret and/or passive interventions.

Among the five countries in our sample we identify the United Kingdom as the country with the lowest intervention activity. Despite the fact that absolute monthly reserve changes are highest in the UK, these changes appear relatively modest when viewed against the degree of openness or the size of the fx market. Also, the reserve level is small compared with the other countries. While this evidence suggests few intervention operations by the Bank of England, this still leaves open the question of how to interpret the remaining reserve changes, however small they are. Hüfner (2000) shows that the decline in the reserves by about 40% is correlated with changes in the GBP/US$ exchange rate. The view of the Bank of England on foreign exchange intervention has been exemplified by Wadhwani (2000). Generally, he writes that sterilised interventions provide a tool to support achieving the inflation target: "However, used judiciously, it [foreign exchange intervention] can sometimes be helpful in terms of achieving our monetary policy objective." (Wadhwani, 2000: 19). However, discussions of the Monetary Policy Committee in 2000 show that the intervention tool is seen controversially among the members.[122] Thus, our result suggests that there may be interventions by the Bank of England albeit on a much smaller scale than what can be observed in other inflation targeting countries. Newswire reports of intervention activity (see Appendix I) indicate that the Bank of England on some occasions participated in concerted intervention operations, e.g. in 1994 buying Deutsche marks versus US dollars or acting on behalf of the Bank of Japan in 1995. This explains some of the reserve changes which are, however, not directly related to the British monetary policy.

On the other hand, New Zealand and Sweden are identified as countries with relatively high intervention operations. Australia and Canada are ranked between the two extremes with no clear order emerging. The high reserve variability of New Zealand is especially puzzling given the fact that the Reserve Bank officially denies any intervention operations. The Deputy Governor of the central bank, Murray Sherwin declares: "[...] our exchange rate regime has been as close to the non-interventionist end of the spectrum as can be found. Since floating the Kiwi dollar in March 1985 there has not been a cent committed to fx market intervention." (Sherwin, 2000). This statement is quite the contrary to our findings.[123] The

---

122 See Bank of England, Minutes of Monetary Policy Committee Meeting 9 and 10 February 2000, available at www.bankofengland.co.uk. Some members of the committee view interventions as a more powerful signal than verbal concerns about the exchange rate. However, it turns out that the majority of committee members is concerned that failed intervention operations would seriously damage the credibility of the central bank.

123 Other studies support our finding of high reserve variability for New Zealand: Levy Yeyati and Sturzenegger (1999) find: "[...] many countries that claimed to run a floating rate displayed little exchange rate volatility coupled with intense foreign exchange market intervention, so that in reality they are closer to a fix exchange rate regime. Brazil and New Zealand appear occasionally in this group as well as some

explanation for the stated policy is that the Reserve Bank of New Zealand does not believe in the efficiency of sterilised interventions and thus concludes that interventions provide an independent tool besides the setting of interest rates for the conduct of monetary policy. Given this background, how can it be explained that New Zealand is found to have a relatively high intervention activity?

One explanation might stem from a different definition of intervention used by the central bank – i.e. that the central bank undertakes operations that it does not consider to be interventions. Indeed, in its Annual Report 1996/97 the Reserve Bank states: "Our presence in the market is now limited to small positions that we initiate. This trading helps our understanding of market dynamics, maintains links with market participants, and ensures that systems and procedures are in place should the bank need to intervene in the foreign exchange market." (p. 12). The main difference between these transactions and official interventions seems to be the fact that the Reserve Bank does not aim at influencing the exchange rate.[124] A further possibility is that these reserve changes reflect passive interventions, i.e. dealings with customers such as the government or other entities, which might nevertheless be used to influence the exchange rate. However, these are only two potential explanations for the obvious divergence of our findings with the official statements. In our review of New Zealand monetary policy under inflation targeting we will study reserve changes and exchange rate movements to see whether the relationship between them is close.

The Reserve Bank of Australia is more optimistic with regard to the efficiency of sterilised interventions. It highlights the importance of the credibility of a central bank when intervening and its ability to change the expectations of market participants (Rankin, 2000). Consequently, one reason why fx interventions are used in Australia is "to give monetary policy greater room for maneuver." Specifically, "intervention can help to ensure that any costs of surprising markets [with rapid changes in interest rates] are minimised, allowing greater room for monetary policy to move ahead of market expectations." (Rankin, 2000). What is especially noteworthy in the case of the Reserve Bank of Australia is its openness regarding intervention operations.[125] A time series including daily intervention transactions

---

Scandinavian economies like Norway, Finland and Sweden." (p. 9). Similarly, Calvo and Reinhart (2000) write: "[...] large swings in foreign exchange reserves appear to be commonplace, consistent with a higher extent of intervention in the foreign exchange market – even relative to what is to be expected a priori from a freely floating exchange rate regime. Nor is this exclusively an emerging market phenomenon – Canada's and New Zealand's reserve changes are about seven times and five times, respectively, as volatile as that of the United States." (p. 20). Both studies do not refer to the statement of the Reserve Bank of New Zealand that it is one of the purest floaters and thus do not attempt to explain this discrepancy further.

124 This interpretation is supported by the fact that there are virtually no news reports of interventions by the Reserve Bank of New Zealand (see Appendix I) – which would be surprising if the central bank is indeed pursuing active intervention operations on a high frequency and scale.

125 This is also reflected by the frequency of news reports about Australian central bank intervention given in Appendix I.

is available for the past twenty years on the central bank website. This helps to enhance transparency which, as mentioned in the second chapter, is one of the key factors of an inflation targeting framework. Thus, the official Australian stance concerning interventions is in line with our findings that this tool has indeed been used.[126]

Similar to other central banks the Swedish Riksbank does not reveal much information about its past intervention operations. When it intervened in June 2001 to stop the depreciation trend of the krona versus the euro the Riksbank published statements that shed some light on the view that the central bank has regarding interventions. Governor Bäckström said: "Currency market interventions are one of the instruments at the disposal of a central bank. For a central bank that targets inflation, the primary instrument is, however, the interest rate. But at a time when the exchange rate is a serious upside risk in the inflation forecast and deviates markedly from a reasonable value, a situation may arise where currency market interventions are motivated as an additional element in the work of continuously ensuring price stability." (Riksbank, 2001a). This statement is very close to the idea that sterilised interventions serve as an additional policy tool besides the interest rate that we suggested. It recognises the fact that exchange rates deviate from fundamental values and can be controlled only insufficiently with interest rate policy. It is also made clear that the use of interventions serves to achieve the inflation target and not to control the exchange rate per se. Thus, the Riksbank seems to comply relatively closely to what can be termed managed floating in a policy of inflation targeting.

Canada is very open with respect to its fx interventions. Although actual intervention data are kept secret, the Bank of Canada publishes the strategy of its intervention operations, known as intervention programs. According to Murray et al. (1996) the objective of these programs was to control short-term movements in the Canadian dollar's value against the US dollar rather than to establish a specific exchange rate target (see Box on next page).[127] Among other objectives a reduced exchange rate volatility should help in the conduct of monetary policy – this is the classical case of 'exchange rate smoothing' in contrast to 'exchange rate targeting'. This objective is different compared with Australia and Sweden. Taken together this suggests that Canadian interventions have not been used primarily to serve as an additional operating target of monetary policy to influence the stance of monetary conditions. Rather, according to the official statements stability of the exchange rate per se was the aim.

---

126 Kim and Sheen (2002) find that the Reserve Bank's interventions were determined by exchange rate trend correction, volatility smoothing, US-Australian interest rate differentials, profitability and reserve inventory considerations. This shows that the Reserve Bank was quite flexible in its approach.

127 In September 1998 the Bank of Canada abolished the intervention programs which triggered intervention in an automatic fashion. Since then, interventions are carried out on a discretionary basis (see Canadian Department of Finance, Annual Report to Parliament on the Operations of the Exchange Fund Account 1999).

The intervention programs of the Bank of Canada

There are two intervention programs that were followed by the Bank of Canada. The objective of both of them was to dampen "short-term movements in the exchange rate, rather than maintaining or reestablishing a specific exchange rate level." (Murray et al., 1996: 312). The first program was in place until 12 April 1995 when the second started. The exact features of the programs were never revealed to the public. Nevertheless, as is mentioned in the literature, foreign exchange traders could easily figure out the procedure since the intervention rule was relatively mechanic. Furthermore, two papers from Bank of Canada economists, Murray et al. (1996) and Beattie and Fillion (1999), provide some background information about the design of the intervention programs.

The old intervention regime

During the old regime intervention took place on 48% of all days. Intervention always occurred when the exchange rate left a non-intervention band that was established each trading day. Once the exchange rate left the band intervention was triggered automatically. Intervention was therefore by construction always conducted in a leaning against the wind manner, e.g. countering the actual trend in the exchange rate. At the end of the 1980s the band was 100 basispoints wide. When the exchange rate moved out of the target range the central bank began buying or selling 4 million US dollars per basis point. Thus, if the exchange rate rose 10 points above the upper ceiling (=depreciation) the Bank of Canada had to sell 40 million US dollars in exchange for Canadian Dollars. On the next day the upper ceiling was set at the last exchange rate where intervention took place.

Old intervention program example

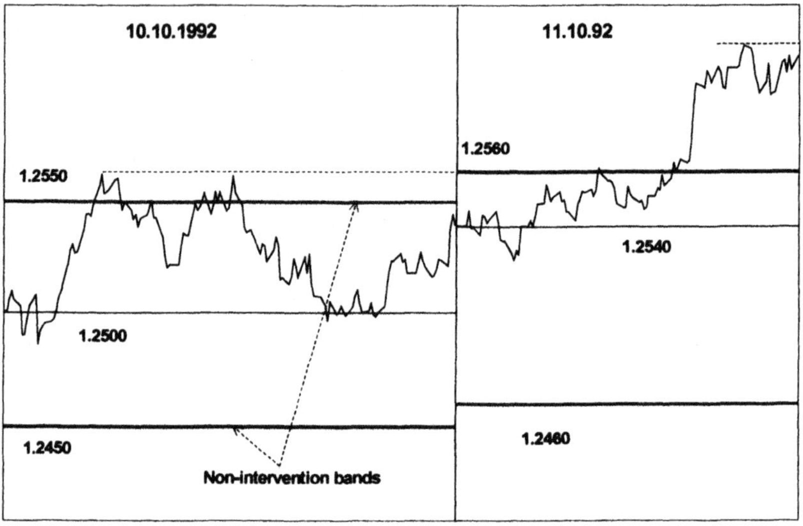

Note: On the first trading day in the example (10.10.1992) the midpoint of the non-intervention zone lies at 1,25 C$/US$. Intervention takes place whenever the exchange rates breaks through the upper ceiling at 1,2550 C$/US$. On the following day the upper ceiling is set at 1,2560 C$/US$, i.e. the exchange rate where the last intervention of the preceding day took place. Source: Own illustration.

The new intervention regime

On 12 April 1995 the intervention program of the Bank of Canada was changed for four reasons (see Murray et al., 1996: 319):

- The frequency of intervention should be reduced,
- To allow for more intense interventions,
- To better achieve the objective of maintaining orderly markets,
- To allow for more discretionary interventions.

In order to give the market more freedom in exchange rate movements, the non-intervention bands were widened. It still encompassed 100 basis points but the mid-point of the intervention band was set near the previous days' close. Thus the exchange rate needed to move at least 50 basis points in each direction before the central bank entered the market. Furthermore, the volume of interventions was increased and it was announced that discretionary interventions would occur more often. Beattie and Fillion (1999) report that intervention under the new regime occurred only on 9% of business days (in contrast to almost 50% under the old regime). Table 8 summarises intervention statistics for the period 12 April 1995 – 30 January 1998.

Intervention statistics Bank of Canada

	April 1995 – September 1997				October 1997 – January 1998			
	Number of interventions		Average absolute amount		Number of interventions		Average absolute amount	
	Mech.	Discr.	Mech.	Discr.	Mech.	Discr.	Mech.	Discr.
All	47	9	148.0	125.7	6	21	196.5	164.7
Buying US$	26	0	146.7	0	1	0	51.0	0
Selling US$	21	9	149.6	125.7	5	21	225.6	164.7

Note: The amount of interventions are measures in mill US$. 'Mech.' and 'Discr.' refer to automatic and discretionary interventions, respectively. Source: Beattie and Fillion, 1999: 27.

Note that in the above example with the exchange rate standing at 1,25 the intervention bands were set at +/- 0,4%. The intervention bands around the currencies in the European Monetary System had been set at +/- 2,5% before they were widened to +/-15%. The bands around the crawling peg of Chile were set at 0,5% in 1984 but were gradually widened to 5% in 1989. Colombia set its crawling band width at 7% and Israel initially introduced a band of +/- 3% around the Shekel's value.[128] These examples show that the intervention rules of Canada were indeed even stricter than in a regime of limited flexibility. The result of this policy has been very little volatility of the Canadian dollar. This is indeed an example of a successful use of foreign exchange intervention in practice.

5.3 The Use of Interventions as an Additional Policy Instrument

So far we have seen differences in the use of foreign exchange interventions among the five inflation targeting countries. What has not been asked, however, is the question how these differences can be explained. To be sure, one could argue that these differences are country-specific, i.e. that some countries had to cope

128 See Williamson, 1996.

more with exchange rate fluctuations than others. The case studies for each country will shed more light on this issue.

This chapter is now dealing with the relationship between intervention activity and interest rate policy. Again, our stylised model of monetary policy in an open economy (Figure 18) illustrates the reasoning for this analysis:

Figure 18: Stylised model of monetary policy in an open economy

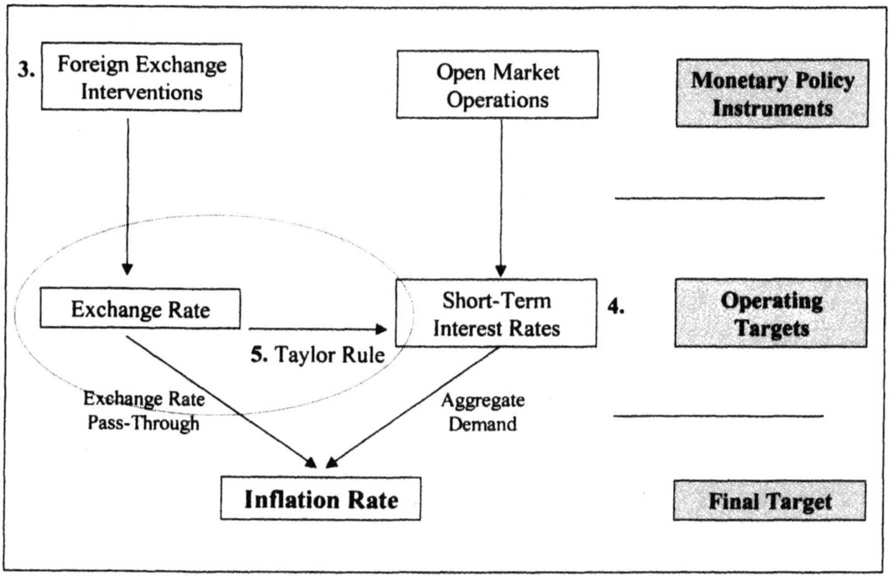

The exchange rate can either be influenced by direct interventions or via interest rate policy. We showed that uncovered interest parity does not hold, i.e. the exchange rate does not react automatically in a predictable fashion to interest rate differentials. Now that we studied intervention behaviour in the prior chapter, we look at which countries incorporate the exchange rate in their interest rate decision process.[129] Our hypothesis is that countries that intervene more heavily do exhibit less variability in interest rates (question 4 of our subjects of inquiry) and react to a smaller extent to exchange rate fluctuations with their interest rate policy than countries that exhibit smaller intervention operations (question 5 of our subjects of inquiry).

So far, these hypotheses have not been tackled in the literature explicitly across countries. As Fischer (2000) states: "The intervention literature has focused primarily on the effectiveness of interventions on the exchange rate and has not considered whether the decision to intervene influences the dynamics of other monetary instruments such as short-term interest rates." (p. 4). As shown previously, sterilised interventions can be viewed as an independent policy instrument for

[129] Note that this relationship is different to uncovered interest parity: if UIP would hold continuously, then central banks would not need to care about the exchange rate since foreign exchange market efficiency would always be guaranteed.

central banks as they leave interest rates unchanged. Thus, one might expect that central banks that intervene more frequently and to a relatively larger extent do not have to rely so much on interest rate policy to cope with exchange rate fluctuations.

5.3.1 Interventions and the Variation of Interest Rates

In a first step to explore the relationship between foreign exchange intervention and interest rate policy we look at the variability of interest rates across countries. If interventions are consequently used as an additional policy instrument then one would expect to see less variation in interest rates since interest rate policy can focus more on domestic factors and thus needs to focus less on the exchange rate.[130] Thus, the hypothesis (issue 4 of our list of issues laid out in the introduction) is that the use of interventions as an additional policy tool leads to a decrease in the volatility of the other policy instrument (short-term interest rates). First evidence for such a behaviour has been put forth by Fischer (2000). He finds that US interventions in the foreign exchange market led to a prolonged duration of the US Federal Funds Rate, i.e. the time period between interest rate changes has been longer in times when the US Federal Reserve intervened. He interprets his findings as evidence that interventions 'smooth' interest rates in the sense of less interest rate variability. This is consistent with the hypothesis that both instruments are complementary. On the other hand, a central bank that relies solely on interest rate policy theoretically might need to follow a more activist policy as it has to react to both domestic and external factors with only one instrument.

5.3.1.1 Interest Rate Volatility Compared

One indicator of interest rate policy activism is the variance of interest rates.[131] Table 18 displays the standard deviation of the 3-month Treasury bill interest rates and the overnight money market rates for all countries since 1993.

---

130 Svensson (2000b), whose model of open economy inflation targeting does not allow for an additional policy tool like sterilised interventions, argues that incorporating the exchange rate into monetary policy under strict inflation targeting leads to more interest rate variability. "[...] under strict inflation targeting [...] the direct exchange rate channel offers a potentially effective inflation stabilisation at a relatively short horizon. Such ambitious inflation targeting may require considerable activism in monetary policy (activism in the sense of frequent adjustments of the monetary policy instrument)[...]" (Svensson, 2000b: 4).

131 See Adam et al., 2001.

Table 18: Standard deviation of short-term interest rates

	Overnight money market rate	3-month Treasury Bill
Australia	1.065	1.095
Canada	1.137	1.227
United Kingdom	1.518	0.792
New Zealand	1.843	1.665
Sweden	2.160	2.113

Note: The sample range is 1993:1 to 2001:1 for all countries. Results refer to daily frequency data and all data are obtained through Thomson Financial Datastream.

It emerges that Sweden has the highest variation among the five countries for both interest rates, followed by New Zealand. The United Kingdom has the lowest variability for the 3-month Treasury bill rate while Australia exhibits the lowest standard deviation for the overnight money market rate. Taken together these results do not suggest a tight relationship between interest rate and reserve variability as would be expected theoretically. Sweden and New Zealand, for example, are identified as having both a large reserve and interest rate variability which suggests no significant substitution of interest rate policy through intervention operations. On the other hand, Australia exhibits a low interest rate variability as well as considerable intervention activity which supports the idea of interventions as an additional monetary policy instrument. According to the hypothesis, the UK would be expected to exhibit a large volatility of interest rates. However, evidence for this relationship remains mixed and depends on the choice of the policy variable in Table 18.

5.3.1.2 Frequency of Policy Rate Changes Compared

To gain more insight into this issue we also analyse the frequency of changes in the monetary policy instrument. In the sense of Fischer (2000), more frequent interventions in the foreign exchange market should 'smooth' interest rates, i.e. lead to less frequent adjustments in the policy instrument. Table 19 compares the number of policy instrument changes across countries as well as the average number of days between them.

Table 19: Frequency of policy instrument changes

	Number of policy rate changes	Average number of days between policy instrument changes
Australia	17	87.8
United Kingdom	27	54.2
Sweden	30	47.4
Canada	36	40.8

Note: The sample range is February 1996 – December 2001. Average number of days between policy instrument changes encompasses only trading days. The policy instruments used are: Bank rate (Canada), Repo rate (Sweden), Cash rate target (Australia), Base rate (UK). Source: Thomson Financial Datastream.

We were not able to include New Zealand in this analysis since the Reserve Bank did introduce the Official Cash Rate Target only in March 1999.[132] Before this date, New Zealand operated a daily settlement cash target which inevitably led to high fluctuations in the money market rate, thus making it extremely difficult to determine concrete policy changes. In order to obtain a sufficiently large number of observation we thus chose to start the sample range in February 1996.[133] Table 19 shows that the most policy instrument changes during the sample period occurred in Canada while Australia is identified as the least activist among the four countries. Accordingly, the Australian Reserve Bank changes its Cash Rate Target on average every 88 days. In Canada, only 41 days lie between changes in the Bank Rate. Both Sweden and the UK exhibit significantly more policy instrument changes than Australia and thus can be said to be more activist in their interest rate policy implementation.

5.3.1.3 Interpretation of the Findings

Coming back to the starting question of our analysis, it can be said that there is weak evidence for the theory that interventions smooth interest rates, i.e. lead to less activist interest rate policy. Both the low variance of money market rates as well as the small number of policy instrument changes in Australia combined with intervention activity that is considerably larger than in the UK suggest that the Reserve Bank of Australia indeed uses interventions as an additional policy tool that substitutes interest rate policy to some extent. However, this cannot be said of the

---

132 See Reserve Bank of New Zealand, 1999.

133 February 1996 is our starting point since the Bank of Canada changed the method of monetary policy implementation which made it easier to determine the Bank's near term policy stance. Before this date, the Bank rate had been set each week as the average interest rate of auctions of 3-month treasury bills. From 26 February on, the Bank rate equals the upper limit of the operating band for the overnight financing rate which means that policy changes can be identified more precisely than before. According to the Bank of Canada, this measure „eliminates the uncertainty and confusion that had existed previously as to which was the key indicator of the Bank's policy stance.“ (Bank of Canada Monetary Policy Report May 1996, p. 14).

Swedish Riksbank: here, considerable intervention activity is combined with high volatility of interest rates and high frequency of interest rate changes. This suggests that Sweden does not substitute interest rate policy with the use of interventions. The same can be said of the Bank of Canada. Given the low intervention activity of the Bank of England one would have expected a much more activist interest rate policy in Great Britain.

However, different variability of interest rates across countries might also be due to country-specific shocks and is not necessarily directly related to intervention activity. In the next step we therefore analyse more in-depth the determinants of interest rate policy in these countries.

5.3.2 Policy Reaction Functions and Exchange Rates

We now turn to the question if inflation targeting countries do react to exchange rate fluctuations with their interest rate policy and whether this behaviour is related to their intervention activity. One way to analyse which factors are determining interest rate decisions of central banks is to estimate policy reaction functions. Kahn and Parrish (1998) define a policy reaction function as "a relationship between the level of the nominal official rate and key economic indicators that policymakers use as information variables in adjusting policy." (p. 21). In an open economy, these variables include – besides data on inflation and output – the exchange rate. Probably the most popular version of such a reaction function is the Taylor rule. We estimate for each country a version of the Taylor rule that contains the exchange rate as an explanatory variable. Comparing the coefficients of the exchange rate variable sheds light on the extent that the central bank incorporates exchange rate fluctuations in their interest rate decision process. The hypothesis is that interest rate policy with regard to exchange rate fluctuations is to some extent replaced by sterilised intervention, i.e. the more a country intervenes, the less the weight of the exchange rate variable in its Taylor rule.

To be sure, we do not expect clear-cut results from the analysis – they might instead just give a first idea about the differences of the central banks in their approach to the exchange rate. Above all, it is not clear that they do already pursue a model that incorporates interventions in the way we propose.[134]

5.3.2.1 Evolution of Taylor Rules

For our purposes we need to ask whether central banks that we identified as using interventions more frequently do apply a different interest rate policy. Specifi-

[134] See for example the discussion of the Swedish interventions in 2001 by the Riksbank executive board meeting (Riksbank, 2001b). The controversy among the board members concerning the efficiency of these interventions as well as questions about the relationship between interventions and interest rate policy demonstrates that in the day-to-day conduct of monetary policy the role of interventions is far from self-evident.

cally, we look at the reaction of short-term interest rates to exchange rate fluctuations. To analyse this question we estimate different versions of a Taylor rule where the short interest rate set by the central bank is explained with deviations of inflation from its target and with the output gap of the country. This is the essence of Taylor (1993) who used the following formula to describe the interest rate policy of the US Federal Reserve

$$r_t = (r^* + \pi^*) + 1.5(\pi_t - \pi^*) + 0.5y_t \tag{5.5}$$

with r_t as the federal funds rate in period t, r^* as the real interest rate, π^* and π_t as the inflation target and actual inflation, respectively, and y_t as a measure of the output gap (difference between actual and potential output). The parameters 1.5 and 0.5 are not essential to the rule – they merely represent the finding of Taylor for the US over a considerable long time span and therefore might vary for other countries. The Taylor rule aims to reduce the complex process of monetary policy to a simple rule. The intuition of equation (5.5) is straightforward: Given an equilibrium nominal short-term interest rate, consisting of the real interest rate plus the target inflation rate, short-term interest rates need to be higher whenever actual inflation is above the target or if output is above potential output (which is equal to a positive value for the output gap).

Equation (5.5) has been refined over the past years into forward-looking models of monetary policy. While the traditional Taylor rule had the interest rate react to current inflation and output, in reality central banks focus more on expected inflation. Furthermore, current output might not be observable by the monetary authorities at the time of decision-making since data like GDP is published with a lag. Thus, equation (5.5) is changed as follows (see Clarida et al., 1998):

$$r_t^* = \bar{r} + \beta(E[\pi_{t+n} / \Omega_t] - \pi^*) + \gamma(E[y_t / \Omega_t] - y_t^*) \tag{5.6}$$

with E as the expectations operator, Ω_t as the information available at time t, $\bar{r}$ as the long-run equilibrium nominal rate and π_{t+n} as the inflation rate n quarters ahead. Since inflation targeting is often described as inflation-forecast targeting, the forward-looking should be able to capture the central bank operations more accurately than the backward-looking or real-time model.

Additionally, more recent models include a lagged dependent variable to capture the tendency of central banks to smooth interest rates, i.e. sudden and large policy reversals are usually avoided. Generally, this is done to avoid disrupting financial markets and to gain credibility (Goodfriend, 1991; Goodhart, 1996). In reality, for example, financial markets usually do not expect the US Federal Reserve to change interest rates by more than 50 basis points. Interest rate smoothing is usually modelled with the following equation

$$r_t = \rho r_{t-1} + (1-\rho) r_t^T + \upsilon_t \tag{5.7}$$

with r_t^T as the target interest rate resulting from the Taylor rule and ρ as the smoothing parameter. Incorporating (5.7) into (5.6), replacing $\alpha \equiv \bar{r}$ and $x_t \equiv y_t - y_t^*$ as the output gap and rewriting (5.6) with realised variables, we get

$$r_t = (1-\rho)\alpha + (1-\rho)\beta(\pi_{t+n} - \pi^*) + (1-\rho)\gamma x_t + \rho r_{t-1} + \varepsilon_t \qquad (5.8)$$

This is the baseline equation which we will estimate for each country separately.

The original Taylor rule was only considering closed economy aspects. The exchange rate is indirectly part of this rule in that it affects future inflation – Taylor (2001) thus argues that his original formula, while the exchange rate is not directly incorporated, also encompasses open economy aspects. In Taylor's view: "What might appear to be a closed economy policy rule is actually just as much an open economy rule as if the exchange rate appeared directly." (Taylor, 2001: 9).

Recently, however, work by Nelson (2001) and Clarida et al. (1998) considered open economy aspects directly in a Taylor-rule-type reaction function. The difference to Taylor (1993) is that the exchange rate is incorporated as a separate variable into the reaction function.[135] It is thus studied if the central bank reacts directly to exchange rate fluctuations in addition to future inflation and output. The rationale behind such an approach might be that the central bank targets a combination of interest rates and exchange rates – a so-called Monetary Conditions Index (MCI) as mentioned before.

To study this question, we will add in a second step the nominal effective exchange rate as an additional explanatory variable to see whether the central banks react directly to exchange rate fluctuations (this approach is similar to Gerlach and Smets (2000)). Thus, we estimate the following equation

$$r_t = (1-\rho)\alpha + (1-\rho)\beta(\pi_{t+n} - \pi^*) + (1-\rho)\gamma x_t + (1-\rho)\delta ex_t + \rho r_{t-1} + \varepsilon_t \qquad (5.9)$$

with ex_t as the nominal effective exchange rate variable.

5.3.2.2 Description of Data and Methods

Following Nelson (2001), the model is estimated with two-stage-least-squares (TSLS).[136] Estimation with TSLS – as a special case of instrumental variable esti-

135 Taylor did not include the exchange rate into his rule for the United States because „simulations of multicountry models led me to believe that if the central bank reacted too strongly to the exchange rate then inflation-output performance would deteriorate." Thus, the Taylor rule should be viewed as a formula specifically designed for the US. As Taylor admits: „However, it is clear that the same conclusion would not necessarily be reached for other countries, especially small open economies." (Taylor, 2000b: 16).

136 This follows the procedure of Nelson (2001). Another method often applied to this kind of problem (see e.g. Clarida et al., 1998) is estimation by GMM. However, results with this method proved to be very unstable – not least because of the relatively

mation – encompasses two steps: In the first step all variables are regressed on all instruments using OLS to find out which portion of the variables can be attributed to the instruments. In the second step the original equation is estimated using the fitted values from the first-stage regression.[137] This is done for two reasons: First, we are dealing with an errors-in-variables approach since the true inflation forecast of the central bank is not known and second, variables on the right hand side (such as the exchange rate) are endogenous. Thus, variables on the right hand side can be expected to be correlated with the disturbance term. The standard approach in cases where right-hand side variables are correlated with the residuals is to estimate the equation using instrumental variables regression. The idea behind instrumental variables is to find a set of variables, termed instruments, that are both (1) correlated with the explanatory variables in the equation, and (2) uncorrelated with the disturbances. These instruments are used to eliminate the correlation between right-hand side variables and the disturbances.[138] As is standard practice in similar Taylor rule studies (e.g. Nelson, 2001; Clarida et al., 1998; Adam et al., 2001; Faust et al., 2001) we use as instruments a constant and lags 1-4 of all right hand side variables.

All data are taken from the IMF International Financial Statistics (obtained through Thomson Financial Datastream). The sample range starts for each country with the introduction of inflation targeting and ends for all countries in 2001:4. As policy variable we use the three-month Treasury bill rate (IFS line 60c) for each country.[139] As inflation variable we use the annual percentage change in the consumer price index (IFS line 64) except for the UK were we use the RPIX (Retail Price Index excluding mortgage interest rates; Datastream code UKRPAXMIF). To construct the inflation gap (i.e. the deviation of actual from target inflation) we use the official inflation target (in case of a target range we use the middle point of the range). Output gaps are constructed using real GDP (IFS line 99b.r) and a Hodrick-Prescott-Filter (smoothing parameter 1600). Our exchange rate variable is measured as the percentage deviation from the logarithm of nominal effective indices (IFS line neu) from a smoothed series (again constructed with a Hodrick-Prescott-Filter). This procedure has two advantages: First, this constructed vari-

short sample. Lotti (2000) notes that TSLS produces more stable, although less efficient estimates than GMM. Adam et al. (2001) apply both methods in their study and results obtained with the different procedures do not differ significantly.

137 See Kennedy, 1998.

138 A more detailed description of the TSLS method is given in the appendix.

139 We chose not to use the overnight interest rate, since New Zealand operated, until 1999, a cash target instead of targeting overnight interest rates directly (see Reserve Bank of New Zealand, 1999). As a consequence, New Zealand overnight interest rates in the first nine years of inflation targeting were highly volatile. Thus, we follow Huang et al. (2001), who in their study of New Zealand monetary policy state: "There is thus no equivalent of the Federal Funds Rate to incorporate but it seems sensible to use the rate that the RBNZ [Reserve Bank of New Zealand] itself referred to, namely, the 90-day bank bill rate, as the best indicator of policy in the context of a Taylor rule." (p. 10). In order to better compare interest rate movements we use the three-month interest rate for all countries.

able is stationary (while exchange rates in levels are well-known as being non-stationary) and second, it measures only permanent, significant deviations of the exchange rates from an underlying trend. This takes account of the fact that exchange rate pass-through is higher when exchange rate changes are permanent. Monetary policy thus does not need to react to short and small quarter-on-quarter changes but only to more persistent movements.[140]

We use quarterly data for two reasons: First, GDP data are only available on a quarterly basis. While one might use industrial production alternatively (usually available on a monthly basis), this measures only an increasingly small portion of the real activity of a country.[141] Second, data on consumer prices for Australia and New Zealand are only available on a quarterly basis. For estimation of the Taylor rules the sample range for each country was adjusted to correspond with the period in which inflation targeting was conducted.

5.3.2.3 Stationarity Tests

To test for the stationarity of the variables in our estimation we applied Augmented-Dickey-Fuller (ADF) tests. By construction the exchange rate and output gap variable are stationary (as they represent deviations from an underlying trend) and thus were not included in the tests. The regression for the ADF test is

$$\Delta y_t = \mu + \gamma y_{t-1} + \sum_{j=1}^{p-1} \delta_j \Delta y_{t-j} + \varepsilon_t \tag{5.10}$$

and the null hypothesis is non-stationarity. The appropriate number of lagged differences Δy to be included on the right-hand side was determined similar to the procedure proposed by Campbell and Perron (1991): Starting with a maximum lag length of k=10 equation (5.10) is estimated. If the last lag included is significant, k=10 is chosen as the appropriate lag length. If not, the number of lagged differences is reduced by one until the coefficient on the last lag is significant on the 10% level. If no lags are significant we chose k=0. We included a trend and/or an intercept into the test equation whenever they were found to be significant.

140 Including the exchange rate in first differences (which would also be stationary) would thus be inferior as it would only measure the central bank's reaction to short-term fluctuations.

141 New Zealand industrial production is available only on a quarterly basis, anyway.

Table 20: Results of stationarity tests

Variable	Lags	No trend	Trend + Intercept	Intercept
I3_AU	1			-3.39**
I3_CN	0			-2.74*
I3_NZ	1			-3.09**
I3_SW	0	-2.03**		
I3_UK	1			-3.21**
PI_GAP_AU	4	-3.05***		
PI_GAP_CN	1		-4.12**	
PI_GAP_NZ	1	-2.78***		
PI_GAP_SW	4	-3.68***		
PI_GAP_UK	0	-2.98***		

Note: Sample range 1990:1-2001:4.***, **, * denote rejection of the null hypothesis "non-stationarity" at the 1, 5 and 10% significance level. I3_ and PI_GAP denote the three-month interest rate and the inflation gap (difference between actual and target inflation rate). Lags denotes the number of differenced lagged variables included in the ADF test.

Table 20 summarises the results: For all variables the null-hypothesis could be clearly rejected and therefore both the three-month interest rates and the inflation gap (difference between actual inflation and inflation target) are stationary for all five countries. Thus, there should be no danger of spurious regressions while using TSLS.

5.3.2.4 Country-Specific Results and Interpretation

Table 21 displays the results of our country-specific Taylor rule estimation of the equation

$$r_t = (1-\rho)\alpha + (1-\rho)\beta(\pi_{t+n} - \pi^*) + (1-\rho)\gamma x_t + (1-\rho)\delta ex_t + \rho r_{t-1} + \varepsilon_t \qquad (5.11)$$

We first estimated a baseline equation (5.8) (i.e. without an exchange rate variable). The appropriate lead n of the inflation forecast term $(\pi_{t+n} - \pi^*)$ was determined on the basis of goodness-of-fit of the regression (see Muscatelli et al., 2000). While we identified a three quarter lead of the inflation forecast for Australia and the UK, for Canada a lead of four quarters was optimal. In the equation for Sweden and New Zealand we found shorter leads with one and two quarters ahead, respectively.[142] The sign of the inflation coefficient is positive for all countries as expected: An increase in future inflation leads to an increase in the policy rate. In all cases the lagged dependent variable is found to be highly significant,

142 We also performed the estimates using contemporaneous inflation variables (as in the original Taylor rule) and the results were worse. This supports the fact that monetary policy of inflation targeting central banks is forward-looking, i.e. that interest rate decision are based on forecasted inflation. The finding that the Reserve Bank of New Zealand focuses more on short term than on long term inflation forecasts is supported by Huang et al. (2001: 24).

thus proving the existence of interest rate smoothing by all four central banks. Among the five countries, the Reserve Bank of Australia exhibits the largest coefficient on the lagged interest rate thus suggesting that Australia appears to smooth rates more than the other countries.[143] In comparing the response of short-term interest rates to future inflation we focus on the long-run response (i.e. adjusted for the smoothing parameter). If the long-run inflation coefficient is below unity then an increase in the inflation rate by 1% is followed by an interest rate increase by less than 1%. Accordingly, the real interest rate decreases and thus the central bank accommodates rather than fights the rise in inflation. As has been shown by Clarida et al. (1999), optimal policy for a central bank requires raising the real interest rate to contract demand whenever the inflation rate is above target.[144] To do this, nominal interest rates need to rise by more than the inflation rate and the long-run inflation coefficient must exceed unity. As can be seen, this long-run coefficient is larger than one in most of the cases except for the Swedish baseline case, where it is slightly below and the Canadian equation including the exchange rate variable.

Accordingly, there is evidence that the majority of these inflation targeting countries respond to increases in inflation with an increase in real interest rates. A further observation is that the output gap is significant only in some cases. While Australia obviously does not respond to output fluctuations, this variable is highly significant for the Swedish Riksbank. In the other three countries results are somewhat inconclusive – with output being significant in only one equation specification.[145] The second column displays the estimation results of equation (5.9) (i.e. the baseline equation plus an exchange rate term).

---

143 This results is in line with the findings of Drew and Plantier (2000) who study interest rate smoothing behaviour in New Zealand, Australia, Canada and the United States.

144 Clarida et al. (2000) show that in the US pre-Volcker period nominal rates were increased by less than the inflation increase. They argue that this caused the macroeconomic instability (i.e. high volatility in both inflation and output development) of the late sixties and seventies compared with the Volcker-Greenspan era.

145 Taken together, our results are supported by related studies like Collins and Siklos (2001). They find for Canada, New Zealand and Australia that "[...] dollar bloc central banks are reasonably well-described as having targeted inflation, pursued heavy interest rate smoothing, and perhaps having little concern over output." (p. 21).

Table 21: Regression results for Taylor rule

Sample range	Australia 93:1-01:1		New Zealand 90:1-01:1		Sweden 93:1-01:1		Canada 91:1-01:1		UK 93:1-01:1	
r_{t-1}	0.95*** (0.08)	0.94*** (0.08)	0.86*** (0.14)	0.66*** (0.07)	0.80*** (0.05)	0.79*** (0.04)	0.87*** (0.09)	0.77*** (0.10)	0.84*** (0.17)	0.71*** (0.13)
π_{t+1}					0.19*** (0.07)	0.22** (0.09)				
π_{t+2}			0.28*** (0.08)	0.43*** (0.08)						
π_{t+3}	0.16*** (0.04)	0.18*** (0.04)							0.30 (0.20)	0.62** (0.27)
π_{t+4}							0.16 (0.15)	0.12 (0.13)		
Long-run Inflation coefficient[a]	3.2	3	2	1.26	0.95	1.05	1.23	0.52	1.88	2.14
x_t	0.04 (0.11)	0.01 (0.09)	0.04 (0.24)	-0.22** (0.09)	0.25*** (0.04)	0.24*** (0.05)	0.26** (0.10)	0.18 (0.11)	0.18** (0.08)	0.03 (0.06)
ex_t		0.01 (0.01)		0.08*** (0.02)		0.004 (0.03)		-0.07 (0.06)		0.05** (0.02)
Adj. R^2	0.90	0.91	0.86	0.89	0.96	0.96	0.72	0.73	0.83	0.85
LM test	0.24	0.33	0.10	0.12	0.69	0.67	0.22	0.14	0.76	0.48
S.E.	0.35	0.34	0.66	0.58	0.43	0.43	0.68	0.65	0.29	0.27
Obs.	32	32	40	40	26	34	34	34	28	30

Notes: *, **, *** indicates significance at the 10/ 5/ 1% level. [a] Long-run response to inflation is calculated as $\beta/(1-\rho)$ with β as the coefficient for the inflation and ρ as the smoothing parameter. Instruments: constant and lags 1-4 of r_t, π_t and x_t. LM-test is for first- to forth-order serial correlation. The UK equation contains an MA(1)-term to correct for first order autocorrelation.

Turning to the exchange rate variable we find the following: Significance at the 1 and 5% level, respectively, is found for New Zealand and the UK while in the other three countries this variable is insignificant.[146, 147] Thus, only the Bank of England and the Reserve Bank of New Zealand seem to incorporate exchange rate fluctuations directly in their interest rate decision process. All three other countries either do not take exchange rate developments into account in formulating policy or they do so only indirectly via their expectations of future inflation.

How does this correspond to our findings of intervention activity? Concerning the UK our hypothesis for interest rate policy is supported: We found the least intervention activity of all five inflation targeters for the Bank of England and at the same time we found a significance of the exchange rate in the interest rate reaction function of the British central bank. Thus, our assumption that without the use of the additional tool of interventions a central bank has to rely more on interest rate policy to influence the exchange rate is supported. In contrast, for Australia, Canada and Sweden no significance of the exchange rate in the Taylor rule coincides with considerable more intervention activity. Consequently, it could be hypothesised that these countries replace their interest rate policy to some extent with the use of interventions. There thus seems to be evidence for the use of interventions as an additional policy tool in these countries. Supporting this findings is a statement of the Swedish Riksbank which says: "In addition to adjusting the interest rate, the Riksbank can resort to interventions in the foreign exchange market [...] for the purpose of maintaining price stability." (Riksbank, 2002: 4).

However, the result for New Zealand contrasts with our earlier finding of reserve variability. Given the relatively high intensity of reserve variations for the Reserve Bank of New Zealand we would have expected – similar to Australia, Canada and Sweden – that this intervention activity replaces to some extent the interest rate response to exchange rate fluctuations. This is not the case. It nevertheless confirms the following statement of Archer and Halliday (1998) from the Reserve Bank's Financial Market Department: "Would concerns about the level of the exchange rate in the context of foreign exchange market crisis better be dealt with by an interest rate response than by direct intervention using reserves? The answer is probably yes [...]. [...] changing interest rates alters directly the return on buying the local currency. In turn, this should impact on the willingness to trade foreign exchange and on the short-term equilibrium exchange rate." (p. 351).

---

146 Gerlach and Smets (2000) report similar results: in their study of Australia, Canada and New Zealand they find that the exchange rate coefficient is insignificant in Australia and significant in New Zealand. In contrast to our study, however, they also report a significant coefficient for Canada. It needs to be noted that their sample range is much smaller than ours (theirs ends in 1997:2).

147 Note that the coefficient on the exchange rate does not necessarily have to be negative which would indicate something like a leaning-against-the-wind behaviour, i.e. raising interest rates when the exchange rate depreciates and vice versa. The central bank might instead choose to support an existing appreciation/depreciation trend if it is in line with the achievement of the inflation target.

Figure 19: Actual and fitted graphs for Taylor rule estimates

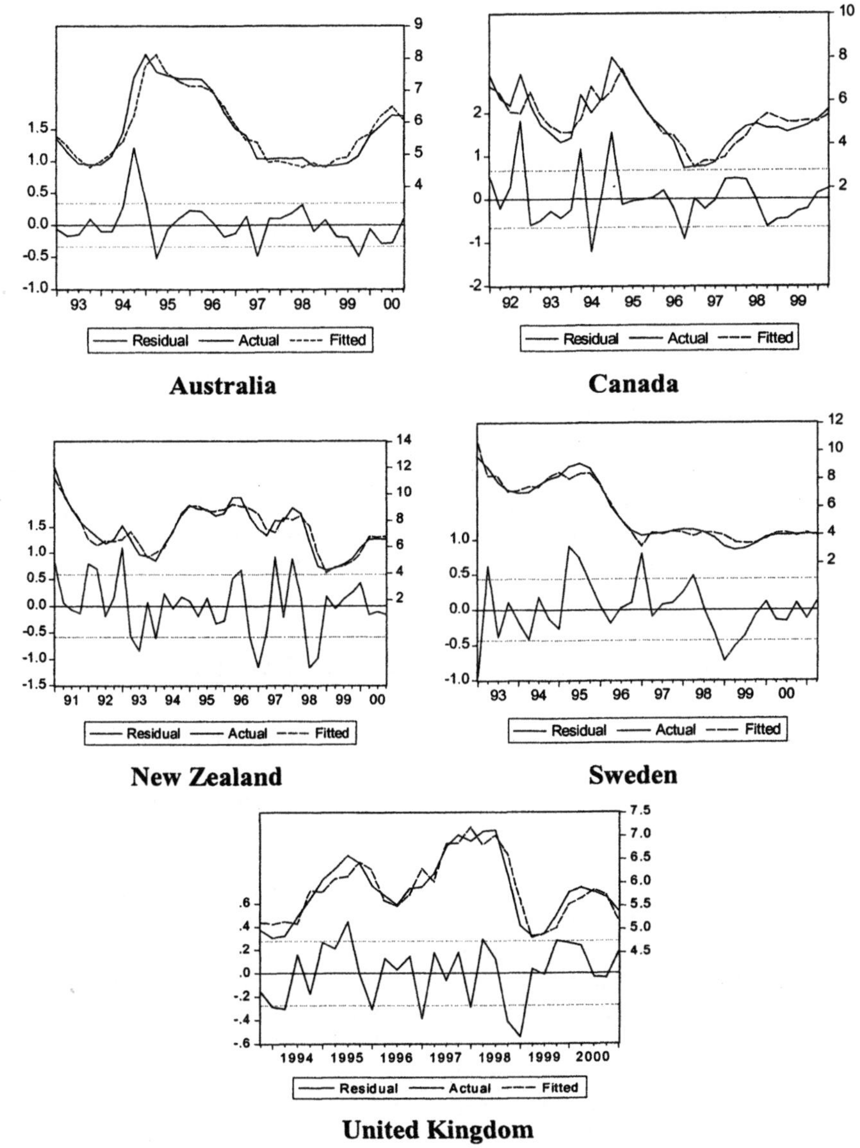

Note: The graphs refer to the Taylor rule specification **including** the exchange rate variable.

This statement shows rather clearly that the Reserve Bank of New Zealand's official approach to the exchange rate is based on the rationale of the uncovered interest parity. Furthermore, our result is in line with the fact that New Zealand used a Monetary Conditions Index as an operating target for some time, which was controlled solely by interest rate changes (see Bernanke et al., 1999: 98).

The puzzling result in the New Zealand case, however, is the fact that reserve variability is still high suggesting also significant transactions in the foreign exchange market. As mentioned New Zealand officially insists not to have intervened in the foreign exchange market and therefore the reserve variability might reflect simply the day-to-day trading of the central bank with no clear intention of influencing the exchange rate. Also, in accounts of New Zealand monetary policy the exchange rate is often named as an important variable in the formulation of the Reserve Banks' interest rate policy. Nevertheless, taken together the New Zealand effect is puzzling.

Taken together, we can summarise that Australia presents a case in point for our theory: Intervention activity is combined with an interest rate policy that does not focus on exchange rate changes and thus is considerably less activist than in other countries. The Bank of England intervenes less in the foreign exchange market and consequently includes the exchange rate in its interest rate policy. While this does not lead to a more activist role than in any other country, the Bank of England is obviously more activist than the Reserve Bank of Australia.

5.4 Short Case Studies of the Country Experiences

Until now, we performed comparative analyses between the five inflation targeting countries. This chapter focuses instead on the individual experience of each country and will give a review of their monetary policy implementation. While the development of reserves suggests some intervention operations in all countries there might be considerable differences in their implementation in monetary policy. For each country we first summarise its interest rate policy and inflation development followed by an analysis of reserve developments. In our analysis of reserve developments we use the following instruments: Levels of foreign exchange reserves (adjusted for valuation effects and interest earnings), bilateral exchange rates and rolling correlations between monthly reserve changes and changes in the nominal effective exchange rate index.[148] Rolling correlations give an impression of the intention that the central bank pursued with the reserve change. A positive correlation (i.e. positive reserve changes coincide with an increase (appreciation) of the exchange rate index) is a signal of leaning-against-the-wind activity while a negative correlation suggests that the central bank intended to support an existing exchange rate trend. Correlations are calculated over a rolling window of 12 months.

---

148 All reserve changes are adjusted for exchange rate valuation effects and interest earnings effects.

5.4.1 New Zealand

New Zealand started its inflation targeting policy in 1990. The target measure is the consumer price index excluding consumer interest rates, energy and commodity prices as well as other effects like changes in indirect taxes. It has remained inside its target bands for most of the time except for short episodes in 1991/92, 1995/96 as well as since the end of 2000. The inflation band was widened from 0-2% to 0-3% in December 1996 as a result of a change in government.

Following Bernanke et al. (1999) monetary policy in New Zealand from 1990 to 1997 can be divided into three different episodes. The last four years since 1997 present a fourth episode. The first episode from 1990 to March 1992 is characterised by disinflation and a gradual lowering of the inflation target bands. Negative GDP growth and rising unemployment led to a fall in the inflation rate even though the exchange rate depreciated slightly. The increase in oil prices following the Gulf crisis had not been reflected in the CPI target measure as it excludes such temporary effects. As inflation was thus steadily falling towards the 0-2% range, which was the stated objective of the Reserve Bank, short-term interest rates were allowed to decrease from over 14% to about 7% at the end of 1991.

Disinflation was achieved at the beginning of the second period which extends to the first quarter of 1994. According to Mishkin and Posen (1997) this period can be best described "[...] by the absence of any challenges to monetary policy." (p. 43) as there was no desire to further reduce inflation. GDP growth rebounded sharply while interest rates declined further to below 5% and the exchange rate started to appreciate. At the end of November 1992 it was agreed that the inflation target should be 0 to 2% for the foreseeable future.

Following this episode is a period starting in early 1994 of rising inflationary tendencies stemming from domestic rather than external sources. This explains the fact that inflation rose although the New Zealand dollar appreciated to an eight-year high against the US-dollar and the Yen. The major factor behind the domestic price increase was a boom in construction. Although interest rates were increased to over 10% during this time, this had not the usual effect since inflation was located in a non-traded sector of the economy and thus, the transmission channel through the exchange rate had little impact. Consequently, interest rates had to rise higher and the exchange rate had to appreciate more to counter inflation. Taken together, these developments led to the breach of the inflation target twice between 1995 and 1996 which, however, did not have consequences for Governor Brash, who remained in office.

Figure 20: Economic indicators New Zealand

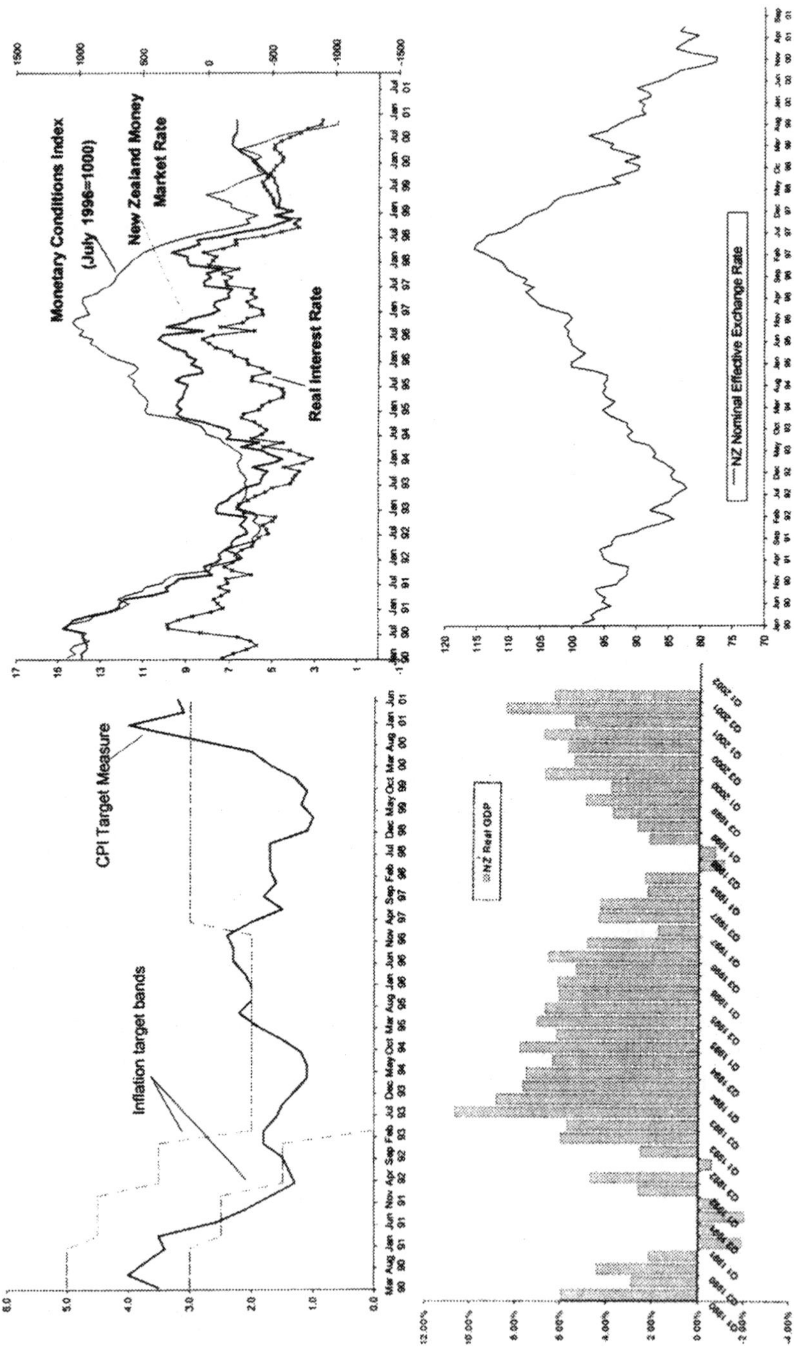

Note: Real interest rates are calculated using consumer prices. Source: International Financial Statistics, Reserve Bank of New Zealand.

The past four years can be seen as the fourth episode of the New Zealand inflation targeting experience. This period is marked by the continued and strong depreciation of the New Zealand dollar from its peak in mid-1997 which was supported by the crisis in emerging markets that disrupted international foreign exchange markets. While the target measure for the inflation rate remained in the middle of the target range until mid-1999 it then began to rise sharply and breached the target ceiling of 3% in the last months of 2000. GDP declined in 1998 as a consequence of lower international demand and contractionary monetary conditions which resulted from the combination of a high exchange rate combined with high interest rates to keep inflation down. However, the contraction of GDP was only short term as both the exchange rate and interest rates were declining sharply and thus promoting economic growth. This easing of monetary conditions as well as rising oil prices also led to the increase in inflation. The breach of the inflation target for the third time in the 1990s was justified by the transient factor of rising energy prices and thus did neither require an interest rate response nor a discussion about the governor to resign. Taken together, this last period was characterised by high volatility in economic activity and in price developments and proved to be a difficult time for monetary policy.

The role of the exchange rate has been highly important in New Zealand policy especially during the third and fourth episode of the inflation targeting time but also in the earlier years.[149] While during the appreciation of the NZ$ (1992-97) the export sector of the economy was depressed, the depreciation of the exchange rate (1997-2000) that followed posed significant problems in terms of imported inflation. The Reserve Bank responded to exchange rate fluctuations with adjustments in short-term interest rates. Bernanke et al. (1999) write: "This was a bit confusing, however, because as long as the Reserve Bank had not specified the degree to which it viewed changes in short-term interest rates and the exchange rate as substitutes, it was unclear whether the exchange rate entered policy decisions as a determinant of future inflation or as a goal unto itself." (p. 98). In response to this criticism, the use of a Monetary Conditions Index (MCI) as an operating target was established in 1996.[150] As can be seen in Figure 20 the appreciation of the NZ$ led to a considerable tightening of monetary conditions in the 1996-1997 pe-

---

149 "In the first half of the 1990s, the exchange rate acted as the principal guide for determining how much policy should be adjusted when the forecast inflation rate deviated from the target range. This was not because significance was attached to the exchange rate level per se, but rather because the exchange rate strongly influences future prices and thus inflation rates in the adjustment period." (Gerlach and Smets, 2000: 1690).

150 The Monetary Conditions Index (MCI) in New Zealand is a combination of the trade-weighted exchange rate index and the 90 day bank bill rate (a 2% increase (decrease) in the exchange rate index is equivalent to a one percentage point increase (decrease) in 90 day rates). A one-point change on this index is equivalent to a 0.01 percentage change in the 90 day rates in the absence of a change in the TWI. See www.rbnz.govt.nz.

riod. The MCI as an operating target was abandoned in 1999 as its implementation lead to a significant increase in the volatility of short-term interest rates.

As mentioned above, New Zealand had to cope with large swings in its exchange rate over the past decade. A period of strong appreciation (about 40%) was followed by a period of strong depreciation (more than 30%). This fact alone suggests that foreign exchange intervention, if pursued, was not really successful in preventing these large swings. Looking at the reserve development against the exchange rate index (upper graph) it emerges that a period of reserve accumulation until mid-1996 was followed by a period of reserve sales. This development coincides with movements in the exchange rate: Foreign exchange was bought during the appreciation period of the NZ$ and reserves were sold when the NZ$ was depreciating from 1997 on. This is the typical picture of leaning-against-the-wind behaviour intended to counter existing trends in the exchange rate. The rolling correlations in the lower graph support this view: Correlations are positive over most of the time indicating a strategy of leaning-against-the-wind. The clustering of positive correlations in 1992-93 suggests that the central bank leaned against the wind during this time, i.e. against the depreciation tendencies (note that the correlation bars refer to the twelve-months period prior (left) from the bar – thus, for interpretation purposes the correlations should be shifted a few months to the left hand side to correspond with the movement of the exchange rate prevailing at this time). The switch from positive to negative correlations at the peak of the appreciation period suggests that interventions were first used to break the trend and afterwards were used to support the existing depreciation trend which would make sense as the central bank was concerned with the negative effects of the strong New Zealand dollar. However, when the depreciation movement became too strong correlations indicate that the central bank bought domestic currency in the course of 1999-2000 to dampen the negative effects on the inflation rate.

Taken together it emerges that the reserve changes correlate with exchange rate changes quite sensibly. Correlation coefficients range between 0,66 and –0,56. Again, this contrasts with the stated aversion of the Reserve Bank against interventions. However, it is in line with the statement that the central bank trades in the market in order to practice for potential future intervention operations.

Figure 21: Reserve level, rolling correlations and exchange rate, New Zealand

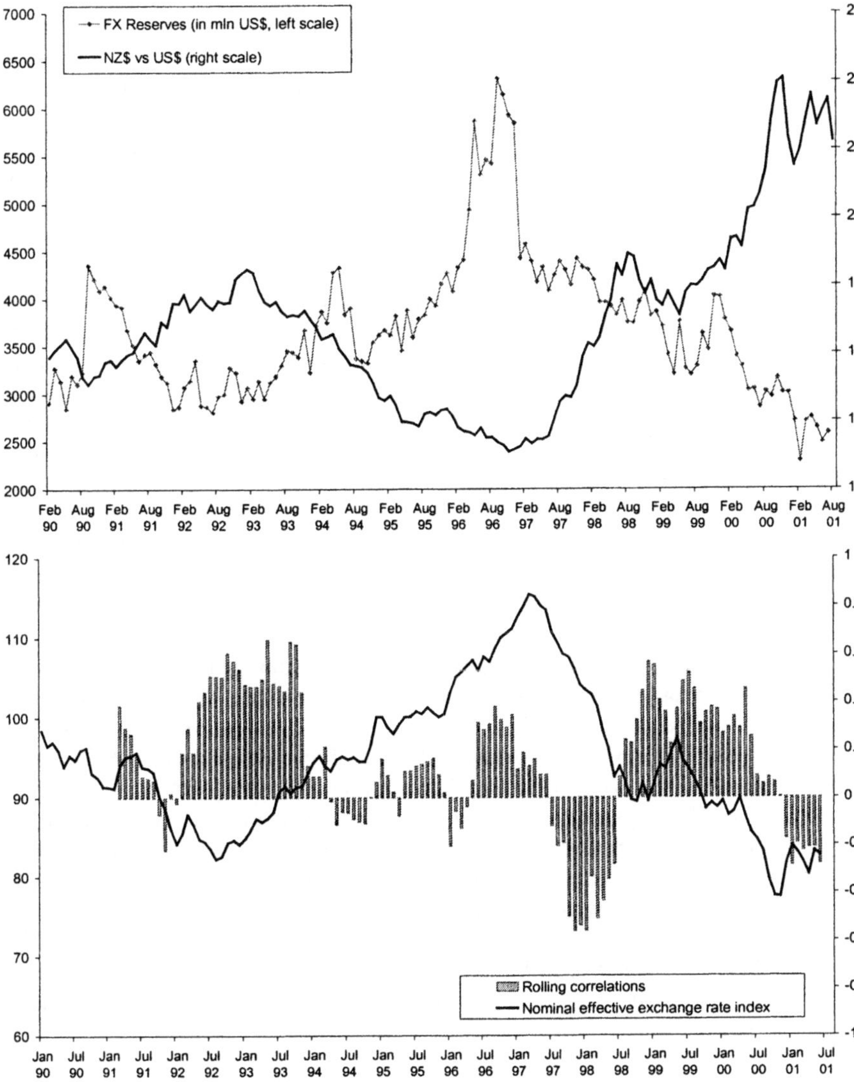

Source: International Financial Statistics, own calculations.

5.4.2 Canada

Canada started its inflation targeting framework in February 1991 as the second central bank after New Zealand. The target is set in terms of headline consumer price inflation although the Bank of Canada stresses the importance of core inflation in the decision making process. Like in New Zealand, the first years of the new framework included gradually decreasing target zones for inflation to promote the process of disinflation. Once low inflation rates were achieved the target bands were set at 1-3% from 1996 on.

Mishkin and Posen (1997) distinguish two periods in the Canadian inflation targeting experience until 1997. The first encompasses the first year which was characterised by a steep decline in the inflation rate. The second period challenged the central bank in that inflation tended to breach the lower band of the inflation target. The most recent two years might be characterised as a third period. Here, inflation picked up like in other countries as a result of rising oil prices and the generally favourably economic situation which created inflationary pressure.

As a consequence of the fact that inflation was even lower than expected and planned over certain periods of time, the Bank of Canada had to deal with mounting criticism from politics. Especially in view of high unemployment in Canada, monetary policy was often accused of being too restrictive. However, it is pointed out that this criticism also led the central bank to become more transparent as it frequently had to justify its policy and explain the benefits of low and stable inflation for the economy in the long run.

As economic growth recovered from the recession in 1991 and also in response to the Mexican Peso crisis, the bank subsequently increased interest rates during 1994 and the first half of 1995. The sharp drop in inflation 1994, when the headline and core measure reached 0% can be attributed to a reduction in the tobacco excise tax. As this was only a one-time effect, the Bank of Canada did not react to it. Beginning in 1995, inflation rose again inside the inflation target bands. Beginning in the second half of 1995 short-term interest rates were reduced significantly in response to worsening forecasts for the economy. This proved to be the right decision also from the point of view of inflation which remained inside the bands and even tended to the lower side of the bands in the following years.

In the last couple of years headline inflation rose as a consequence of rising energy prices and the continued low level of the Canadian dollar. Core inflation, however, remained stable inside the bands. In view of the upcoming weakness of the economy and following the interest rate cuts by the US Federal Reserve in 2001 the Bank of Canada continuously reduced its short-term interest rate. This again proved the flexible approach that the Canadians are pursuing within their inflation targeting framework by also putting some weight to output developments in the recent past.

Figure 22: Economic indicators Canada

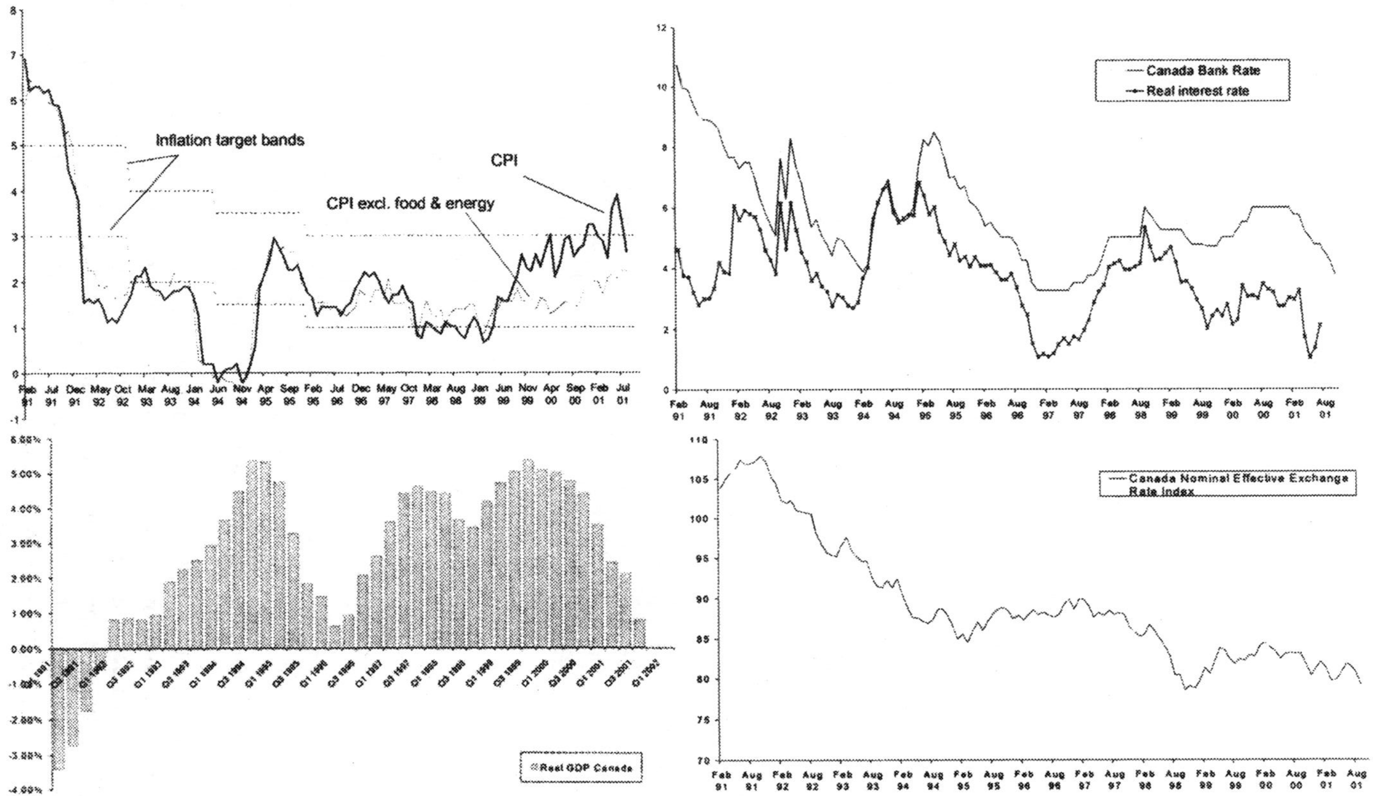

Note: Real interest rates are calculated using consumer prices. Source: International Financial Statistics, Bank of Canada.

Figure 23: Reserve level, rolling correlations and exchange rate, Canada

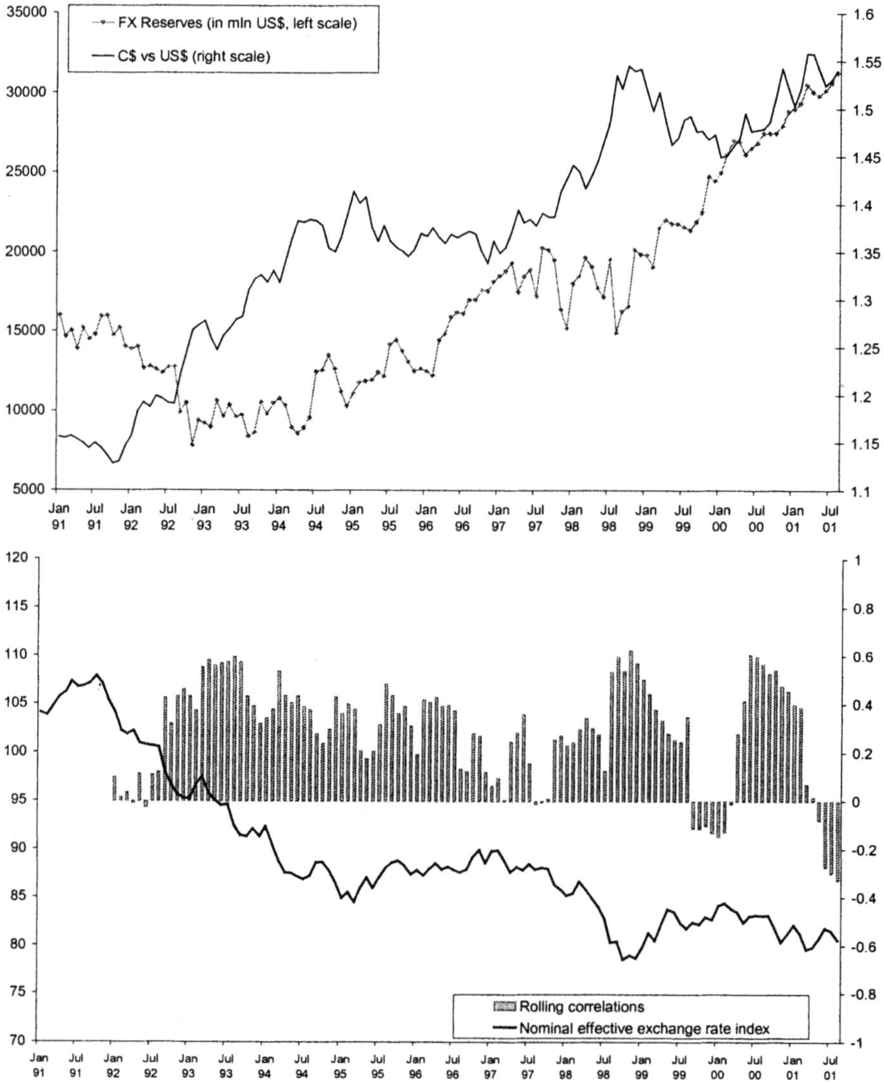

Source: International Financial Statistics, own calculations.

The development of the Canadian dollar in the past is characterised by a continued depreciation of about 28% versus the major trading partners. Negative reserve changes occur more often than positive changes suggesting that the Bank of Canada countered the downward trend in its exchange rate by buying domestic currency and selling US dollar reserves. These transactions can especially be observed in the third and fourth quarters of 1997 and the first quarters of 1998 – a period when the Bank of Canada intervened as a consequence of the shake-up in foreign exchange markets in the wake of the Asian crisis.[151] In November 1997 the Canadian dollar fell to a 12-year low. During this time the rolling correlations also indicate strong leaning-against-the-wind behaviour with correlations over 0,6. At the same time short-term interest rates were increased as an additional manner to tighten the monetary policy stance which had become easier as a result of the weak exchange rate. Following this period of strong intervention operations, the Bank in September 1998 abandoned its earlier policy of automatic intervention whenever exchange rates moved outside daily non-intervention bands. Future interventions would be made on a more discretionary basis. Correlation is especially high during times of more dynamic depreciation while it is lower and sometimes negative whenever the exchange rate seems to stabilise (such as in 1999 or 2001).

Despite the finding of the rolling correlations analysis that Bank of Canada intervened to counter the depreciation trend of the C$, the level of foreign exchange reserves increased significantly (about 400% from 1992 to 2001). As mentioned earlier, the policy of the central bank was to generally increase the reserve level which was thought to be too low. Obviously, the Bank was conducting purchases of foreign exchange at times of relative strength in the currency, thereby preventing a continued appreciation. Taken together, the Canadian case demonstrates that one drawback of the instrument of foreign exchange intervention is the dependency on the reserve level. According to the Bank of Canada, inventory considerations played a role in its reserve management and thus might have prevented a more effective countering of the depreciation of its currency.

5.4.3 Australia

Inflation targets in Australia differ from other countries in that the Reserve Bank does not view them as a strict range but they rather serve to indicate where the central bank would like to see the average rate of inflation over the medium run. Thus, while the inflation target range of 2-3% seems to be rather narrow, this has to be viewed in the flexible spirit of the Australian monetary authority.

Although geographically close, New Zealand and Australia differ to some extent in their inflation targeting policies. As mentioned before, the introduction of inflation targets in Australia has been much less formal than in other countries and "in sharp contrast to New Zealand [...] the Reserve Bank of Australia emphasised flexibility in all aspects of its operations [...]" (Bernanke et al., 1999: 223). When Australia introduced inflation targeting in early 1993, the recession of 1991 was already replaced by strong growth in GDP.[152] Prior to 1993 the A$ had depreciated markedly and the Reserve Bank had countered this trend by intervening heavily in

151 The Bank of Canada spent about US$ 5,8 billion in August 1998 in support of the Canada dollar (see Bloomberg news, September 30, 1998, "BANK OF CANADA CHANGES INTERVENTION POLICY FOR CANADIAN DOLLAR").

152 As mentioned earlier there is some discussion about the formal start of inflation targeting. The Reserve Bank defines early 1993 as the start.

foreign exchange markets. As the fall in the exchange rate had been stopped, its effects on inflation remained low and the inflation target was not breached significantly. After a few months of high GDP growth the central bank became concerned about upcoming inflationary pressures and increased short-term interest rates quite dramatically from 4,75% to 7,5% within a short time interval. Nevertheless, and also supported by a weakening of the exchange rate, underlying inflation rose over 3% during the second half of 1995 and remained above target until mid-1996. While GDP growth continued to be high, inflationary pressures subdued and inflation decreased over the next years. In contrast to New Zealand, Australia did not experience a recession in 1998 but instead enjoyed a remarkable steady growth in economic activity. Thus, it suffered relatively less from the crisis in East Asia than other countries. The surge in underlying inflation in 2000 is mostly related to the introduction of a new goods and service tax (GST). Contributing to this was the rise in oil prices as well as the continued weakness of the exchange rate. In accordance with other major central banks and in view of the continued strength of the Australian economy, the Reserve Bank increased short-term interest rates in the year 2000 to counter upcoming inflationary pressures.

The Reserve Bank of Australia (RBA) has been remarkably open with respect to its operations in foreign exchange markets – especially when compared with the other inflation targeting central banks. As shown in Appendix I, reports of RBA intervention clearly outnumber all other countries. While this does not signal that other central banks intervened to a smaller extent than the RBA, it nevertheless is a sign of openness.[153] Two periods of significant reserve changes are visible: during 1995/96 and during 1997/98. In both cases foreign currency was sold to stop a depreciation trend of the A$. On the other hand, the appreciation period that followed in 1996 was countered with a brief intervention that brought this trend to a halt. In comparison with New Zealand, whose currency closely follows the A$, this appreciation trend has been less severe in Australia and subsequently GDP growth was not as badly affected as in New Zealand. The RBA again intervened on many occasions in 2001 as the currency dropped significantly.[154]

From the analysis of the rolling correlations the intervention policy of the RBA can be detected. During the first four years of the inflation targeting regime, the central bank tried to appreciate the A$. This becomes evident from negative correlations whenever the currency appreciated and a brief period of positive correlations (i.e. leaning-against-the-wind) at a time of depreciation at the beginning of 1995.

---

153 As mentioned before, the RBA also published time series of its daily intervention operations with a time lag.

154 While this is not yet evident from the reserve developments, it is reflected in news reports (Appendix I).

Figure 24: Economic indicators Australia

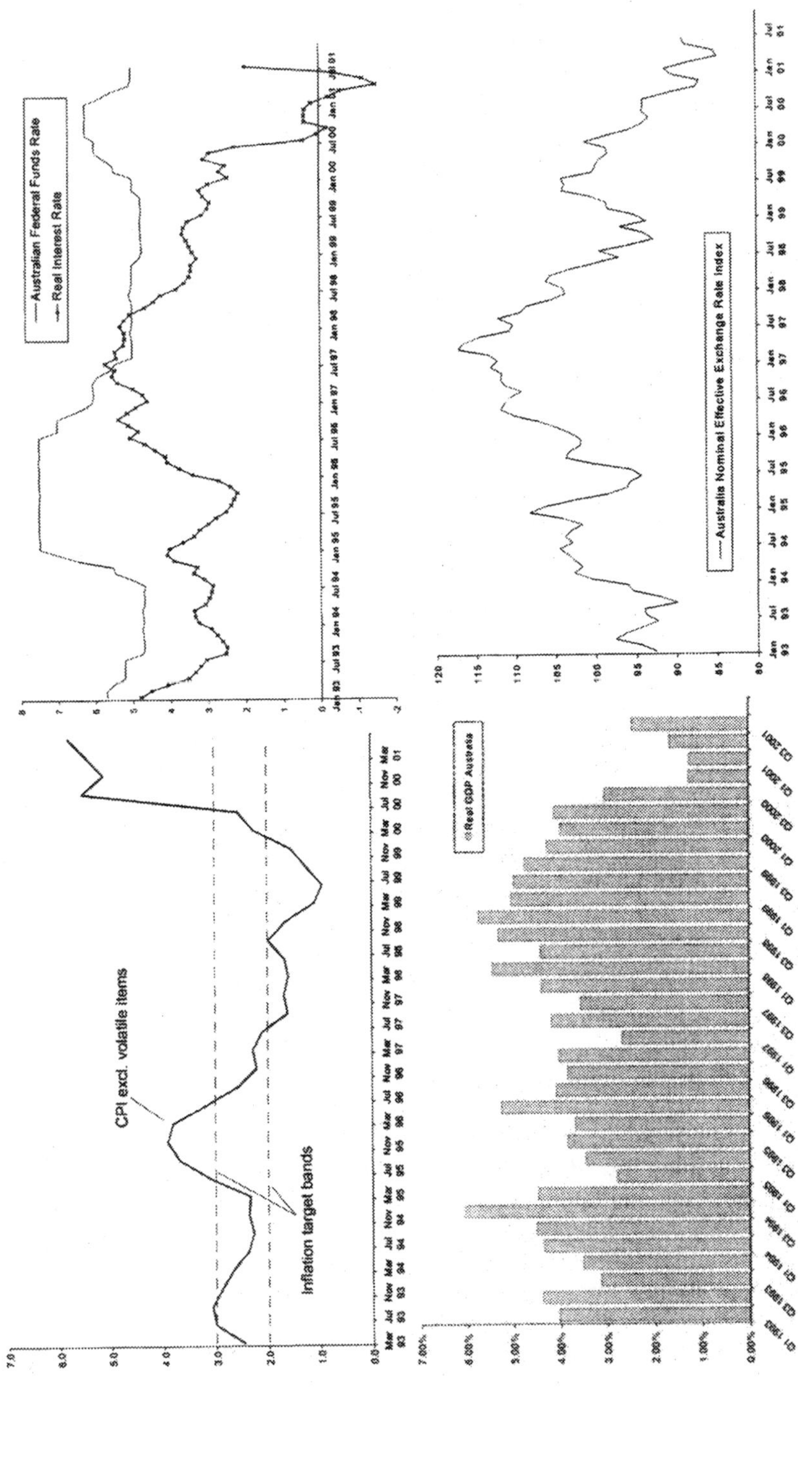

Note: Real interest rates are calculated using consumer prices. Source: International Financial Statistics, Reserve Bank of Australia.

Figure 25: Reserve level, rolling correlations and exchange rate, Australia

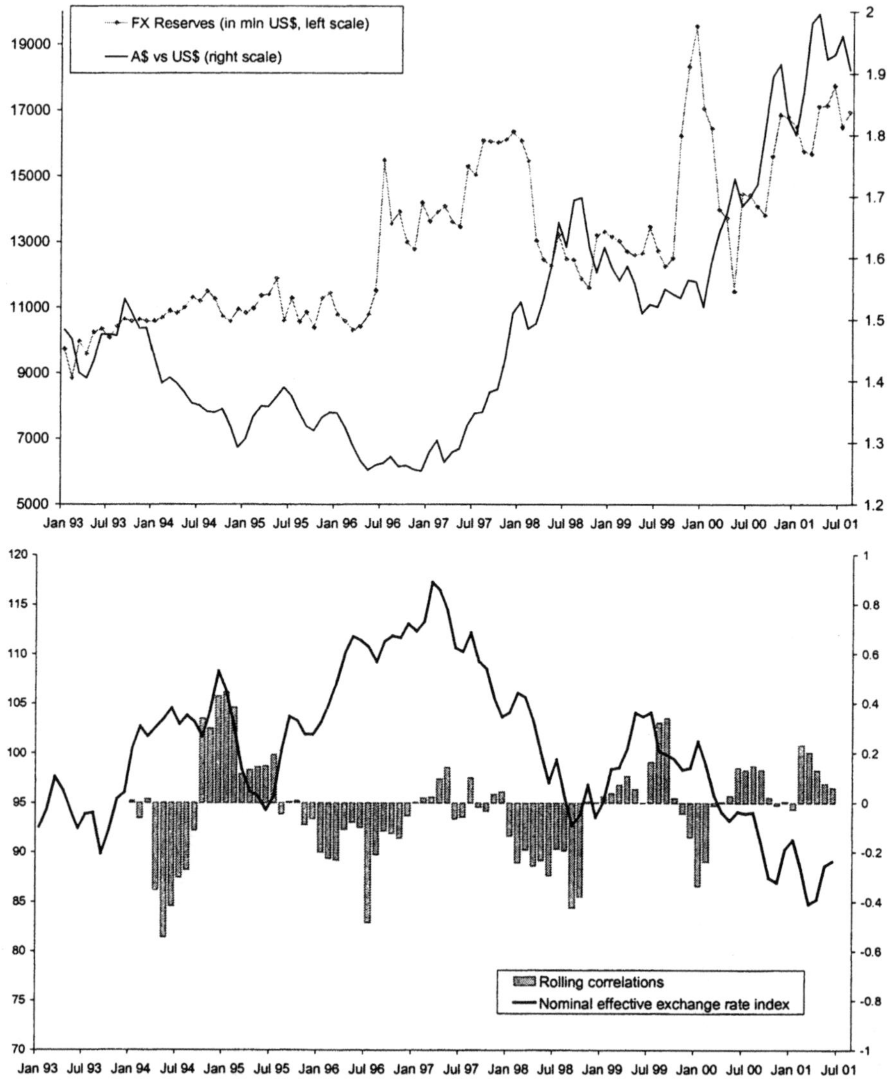

Source: International Financial Statistics, own calculations.

This corresponds with the stated intention to keep the inflation rate inside the target bands and is in line with the significant increase in short-term interest rates to tighten monetary conditions. This policy, however, changed in 1997 with inflation at the lower end of the target range and easing of interest rates. At that time, the RBA seemed to be interested in a depreciation of the currency and thus purchased foreign exchange. Consequently, negative correlations indicate that the depreciation trend that began in early 1997 was successfully supported. Only as the currency has fallen significantly, correlations turn positive to prevent a further decline of the exchange rate (also because a tightening of monetary conditions was desirable at a time of rising inflation rates).

Taken together, the analysis shows that interest rate and intervention policy in Australia seem to be in line. This further supports the earlier findings that the Reserve Bank of Australia makes active use of sterilised interventions as an additional monetary policy instrument.

5.4.4 United Kingdom

Following the foreign exchange crisis in September 1992, the UK introduced inflation targeting and thus ended the period of exchange rate targeting that had been conducted since 1987.[155] The target is measured against the retail price index excluding mortgage interest payments (RPIX). Thus, it does include energy and other volatile items and thereby is comparable to a measure of headline inflation. While initially inflation targets were announced that included bands, the Bank of England switched to a point target in June 1995. It now is the only inflation targeter in our sample that chooses to target an inflation rate of 2,5% without bands. The reason for this lies in the experience of other banks that the bands take a life of their own.[156] Bands around the desired inflation target actually served to admit that monetary policy has imperfect control over inflation. However, once set they were often perceived as binding for the central bank. A further unique feature of the UK is that the Bank of England only gained its independence in May 1997 following the election of the new Labour government. Thus, the British experience shows that inflation targeting does necessarily need to be associated with an independent central bank.

The first 24 months after the exit from the ERM presented a favourable economic environment in the UK which allowed monetary policy to be rather expansionary. As it was no longer required to shadow the high interest rates of Germany the base rate was reduced from 8% in October 1992 to 5,25% in mid-1994. Rather unexpected by the Bank of England but nevertheless interpreted as a success of the inflation targeting framework, exchange rate pass-through from the steep depreciation of the Pound Sterling during the crisis has been nearly non-existent. Furthermore, the Pound stabilised in the first months of 1993 and began appreci-

---

155 According to George (1998), the Governor of the Bank of England, there have been two periods since the breakdown of Bretton Woods in which the Sterling exchange rate was targeted. The first period extends from 1987 to 1988 when the Bundesbank policy was shadowed in order to import stability. Sterling's participation in the European Monetary System from October 1990 to September 1992 can be seen as the second attempt to target the exchange rate.

156 As Bernanke et al. (1999) note: "Arguably the United Kingdom's point target allows some flexibility to policy by permitting some short-run deviations from target without causing the public to focus unduly on whether the official target range has been breached." (p. 154).

ating so that there was little inflationary pressure. Inflation during these first two years was on a continuous downward trend and bottomed in 1994 at about 2%. GDP growth, which had picked up shortly after the UK's exit from the ERM, remained very strong throughout 1993 and 1994 and the Bank of England increased its base rate in response to inflationary pressures. Although inflation started to rise in the beginning of 1995, the increase in the RPIX was limited to about 3% throughout 1996. Economic growth declined slightly but still remained at about 2%. The crisis in emerging markets in 1998 put downward pressure on prices and inflation fell below the 2,5% target in 1999. The Bank of England responded with a series of rate cuts starting in the end of 1998. Inflation started to rise again only in the end of 2000 because of rising energy prices as in many other countries. Taken together, the inflation performance measured against the target of 2,5% has been rather impressive for the UK in the past years.[157]

Almost during the whole period of inflation targeting the British Pound tended to appreciate, above all after 1996. Foreign exchange reserves show some fluctuation, although the correlation is relatively low. From 1996 on they indicate leaning-with-the-wind behaviour, i.e. the appreciating currency was supported by subsequent sales of foreign exchange. Hüfner (2000) offers a possible explanation for this phenomenon: While the other European countries have depreciated against the US$ since the mid-1990s, the British Pound remained remarkably stable against the US currency. At the same time, the British foreign exchange reserves declined continuously by more than 40%. One hypothesis is that the Bank of England might have sold parts of their foreign exchange holdings in order to prevent a depreciation of its currency against the US currency.

157 In an interview Bank of England Governor Sir Edward George even admitted when speaking about UK inflation rates in the past years: "[...] I'm still surprised that it [inflation] has stayed as close to 2½% as it has: you can't guarantee that at all." (Financial Times, 7 May 2002, p. 9).

Figure 26: Economic indicators United Kingdom

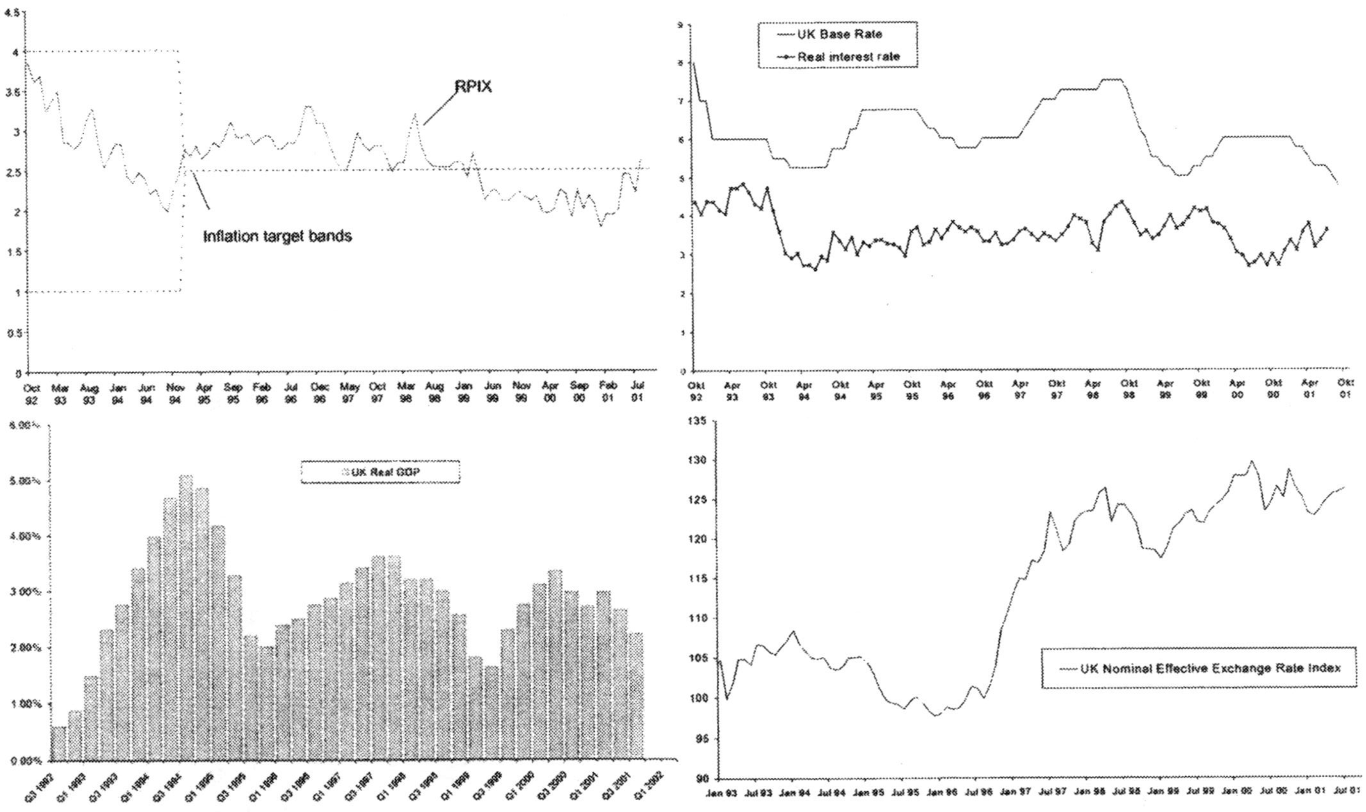

Note: Real interest rates are calculated using consumer prices. Source: International Financial Statistics, Bank of England.

Figure 27: Reserve level, rolling correlations and exchange rate, United Kingdom

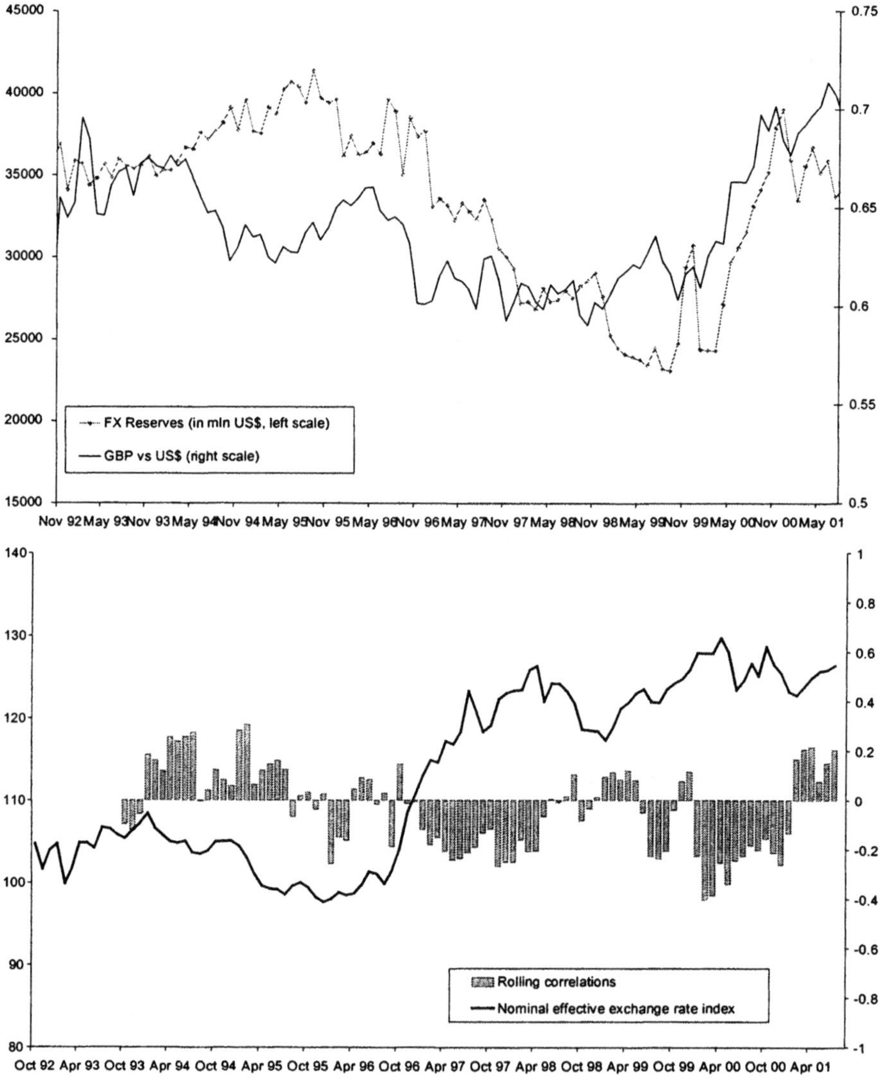

Source: International Financial Statistics, own calculations.

Figure 28: Rolling correlations and the US$/GBP exchange rate

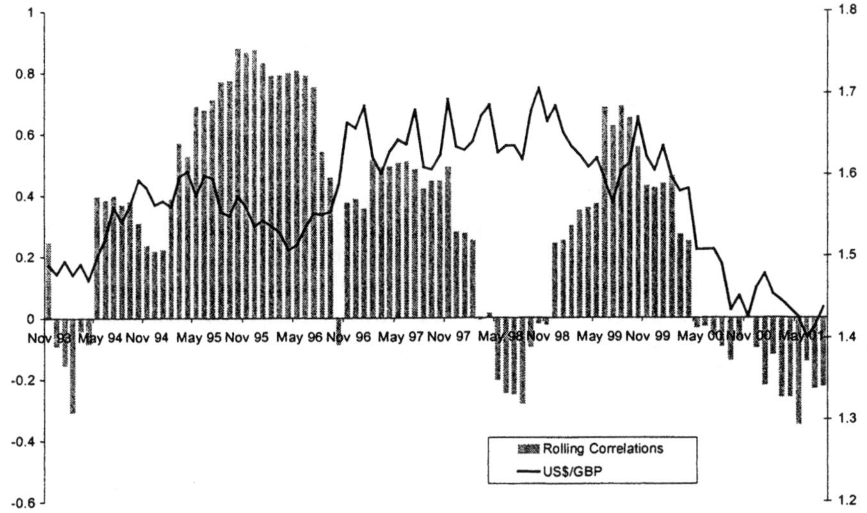

Source: International Financial Statistics, own calculations.

Indeed, correlations between reserve changes and the US$/Pound Sterling exchange rate support this hypothesis (see Figure 28). Over most of the inflation targeting period they indicate leaning-against-the-wind behaviour. Positive correlations are especially high in times of depreciation tendencies of the currency in 1995 and in 1999. As soon as intervention activity stopped in 2000 (indicated by the decline in correlations), the Pound Sterling depreciated. As can also be seen in an increase in the reserve level, the strategy of preventing a fall in the currency versus the US$ was dropped. Thus, one could argue that the sale of foreign exchange reserves prevented the exchange rate from falling against the US$ during most of the 1990s while other European currencies depreciated markedly. As a result of this effort the volatility of the Pound Sterling against the US$ has been relatively lower compared with other US$ cross rates.

Taken together, the intervention activity of the Bank of England seemed to have focussed on the exchange rate versus the US$. However, it has been considerably lower than in the other inflation targeting countries – a fact that is also supported by relatively few news reports about foreign exchange operations (see appendix 1). Some of the reported interventions have been undertaken on behalf of other central banks such as the Bank of Japan (in 1996) or the US Federal Reserve (in 1995) and therefore are not directly related to the British domestic monetary policy.

5.4.5 Sweden

Sweden's inflation target is measured in terms of headline CPI inflation. The band from 1-3% has not been changed since the introduction of the framework on January 15, 1993.[158] Like in the UK, the choice of inflation targeting in Sweden arose from the ERM crisis which led to the floating of the krona in November 1992. Thus, the implementation of the new strategy was conducted within a very short time span.

As in some of the other countries, monetary policy in Sweden can be divided into different time periods. The first period is characterised by significant disinflation after the initial rise in inflation resulting from the exchange rate devaluation. At the same time GDP growth was turning positive. Continued economic strength led to an increase in short-term interest rates from mid-1994 on which was also the turning point for the downward trend in inflation.

Headline inflation rose to the upper band of the inflation target during 1995. At the same time the krona began appreciating sharply and contributed to keeping inflation inside the bands. However, the Riksbank misjudged the following disinflation phase which took the inflation rate close to zero (although it was argued that a measure of underlying inflation that excluded interest rate effects remained stable inside the inflation bands). Nevertheless, monetary policy became very expansionary with the repo rate falling from around 9% to 4% during 1996. This also stopped the exchange rate from appreciating further, GDP growth remained positive and the inflation rate was brought back to levels of 1-2%. The last years of the Swedish inflation targeting experience are characterised by declining GDP growth (along with the downturn in the world economy), a depreciation of the krona and increases in inflation (albeit within the 1-3% band). Figure 29 displays that the inflation target of the Riksbank was undershot twice with both times – 1996 and 1998 – deflationary pressures. One explanation for missing these targets is that the Riksbank has been more flexible in the interpretation of the target: As Bernanke et al. (1999) mention: "Unlike the Reserve Bank of New Zealand, the Riksbank treated target breaches as less of a problem than the sharp movements in monetary-policy instruments that would be necessary to prevent such breaches." (p. 196).

---

158 While inflation targeting was officially introduced in 1993, the policy of the Riksbank for 1993 and 1994 was focussed on generally limiting inflationary pressures resulting from the depreciation of the krona (of about 14%) after the fixed exchange rate had been abandoned. Thus, formally the inflation target of 1-3% started in 1995 (see Bernanke et al., 1999: 174).

Figure 29: Economic indicators Sweden

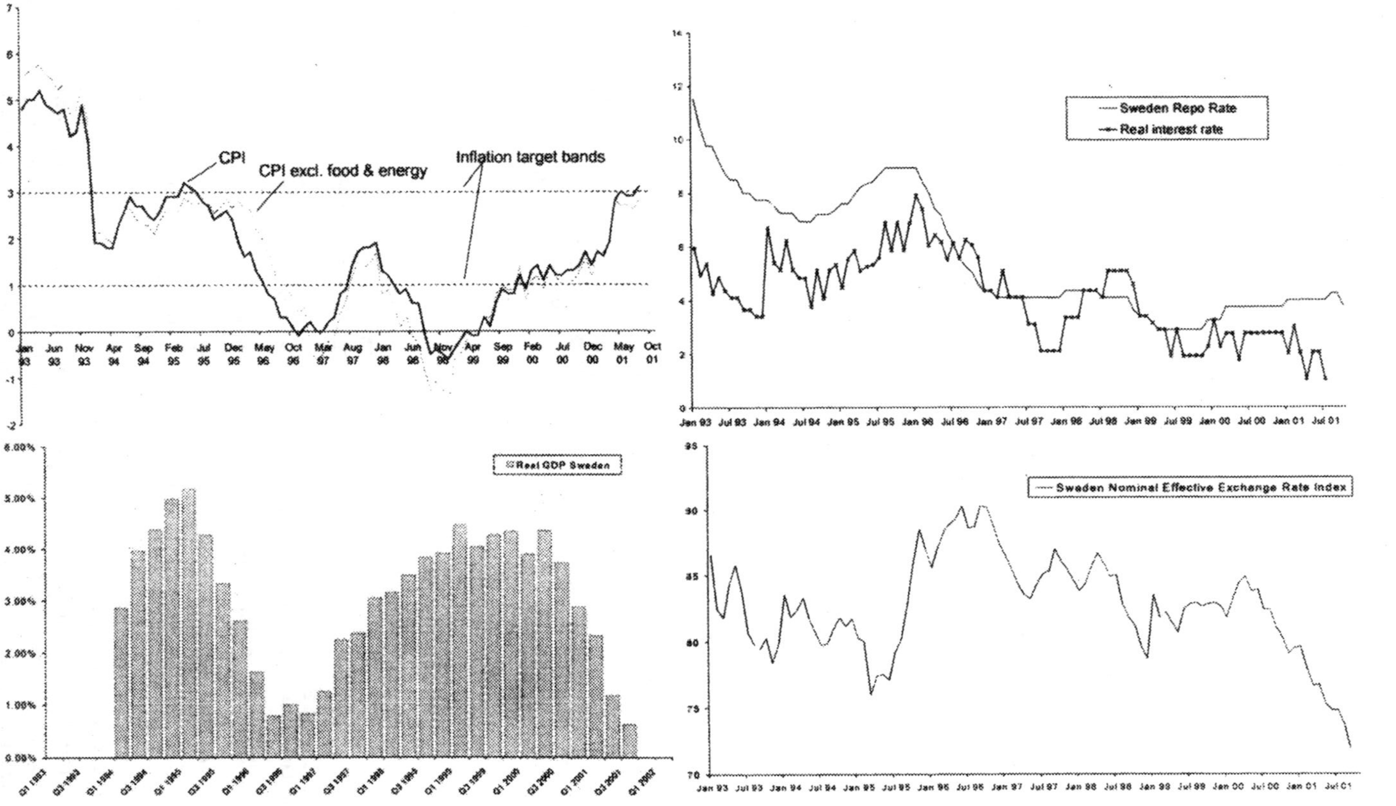

Note: Real interest rates are calculated using consumer prices. Source: International Financial Statistics, Riksbank.

Figure 30: Reserve level, rolling correlations and exchange rate, Sweden

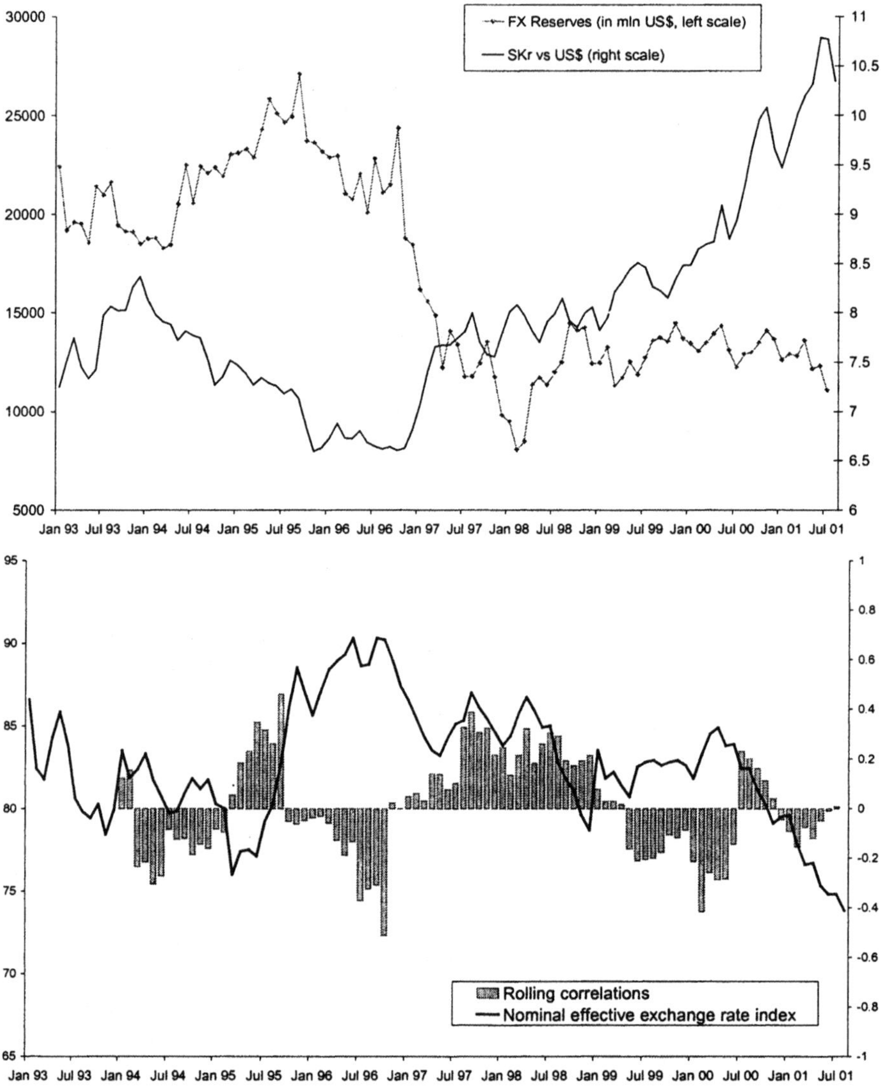

Source: International Financial Statistics, own calculations.

The exchange rate has historically been an important factor in Swedish monetary policy as Sweden had pursued a fixed exchange rate regime from the 1930s until November 1992 when the krona was allowed to float freely.[159] During the

159 From 1933 on the krona was pegged to the UK Pound sterling and from 1939 on it was fixed to the US dollar. Sweden joined the Bretton Woods system in 1951 and after its breakdown in 1973 participated in the European Currency Snake. From 1977

turbulence in European currency markets in 1992 the Riksbank tried to maintain the parity of the krona by raising overnight interest rates drastically to 500% in September and by intervening heavily in foreign exchange markets. After several months of speculative attacks the krona was allowed to float freely in November 1992 and it immediately depreciated by about 10%.

Concerning the development of the krona since 1993 one can also distinguish two different phases: an appreciation period until mid-1996 followed by a continued depreciation period thereafter. Looking at the development of the reserve level gives a first hint at the intervention strategy of the Riksbank: During the first (appreciation) period there was a tendency to accumulate reserves (reserve holdings increased by about 25% in the first years of inflation targeting) which suggests that the intention was to dampen the exchange rate movement. Rolling correlations support this to some extent.

A striking change in intervention behaviour, however, can be observed from mid-1996 on when the krona began to depreciate. Rolling correlations turn positive, suggesting that the Riksbank tried to counter the trend by selling foreign exchange. Foreign exchange reserves as a consequence declined markedly. Figure 31 shows rolling correlations versus the US$ which exemplifies the different periods of the Riksbank's intervention policy.

Figure 31: Rolling correlations and the US$/SEK exchange rate

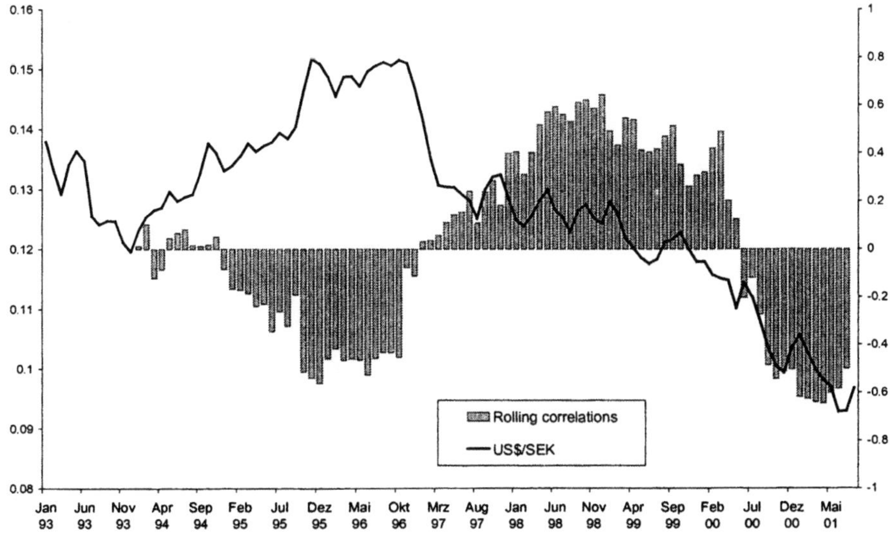

Source: International Financial Statistics, own calculations.

One of the reasons why the decline in the krona was not prevented and correlations declined eventually can be found by looking at the reserve level again. In

---

on it pegged the krona unilaterally to a weighted basket of currencies and from May 1991 on to the ECU.

1998 reserve holdings dropped below 10 billion US dollars which obviously forced the Riksbank to stop its intervention operations temporarily. This exemplifies that inventory considerations play a role in intervention policy when the intention is to counter a depreciation trend of the currency.

Taken together, the Swedish evidence is in line with our finding of relatively intense intervention activity found above and is supported by Heikensten (1999), who states that "in recent years the Riksbank has therefore occasionally chosen to intervene in the foreign exchange market in order to underscore its appraisal of the situation." (p. 3).

6 Performance of Inflation Targeting: An Evaluation

The last chapter is concerned with the performance of inflation targeting countries. Specifically, we try to find out whether there is any connection between the use of sterilised foreign exchange interventions and the performance of a central bank (this is point 6 of our subjects of inquiry). This will be done by calculating different types of loss functions across countries over time. Surely, since the period under investigation is rather short, the results need to be interpreted with care.

In order to measure the success of monetary policy, the precise goals of this framework need to be known. If inflation targeting is taken simply by its name, the goal is to minimise deviations of actual inflation from a given inflation target over a certain time horizon. This is called *strict inflation targeting* in the literature. However, there is widespread agreement that inflation targeting in fact has to be pursued in a *flexible* manner, which means that the central bank also takes into account output fluctuations.[160] Typically, output fluctuations are represented by the output gap, i.e. the difference between actual and potential output. A loss function includes both deviations from the inflation target as well as the output gap:

$$L_t = (1-\lambda)(\pi_t - \pi^*)^2 + \lambda x_t^2 \tag{6.1}$$

where π_t is inflation in period t, π^* is the inflation target, x_t denotes the output gap and $\lambda > 0$ is the relative weight on output fluctuations ($\lambda = 0$ thus characterises the loss function for *strict* inflation targeting).[161] Both inflation and output deviations are squared so that both positive and negative deviations from target are penalised. Furthermore, due to its quadratic form the marginal loss increases with the extent of the target deviation.[162] The exchange rate is not a goal in itself in a strategy of inflation targeting – the fact that it occurs in some specifications of central bank reaction functions simply signals that the exchange rate is used to forecast and to influence future inflation in order to achieve the given target.
We report two different loss functions – one for *strict* inflation targeting ($\lambda = 0$) and one for *flexible* inflation targeting, where we set $\lambda = 0.5$ (deviations from inflation target and output gaps are weighted equally) for all countries. The analysis covers the period 1993-2000 where all five countries pursued inflation targeting.

---

160 See e.g. several contributions in Federal Reserve Bank of Kansas City (1996).

161 The relative weight may be different across countries and is not known. Svensson (2002a) argues that central banks should specify explicit loss functions and publish them in order to become more transparent.

162 See Svensson, 2002a.

For countries with an inflation target range we use the midpoint of the range as π^*.

Table 22 shows the results for each country for each year as well as the average for the period 1993-2000. Generally, all countries display a lower average loss in the flexible inflation targeting specification of the loss function. As can be seen, the United Kingdom exhibits the smallest loss in both strict and flexible inflation targeting measured as the average loss over the seven years. It is closely followed by Australia. In contrast, Sweden obviously performed worse with losses much higher than in the other countries for both loss function specifications. One explanation for the good British performance may lie in the use of the inflation target variable: While the United Kingdom has a point target, all other countries have range targets. Thus, it might be argued that the Bank of England is more focussed on its point target while the other central banks may allow the inflation rate to fluctuate within the bands. As a consequence, the loss for the United Kingdom is smaller, as we included the mid-point of the range in the loss functions.

There is considerable discussion about whether to include an interest-rate smoothing term of the form $(i_t - i_{t-1})^2$ into the loss function. This would penalise overly volatile interest rate policy. Including such a term into the loss function means that interest rate stabilisation is a monetary policy objective in itself besides output stabilisation and keeping inflation on target. Such an objective might be justified to prevent tensions on financial markets that would result from overly volatile interest rates. In fact, this argument has been put forth in discussions about the observed practice of interest rate smoothing by central banks (Goodfriend, 1991; Goodhart, 1996).[163]

[163] A further explanation for interest rate smoothing behaviour is that central banks who control short-term money market rates try to influence 3-month and 6-month interest rates, which are more important for output and price developments than overnight interest rates. Since such longer term rates are also influenced by market expectations, the smoothing of interest rates contributes to keeping these rates on the same path as the short-term rates (Goodfriend, 1991). Svensson (2001d) does not find these arguments convincing except in countries with an "exceptionally weak financial sector." (p. 46).

Table 22: Loss functions 1993-2000

	Strict IT $\lambda = 0$					Flexible IT ($\lambda = 0.5$)				
	New Zealand	Australia	Canada	Sweden	United Kingdom	New Zealand	Australia	Canada	Sweden	United Kingdom
1993	0.160	0.160	1.300	7.290	0.150	4.107	1.756	10.374	24.010	3.936
1994	0.250	0.010	8.066	0.090	0.715	0.125	0.008	5.826	7.503	0.586
1995	1.210	0.490	0.109	0.640	0.055	0.793	0.335	1.033	1.996	0.086
1996	1.690	0.160	0.176	1.440	0.004	1.022	0.357	2.393	3.453	0.017
1997	0.090	0.360	0.144	1.210	0.116	0.046	0.343	0.668	3.225	0.618
1998	0.810	0.640	1.020	2.560	0.205	3.155	0.996	1.275	2.605	0.416
1999	0.490	1.690	0.073	2.890	0.668	0.810	1.639	0.125	1.506	0.434
2000	3.610	1.690	0.533	0.490	0.515	1.983	1.438	0.453	1.175	0.745
Average 1993-2000	1.039	0.650	1.428	2.076	0.303	1.505	0.859	2.768	5.684	0.855

Note: The country-specific inflation targets in the respective years are used in computing the loss functions. Output gaps are obtained from the OECD Fiscal Positions and Business Cycles 2000.

Table 23: Loss functions including interest rate volatility term 1993-2000

$$L_t = 0.5*(\pi_t - \pi^*)^2 + 0.5*x_t^2 + 0.5*(i_t - i_{t-1})^2$$

	New Zealand	Australia	Canada	Sweden	United Kingdom
1993	10.05837	2.6407305	14.8739	67.62776	11.658659
1994	8.326251	0.010492	7.35767	8.981722	0.8307741
1995	0.794135	3.0265125	1.04750	2.692481	0.8300271
1996	1.522013	0.401768	6.03800	6.00692	0.0213714
1997	0.451201	1.7880205	1.55288	5.367211	0.8421892
1998	11.559513	1.1263345	1.57158	2.60564	0.5564347
1999	0.989985	1.66085	0.18632	2.110901	2.3939733
2000	3.107608	2.0651605	0.9933	1.399698	0.9246281
Average 1993-2000	4.60113438	1.589984	4.20264	12.0990	2.257257

Note: For calculation of the interest rate changes we used money market rates from the IFS.

Table 23 displays the loss function for flexible inflation targeting including a term for interest rate variability (weighted arbitrarily with a factor of 0.5). It emerges that the UK exhibits a higher loss in this specification than in the other two loss functions.[164] Australia, on the other hand, has the smallest loss and Sweden again proves to be least successful in achieving the monetary policy objectives.

Taken together we have a mixed picture concerning the success of monetary policy when put into context with our analysis of intervention policy: On the one hand Australia, which we identified as using interventions as an additional policy tool (relatively intense intervention activity combined with a non-significance of the exchange rate in its policy reaction function and low volatility of short-term interest rates) shows a relatively good performance. On the other hand, the United Kingdom, whose regime is characterised by relatively less intervention transactions has performed equally well. Thus, results of the loss functions are not able to prove that using interventions as an additional policy tool leads to better outcomes and more successful monetary policy.

However, it might be asked if the inclusion of output fluctuations in the loss function is indeed a useful measure for the success of monetary policy. Consider the case where a certain central bank policy leads to an increase in the growth potential of a country but causes more output fluctuations. Such a policy would be penalised in the usual loss functions while a central bank that minimises fluctuations around a lower potential growth path would yield better results. While this is not the place to discuss more in-depth whether monetary policy has an effect on the potential growth rate of a country, one can argue that a significant change in a monetary policy regime might have an effect on growth by altering the environment under which the economy operates (e.g. price stability reduces uncertainty about future incomes and improves the spread of information through the price

164 Admittedly, this stems from the loss in 1993 which is caused by the large interest rate reduction after the Pound Sterling left the EMS. The same holds true for Sweden where the fixed exchange rate was also abandoned in late 1992.

system).[165] Using sterilised foreign exchange intervention as an additional policy instrument helps the central bank to cope more effectively with exchange rate fluctuations which in turn might contribute positively to long-term growth. With this background it is interesting to compare the long-term growth rates of Australia and the United Kingdom: While Australian GDP growth rates averaged 4.0% over the period 1993-2001, growth rates in the United Kingdom averaged 2.9%. Using long-term growth as an additional performance measure thus leaves the Australian monetary policy better off.

Nevertheless, it must be kept in mind that the time horizon studied is very short and therefore results should be interpreted with care.

165 See e.g. Reserve Bank of New Zealand, 2001.

7 Conclusion and Outlook

The goal of this study was twofold: to provide a rationale for the use of sterilised interventions in a framework of inflation targeting and to find evidence whether inflation targeting countries use sterilised interventions as an additional monetary policy instrument. Turning again to our simple model of monetary policy we summarise our main findings in the following.

Figure 32: Stylised model of monetary policy

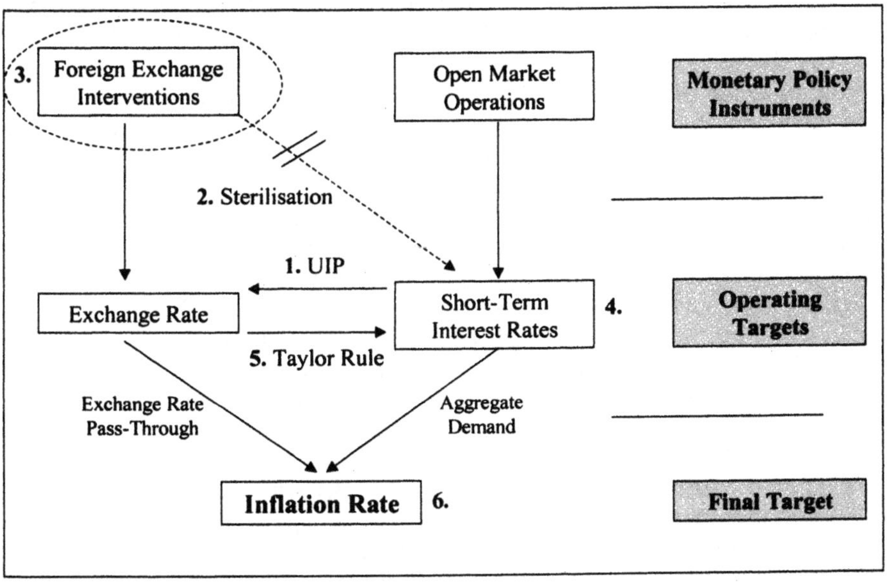

Note: UIP denotes uncovered interest parity.

We began our analysis with a survey of the main characteristics of inflation targeting in order to distinguish this strategy from other monetary policy strategies, thereby highlighting the lack of an intermediate target in this strategy. A review of the existing theoretical literature showed that inflation targeting models for an open economy rely on the assumption of uncovered interest parity to describe the relationship between short-term interest rates and the exchange rate (link 1 in Figure 32). In an empirical analysis for inflation targeting countries, however, we rejected the hypothesis of UIP for all countries in our sample (Australia, Canada, New Zealand, Sweden and United Kingdom) for the period of inflation targeting.

As a consequence, control of the exchange rate with interest rate policy in reality is not perfectly possible as assumed in theoretical models. Thus, our first result is that one of the main pillars of most open-economy models is an empirical failure.

Therefore we argued that it might be useful for a central bank to use a second policy instrument that is independent from interest rate policy, namely sterilised foreign exchange interventions. By intervening in the foreign exchange market a central bank has direct influence over the exchange rate. However, in order to be an independent tool, sterilisation of these operations is a central requirement. In our second empirical analysis we therefore estimated sterilisation equations for each country (this refers to link 2 in Figure 32). For all countries we found evidence of sterilisation of foreign exchange operations which means that interventions do not alter the money base and thus leave short-term interest rates unchanged. Consequently, sterilised interventions can be seen as an additional monetary policy tool in inflation targeting countries. A review of the recent literature illustrated that these interventions can indeed be effective. Particularly the noise-trader and microstructure approach offer explanations for the effectiveness of sterilised interventions while traditional monetary models are unable to deal with this phenomenon.

In a third step we explored to which extent interventions are used in inflation targeting countries (point 3 in Figure 32). We motivated the use of foreign exchange reserves as an intervention proxy and argued that this variable encompasses both active and passive intervention operations that are able to influence the exchange rate. By adjusting for valuation and interest earning effects we eliminated exogenous influences on the reserve levels. Introducing and comparing different measures we found relatively low intervention activity for the United Kingdom. The four other countries show evidence of considerably more intervention activity with New Zealand and Sweden exhibiting the largest reserve variations. A look at news reports of intervention activity (see appendix) revealed that most headlines were found for Australia, Sweden and Canada. We interpreted this as an indication that these countries rely more on active interventions as opposed to New Zealand which seems to rely more on passive interventions.

In a further step we analysed which central banks actually use interventions as an *additional* policy instrument besides open market operations to control interest rates. A first result was found in an analysis of the volatility of short-term interest rates (point 4 in Figure 32). Our hypothesis that more intervention activity leads to a decline in interest rate volatility was only weakly supported: We found the lowest volatility for both Australia and the United Kingdom – two countries with distinctly different intervention activity. Australia, which has considerably higher intervention activity than the United Kingdom, however, exhibits the lowest frequency of interest rate changes. This supports the hypothesis that by using interventions as an *additional* policy tool, interest rate policy needs to be less activist, i.e. interventions *smooth* interest rates.

By looking at the influence of the exchange rate on the interest rate setting of the central banks (link 5 in Figure 32) we analysed whether intervention intensity has an influence on the policy reaction function. We estimated an open-economy version of a Taylor rule and found that the exchange rate variable was significant in the United Kingdom and New Zealand and insignificant in all other countries. We interpreted this as evidence that countries with a lower intervention activity (United Kingdom) have to incorporate exchange rate fluctuations more in their interest rate decisions than countries with a higher intervention activity (Australia, Canada, Sweden). The result for New Zealand does not support this hypothesis. It is, however, in line with official statements of the Reserve Bank of New Zealand concerning its interest rate policy.

The result of our performance analysis (point 6 in Figure 32) once again shows some dichotomy: Both Australia and the United Kingdom were found to be the best performers among all countries when loss functions were compared. Thus, we were not able to disentangle a direct positive influence of the use of foreign exchange intervention on the overall performance of monetary policy. One explanation for the good performance of the United Kingdom might be the focus on a point target in contrast to a target range for the inflation rate. Central banks with a target range, on the other hand, may choose to let inflation fluctuate inside the bands, thus worsening the performance measured with a loss function that incorporates the mid-point of the range as the target inflation rate. The result is also influenced by the short period available for study. However, we showed that Australia exhibits considerably higher long-term growth rates than the United Kingdom. This can be interpreted as evidence that monetary policy positively affected growth potential in Australia.

Our interpretation of the results is as follows:

First, sterilised foreign exchange intervention is used in industrial inflation targeting countries, albeit to a differing extent. The reason for its use might lie in the empirical failure of uncovered interest parity which highlights the need for a further policy instrument. Thus, the rationale for using sterilised interventions seems to be the insufficiency of the interest rate instrument in coping with exchange rate fluctuations.

Second, sterilised interventions are used across countries and there is some evidence that interventions change the way interest rate policy is implemented, i.e. that they are consequently used as an *additional* policy instrument. However, significance of this phenomenon remains weak. For example, countries that intervene might also react to exchange rate fluctuations by changing their interest rates (New Zealand) and countries that intervene less might also exhibit low interest rate volatility (United Kingdom).

Third, it was shown that no country actually conducts inflation targeting in exactly the way prescribed by theoretical models. Either they use interventions, which are not part of the models, and/or they include the exchange rate explicitly in their policy reaction functions. The latter would not be necessary if uncovered interest parity – the main building block of theoretical models – would hold in practice.

Fourth, the use of sterilised foreign exchange intervention as an additional policy tool is practised most obviously in Australia. High intervention activity together with low interest rate volatility and an interest rate policy that focuses on domestic factors are all characteristics of this strategy. Additionally, Australia has also been one of the best performers among inflation targeting countries over the past decade.

Our analysis also has some drawbacks: The time period for analysis is rather short with at most ten years (in the case of New Zealand) available for research. This significantly limits the tools available for analysis and the interpretation of results. Furthermore, the idea of sterilised interventions as an *additional* policy tool is far from being standard knowledge in economics – rather, it represents a significant departure from many existing theoretical models. Thus, central banks cannot be expected to employ this tool in a perfectly predictable manner. Both interventions and interest rate policy are mostly being used without a clear separation (in the sense that sterilised interventions control the exchange rate and interest rate policy focuses on domestic factors). Only the Reserve Bank of Australia seems to serve as a role model for the use of sterilised interventions as an additional monetary policy instrument.

Our findings suggest the following interpretation of the current status of inflation targeting: In practice, rather than making strict division between interventions and interest rate policy, a mix of both can be observed. In other words, if the exchange rate is believed to be out of line with fundamentals and provides a threat to the inflation target, then both interventions and short-term interest rates are used to influence the currency. An example provides the Swedish Riksbank in 2001: In response to a sharp weakening of the krona the Riksbank intervened a couple of times *and* then additionally increased its policy interest rates. Similarly, the European Central Bank (while not being a full-fledged inflation targeter) in autumn 2000 first intervened in support of the Euro *and* then increased its main refinancing rate.

An important conclusion can be drawn for the conduct of inflation targeting. As was highlighted in the beginning this strategy is characterised by a high degree of transparency that is due to the lack of an intermediate target. With respect to foreign exchange interventions, many central banks still retain a high degree of secrecy. It would be desirable for researchers as well as for the public if inflation targeting central banks would be more open with regard to their foreign exchange operations and communicate the usefulness of these operations in achieving price stability in an open economy.

According to Alan Blinder (1997) "central banking in practice is as much art as science. Nonetheless, while practising this dark art, I always found the science quite useful." (p. 17). In his article "What central bankers could learn from academics – and vice versa" Blinder mentions many scientific features that practical central bankers should learn from academics. However, sometimes it might be quite useful for academics to take a look at central banking practice and try to learn from it. Lars Svensson, one of the main academic advocates of inflation targeting, admits that "the credit for the initial rise of inflation targeting goes mostly to insightful central-bank and finance-department officials rather than academics." (Svensson, 2001a: 1). Maybe this will also hold for the rise of sterilised foreign exchange interventions as an additional policy tool in inflation targeting. The example of the Reserve Bank of Australia suggests that the actual conduct of monetary policy differs significantly from the conventional prescriptions of academics.

Appendix

News Reports of Interventions

Date	Source	Report
Canada		
September 22, 2000	B	CANADIAN DOLLAR FALLS AFTER BANK OF CANADA JOINS EURO EFFORT
August 26, 1998	B	CANADIAN DOLLAR PLUMMETS TO HISTORIC LOW; BOC BUYS
August 21, 1998	B	CANADIAN DOLLAR FALLS BELOW 65 U.S. CENTS; BOC BUYS
August 12, 1998	B	CANADA DOLLAR RISES; CENTRAL BANK BUYS DOLLARS AGAIN
August 11, 1998	B	CANADA DOLLAR FALLS ON CONCERN ABOUT JAPAN; BOC BUYS
August 10, 1998	B	CANADA'S CENTRAL BANK PURCHASES DOLLARS, BOOSTING CURRENCY
August 7, 1998	B	CANADA DOLLAR RISES AS BANK OF CANADA BUYS CURRENCY
August 6, 1998	B	CANADIAN DOLLAR FALLS TO NEW LOW AS BOC INTERVENTION FAILS
July 31, 1998	B	CANADA DOLLAR FALLS AFTER GDP DATA; BOC ENTERS MARKET
April 13, 1998	B	CANADA DOLLAR SLIDES AS NO RATE RISE SEEN; BOC BUYS
February 4, 1998	B	Government currency market intervention decreased reserves by $ 1.610 billion as the Bank of Canada tried to prop up the Canadian dollar.
December 19, 1997	B	CANADA DOLLAR PLUMMETS TO 12-YEAR LOW; BOC INTERVENES
November 7, 1997	B	CANADIAN DOLLAR SLIDES AS STOCKS FALL; BOC INTERVENES
October 28, 1997	B	CANADIAN DOLLAR PLUMMETS; BANK OF CANADA TEMPERS FALL
October 27, 1997	B	CANADIAN DOLLAR SINKS TO 2 1/2-YR LOW; BOC INTERVENES
May 1, 1997	B	BANK OF CANADA INTERVENES TWICE AS DOLLAR RALLIES

September 13, 1995	B	CANADIAN DOLLAR DROPS EVEN WITH BANK INTERVENTION
November 29, 1994	B	Yesterday's round of currency intervention by the Bank of Canada has done little to turn sentiment around, analysts at MMS International said in a commentary.
December 22, 1993	A	This prompted intervention by the Bank of Canada which stepped in to try to support its currency.
October 6, 1993	A	Amidst rumors of intervention by the Bank of Canada, the Canadian dollar firmed to 1.3355 to the U.S. dollar,
February 1, 1993	B	BANK OF CANADA BOUGHT U.S. DOLLARS AT C$ 1.2625, TRADERS SAY
September 28, 1992	B	The dollar strengthened to 1.2489 Canadian dollars from 1.2409 despite at least two rounds of intervention by the Bank of Canada
September 22, 1992	B	The dollar finished at 1.2358 Canadian dollars, up from 1.2308 despite repeated intervention by the Bank of Canada aimed at slowing the U.S. dollar's rise.
September 9, 1992	B	BANK OF CANADA BUYS CANADIAN DOLLARS AT C$ 1.2095, TRADERS SAY
Australia		
November 11, 2001	B	RESERVE BANK OF AUSTRALIA INTERVENES TO BUOY FLAGGING DOLLAR
September 28, 2001	B	AUSTRALIAN DOLLAR RISES ON TALK CENTRAL BANK BUYS CURRENCY
July 13, 2001	B	WESTPAC'S MYERS ON AUSTRALIAN DOLLAR, RBA INTERVENTION: COMMENT
July 12, 2001	B	AUSTRALIAN DOLLAR RISES ON SPECULATION CENTRAL BANK INTERVENED
March 14, 2001	B	AUSTRALIA CENTRAL BANK BUYS A$115 MLN MORE THAN IT SELLS IN FEB
March 13, 2001	B	AUSTRALIAN DOLLAR HOVERS NEAR LOW; TALK OF RBA BUYING
February 14, 2001	B	AUSTRALIA CENTRAL BANK BUYS A$150 MLN MORE THAN IT SELLS IN JAN
February 11, 2001	B	RESERVE BANK INTERVENES 'SEVERAL' TIMES TO BUOY CURRENCY
September 8, 2000	B	AUSTRALIAN DOLLAR FALLS AS CENTRAL BANK SUPPORT PROVES FLEETING
September 6, 2000	B	AUSTRALIA DOLLAR RISES FROM 2-YR LOW; CENTRAL BANK BUYING SEEN
August 18, 1998	B	AUSTRALIAN CENTRAL BANK SPENT A$ 2.6 BLN IN BID TO PROP UP DOLLAR
June 4, 1998	B	AUSTRALIAN CENTRAL BANK STEPS IN AGAIN TO BUY DOLLARS

June 05, 1998	A	The Reserve Bank of Australia entered the market for the second straight day Friday to shore up the Aussie dollar against speculative attacks by US funds, dealers said.
June 8, 1998	B	Meantime, the Reserve Bank of Australia has been buying the Australian dollar during the past week, amid concern its fall has been too rapid, and that the lower dollar could herald a pickup in inflation.
June 15, 1998	B	AUSTRALIA'S CENTRAL BANK BOUGHT A$ 577 MLN NET IN MAY
June 16, 1998	B	AUSTRALIA CENTRAL BANK FAILED TO BOOST CURRENCY
May 19, 1998	B	AUSTRALIAN CENTRAL BANK BUYS DOLLARS TO CURB FALL, DOES FOR NOW
May 18, 1998	B	AUSTRALIAN DOLLAR DECLINE STEMMED BY RESERVE BANK
February 16, 1998	B	RESERVE BANK SPENT A$ 400 MLN ON AUSTRALIAN DOLLARS RECENTLY
January 9, 1998	B	AUSTRALIA'S CENTRAL BANK SEEN STEMMING LOCAL CURRENCY'S PLUNGE
September 1, 1997	B	AUSTRALIA RESERVE BANK STOCKS UP ON U.S. DOLLARS IN 1996/97
May 5, 1994	B	AUSTRALIAN BONDS, DOLLAR LITTLE CHANGED AFTER CENTRAL BANK ACTION
September 30, 1993	B	BONDS DROP, AUSTRALIA DOLLAR STEADY AFTER CENTRAL BANK BUYING
June 16, 1993	B	AUSTRALIAN CENTRAL BANK SPENT A$ 760 MLN IN MARKETS LAST MONTH
June 8, 1993	A	Australian dollar plunges despite central bank intervention
May 19, 1993	B	AUSTRALIAN BOND PRICES RISE AS BANK INTERVENTION SETTLES DOLLAR
May 18, 1993	B	Intervention by the Reserve Bank of Australia today failed to half the unit's slide, traders said.
May 17, 1993	B	AUSTRALIAN CENTRAL BANK REPORTED IN MKT AS LOCAL DOLLAR PLUNGES
March 3, 1993	B	AUSTRALIAN CENTRAL BANK GOVERNOR DEFENDS CURRENCY INTERVENTION
February 16, 1993	B	AUSTRALIAN CENTRAL BANK SPENT A$ 1.37 BLN INTERVENING LAST MONTH
January 21, 1993	B	AUSTRALIA TREASURER DAWKINS DEFENDS CENTRAL BANK INTERVENTION
January 20, 1993	B	CENTRAL BANK INTERVENES ON AUSTRALIAN DOLLAR, STOCKS STALLED
January 6, 1993	B	The Reserve Bank of Australia intervened in foreign exchange markets as the dollar tumbled toward a level of 67 U.S. cents, traders said.
December 29, 1992	B	AUSTRALIA BONDS, DOLLAR LITTLE CHANGED AMID INTERVENTION RUMORS
December 22, 1992	B	AUSTRALIAN CENTRAL BANK SPENT A$ 670 MLN IN MKTS LAST MONTH

November 19, 1992	B	AUSTRALIAN CENTRAL BANK SPENT A$ 10.6 BLN SUPPORTING DOLLAR
November 18, 1992	B	AUSTRALIA CENTRAL BANK SPENT A$ 1.04 BLN TO LIFT DOLLAR IN OCT
September 30, 1992	B	AUSTRALIA BONDS OPEN WEAKER, DOLLAR FALLS DESPITE INTERVENTION
August 12, 1992	B	AUSTRALIAN DOLLAR CONTINUES TO FALL DESPITE INTERVENTION
August 11, 1992	B	The central bank's intervention earlier in the day failed to hold the dollar above 73.50 U.S. cents, traders said.

Sweden

November 30, 2001	B	SWEDISH CENTRAL BANK DOES NOT RULE OUT FURTHER INTERVENTION
June 25, 2001	B	RIKSBANK BUYS SWEDISH KRONOR TO STEM WEAKENING OF CURRENCY
June 18, 2001	B	RIKSBANK BUYS SWEDISH KRONOR TO STEM WEAKENING OF CURRENCY
June 15, 2001	B	SWEDISH 2-YEAR YIELD AT 8-MONTH HIGH AFTER RIKSBANK BUYS KRONOR
October 8, 1998	B	Central bank governor Urban Baeckstroem said yesterday in a seminar sponsored by Svenska Handelsbanken in New York. "The Riksbank has chosen to use currency interventions to underscore that the movements in the krona's exchange rate have been unduly abrupt and exaggerated."
September 26, 1995	A	...the Swedish krona to 4.875 to the mark, as some operators reported intervention by the Swedish central bank.
September 20, 1995	A	The Swedish central bank on Wednesday intervened to support the krona, strengthening it slightly, dealers said. The bank entered the market bought krona for German marks at 4.7930 kronor to the mark. One dealer said he estimated that the bank had bought kronor worth about 50 million marks (33.6 million dollars).
May 31, 1995	B	SWEDISH, SWISS CENTRAL BANKS SAY THEY'RE BUYING DOLLARS AGAIN
March 3, 1995	B	SWEDISH CENTRAL BANK SAYS IT'S INTERVENING TO SUPPORT DOLLAR
May 4, 1994	B	BUNDESBANK AND EUROPEAN CENTRAL BANKS BUY DOLLARS WITH FED
September 29, 1993	B	SWEDISH CENTRAL BANK SAYS IT BOUGHT KRONOR
September 20, 1993	B	SWEDISH CENTRAL BANK SAYS IT'S BUYING KRONOR TO HALT DECLINE

September 9, 1993	B	SWEDISH CENTRAL SAYS BUYS KRONOR FOR DEUTSCHE MARKS
September 6, 1993	B	Without the interest rate weapon, the Riksbank has intervened on several occasions to buy kronor in recent weeks to try to prevent it falling 4.88 against the mark, but all in vain.
September 3, 1993	B	SWEDISH CENTRAL BANK BUYS KRONOR TO HALT CURRENCY'S DECLINE
September 2, 1993	A	Despite intervention by the Swedish central bank, the Riksbanken, the Swedish krona continued to fall, opening at 4.96 kronor for one mark before climbing back to 4.94, still off its 4.9 kronor/mark close on Wednesday.
August 31, 1993	B	SWEDISH CENTRAL BANK BUYS KRONOR AS THE CURRENCY FALLS
January 14, 1993	B	SWEDISH CENTRAL BANK SAYS IT'S BUYING KRONOR

United Kingdom

September 22, 2000	B	BRITISH POUND POISED TO GAIN VS DOLLAR; MORE INTERVENTION SEEN
March 17, 2000	B	BOE'S SUSHIL WADHWANI SAYS INTERVENTION ON POUND STILL POSSIBLE
April 03, 1998	A	Sterling suffered substantial losses Friday after-noon on the London forex market due to rumors of intervention by the Bank of England
February 27, 1996	B	DOLLAR REBOUNDS AMID TALK BANK OF ENGLAND ACTED ON BOJ'S BEHALF
March 3, 1995	B	BANK OF ENGLAND INTERVENES TO BUY DOLLARS, CURRENCY TRADERS SAY
February 15, 1995	B	BRITISH POUND RISES AMID TALK OF U.K. CENTRAL BANK INTERVENTION
March 01, 1994	A	Sterling closed generally higher after intervention by the Bank of England, Donald said, adding that the central bank wanted to avoid a speed-up of the pound's depreciation
May 4, 1994	B	BANK OF ENGLAND BUYING DOLLARS FOR DEUTSCHE MARKS, TRADERS SAY
February 2, 1994	B	STERLING DOWN VS MARK AS U.K. RESERVES SHOW BANK INTERVENTION
February 12, 1993	B	BANK OF ENGLAND BOUGHT POUNDS FOR DOLLARS TODAY, TRADERS SAID

New Zealand*

August 10, 1995	B	NZ CENTRAL BANK SQUEEZES CASH TO PROP UP CURRENCY
December 14, 1992	B	NEW ZEALAND CENTRAL BANK INTERVENES TO SHORE UP LOCAL DOLLAR

Note: * Reports of New Zealand intervention refer to intervention in the money market, not the foreign exchange market. Source: [A]: Agence France Press (AFP), [B]: Bloomberg news headlines 1992-2002, obtained through LexisNexis.

Instrumental Variables and Two-Stage-Least-Squares (TSLS)

Generally, in a standard regression analysis the causal effects of one variable on another variable is of interest.[166] A fundamental assumption is that the right-hand side variables are uncorrelated with the disturbance term. There are situations, however, where the standard procedures lead to biased estimates of the true underlying causation. Stock (2001) mentions four situations which are of particular importance:

Omitted variable bias if there are additional unmeasured effects that are not included in the regression

Simultaneous equations bias if there is a reverse causality between the dependent variable and an independent variable

Selection bias in the sample choice

Measurement error in the regressors.

All these four problems lead to the same consequence: the independent variable will be correlated with the disturbance term. Consider the following equation:

$$y = \alpha + \beta x + \varepsilon \tag{8.1}$$

In the presence of one of the above biases, the correlation between x and ε will be nonzero and consequently, the OLS (ordinary least squares) estimator β will be biased. To see why the correlation is non-zero, consider problem (4) – the errors in variables (measurement error): suppose that (8.1) is the true relationship, but that x is measured with error as z with

$$z = x + u \tag{8.2}$$

or

$$x = z - u \tag{8.2'}$$

Then (8.1) becomes

$$y = \alpha + \beta(z - u) + \varepsilon \tag{8.1'}$$

or

$$y = \alpha + \beta z + (\varepsilon - \beta u) \tag{8.1''}$$

Now the disturbance term as well as variable z contain u and both are thus correlated. The most common way to handle this problem is by using instrumental variable estimation. This is done by introducing a second equation

$$x = \phi + \pi x^{i} + \vartheta \tag{8.3}$$

i.e. by regressing the independent variable on an instrument x^{i}. The key idea of instrumental variable estimation is that because x^{i} is uncorrelated with u, x^{i} can

[166] The following draws on Stock (2001) and Kennedy (1998).

be used to estimate β. x^i is then called an instrument and is used to eliminate the correlation between x and the disturbance term. In order to serve as an instrument, x^i needs to be (a) uncorrelated with u (i.e. the instrument must be exogenous) and (b) highly correlated with x (i.e. the instrument must be relevant).

Possible instruments includes the lags of the independent variable x. They are usually correlated with the original independent variable but not *contemporaneously* correlated with the disturbance term (because it is lagged) (see Kennedy, 1998: 142).

The Two-Stage-Least-Squares estimation procedure calls for an estimation in two steps: in the first step equation (8.2) is estimated by OLS which produces the predicted value $\hat{x}$. In the second step equation (8.1) is estimated using the predicted value $\hat{x}$ and the exogenous variable as independent variables. The resulting estimator of the procedure is β^{2SLS}.

List of Figures

List of Tables

Bibliography

ADAM, C./D. COBHAM/E. GIRARDIN (2001): *External Influences and Institutional Constraints on UK Monetary Policy, 1985-2000*, University of St. Andrews Discussion Paper 0116.

ADAMS, D.B./D.W. HENDERSON (1983): *Definition and Measurement of Exchange Market Intervention*, Board of Governors of the Federal Reserve System, Staff Studies 126.

AGUILAR, J./S. NYDAHL (2000): Central Bank Intervention and Exchange Rates: The Case of Sweden, *Journal of International Financial Markets, Institutions & Money* 10, 303-322.

ALLEN, H./M.P. TAYLOR (1990): Charts, Noise and Fundamentals in the London Foreign Exchange Market, *The Economic Journal* 100 (400), Conference Papers, 49-59.

AMATO, J.D./S. GERLACH (2001): *Inflation Targeting in Emerging Market and Transition Economies: Lessons After a Decade*, CEPR Working Paper 3074.

ARCHER, D./J. HALLIDAY (1998): The Rationale for Holding Foreign Exchange Reserves, *Reserve Bank of New Zealand Bulletin* 61 (4), 346-354.

BAILLIE, R.T./O.F. HUMPAGE/W.P. OSTERBERG (1999): *Intervention as Information: A Survey*, Federal Reserve Bank of Cleveland Working Paper 99/18.

BAILLIE, R.T. (2000): Central Bank Intervention, *Journal of International Financial Markets, Institutions & Money* 10, 225-228.

BALL, L. (1999): Policy Rules for Open Economies, in: TAYLOR, J.B. (ED.): *Monetary Policy Rules*, Chicago, 127-144.

BANK FOR INTERNATIONAL SETTLEMENTS (BIS) (1998): *Enhancing Transparency Regarding the Authorities' Foreign Currency Liquidity Position*, Basle, 28th September 1998, <www.bis.org>.

BANK FOR INTERNATIONAL SETTLEMENTS (BIS) (2001): *Central Bank Survey of Foreign Exchange and Derivatives Market Activity in April 2001*, Basle, October 2001.

BARRO, R.J./D.B. GORDON (1983): A Positive Theory of Monetary Policy in a Natural Rate Model, *Journal of Political Economy* 91 (4), 589-610.

BATINI, N./A.G. HALDANE (1999): Forward-Looking Rules for Monetary Policy, in: TAYLOR, J.B. (ED.): *Monetary Policy Rules*, Chicago, 157-192.

BEATTIE, N./J.-F. FILLION (1999): *An Intraday Analysis of the Effectiveness of Foreign Exchange Intervention*, Bank of Canada Working Paper 99-4.

BERNANKE, B.S./I. MIHOV (1997): What Does the Bundesbank Target?, *European Economic Review* 41, 1025-1053.

BERNANKE, B.S./F.S. MISHKIN (1997): Inflation Targeting: A New Framework for Monetary Policy?, *Journal of Economic Perspectives* 11 (2), 97-116.

BERNANKE, B.S./M. WOODFORD (1997): *Inflation Forecasts and Monetary Policy*, NBER Working Paper 6157.

BERNANKE, B.S. ET AL. (1999): *Inflation Targeting: Lessons from the International Experience*, Princeton.

BHARUCHA, N./C. KENT (1998): *Inflation Targeting in a Small Open Economy*, Reserve Bank of Australia Research Discussion Paper 9807.

BLEJER, M.I./A. IZE/A.M. LEONE/ S. WERLANG (EDS.) (1999): *Inflation Targeting in Practice – Strategic and Operational Issues and Application to Emerging Market Economies*, Proceedings of an IMF seminar held in Rio de Janeiro, Brazil, May 3-5, 1999, <www.imf.org>.

BLINDER, A.S. (1997): What Central Bankers Could Learn from Academics – and Vice Versa, *Journal of Economic Perspectives* 11 (2), 3-19.

BLUSTEIN, P. (2001): *The Chastening: Inside the Crisis that Rocked the Global Financial System and Humbled the IMF*, New York.

BOFINGER, P. (2000A): *Inflation Targeting: Much Ado About Nothing (New)*, Paper presented at the annual meeting of the Ausschuss für Geldtheorie und Geldpolitik des Vereins für Socialpolitik, 25 February 2000.

BOFINGER, P. (2000B): Pro Inflation Targeting: Yes, but ..., *CESifo Forum* (2), 37-38.

BOFINGER, P. (2000C): *Inflation targeting: was kann die EZB daraus lernen?*, Deutsche Bank Research EWU-Monitor 83.

BOFINGER, P. (2001): *Monetary Policy – Goals, Institutions, Strategies, and Instruments*, Oxford.

BOFINGER, P./T. WOLLMERSHÄUSER (2001): *Managed Floating: Understanding the New International Monetary Order*, CEPR Discussion Paper 3064.

CALVO, G.A./C.M. REINHART (2000): *Fear of Floating*, NBER Working Paper 7993.

CAMPBELL, J.Y./P. PERRON (1991): *Pitfalls and Opportunities: What Macroeconomists Should Know About Unit Roots*, NBER Technical Working Paper 100.

CHEUNG, Y.-W./M.D. CHINN (2001): Currency Traders and Exchange Rate Dynamics: A Survey of the US Market, *Journal of International Money and Finance* 20, 439-471.

CHEUNG, Y.-W./C.Y.-P. WONG (2000): A Survey of Market Practitioners' Views on Exchange Rate Dynamics, *Journal of International Economics* 51, 401-419.

CLARIDA, R./J. GALI/M. GERTLER (1998): Monetary Policy Rules in Practice: Some International Evidence, *European Economic Review* 42, 1033-1067.

CLARIDA, R./J. GALI/M. GERTLER (1999): The Science of Monetary Policy: A New Keynesian Perspective, *Journal of Economic Literature* XXXVII, 1661-1707.

CLARIDA, R./J. GALI/M. GERTLER (2000): Monetary Policy Rules and Macroeconomic Stability: Evidence and Some Theory, *Quarterly Journal of Economics* 115 (1), 147-180.

COLLINS, S./P.L. SIKLOS (2001): *Optimal Reaction Functions, Taylor's Rule and Inflation Targets: The Experiences of Dollar Bloc Countries*, Wilfrid Laurier University, mimeo, <www.wlu.ca/~wwwsbe/faculty/psiklos/home.htm>.

CORBO, V./O.L. MORENO/K. SCHMIDT-HEBBEL (2001): *Assessing Inflation Targeting After a Decade of World Experience*, Paper presented at the workshop "Exchange rates and monetary policy issues", 19-20 April 2001, Institute for Advanced Studies, Vienna.

CZECH NATIONAL BANK (2002): *Strategy for Dealing with the Exchange Rate Effects of Capital Inflows from Privatisation of State Property and from other Foreign Exchange Revenues of the State*, Press release 17 January 2002, <www. cnb.cz>.

DAL BOSCO, E. (1998): Central Banks' Management of Foreign Exchange Reserves, *Open Economies Review* 9 (1), 295-313.

DEBELLE, G. (1997): *Inflation Targeting in Practice*, IMF Working Paper 97/35.

DE GRAUWE, P./M. POLAN (2001): *Is Inflation Always and Everywhere a Monetary Phenomenon?*, CEPR Discussion Paper 2841.

De León, J. (2000-2001): The Bank of Canada's Management of Foreign Currency Reserves, *Bank of Canada Review*, Winter 2000-2001, 13-31.

Deutsche Bundesbank (1997): *Weltweite Organisationen und Gremien im Bereich von Währung und Wirtschaft*, Frankfurt/Main.

Djoudad, R./J. Murray/T. Chan/J. Daw (2000): *The Role of Chartists and Fundamentalists in Currency Markets: The Experience of Australia, Canada and New Zealand*, Proceedings of the conference "Revisiting the case for flexible exchange rates", 2-3 November 2000, Bank of Canada, <www.bankofcanada.ca>.

Dominguez, K.M./J. Frankel (1993a): *Does Foreign Exchange Intervention Work?*, Institute of International Economics, Washington, D.C.

Dominguez, K.M./J. Frankel (1993b): Does Foreign Exchange Intervention Matter? The Portfolio Effect, *American Economic Review* 83, 1356-1369.

Dominguez, K.M. (1999): *The Market Microstructure of Central Bank Intervention*, NBER Working Paper 7337.

Dornbusch, R. (1976): Expectations and Exchange Rate Dynamics, *Journal of Political Economy* 84 (6), 1161-1176.

Dornbusch, R. (1987): Exchange Rates and Prices, *American Economic Review* 77, 93-106.

Drew, A./L.C. Plantier (2000): *Interest Rate Smoothing in New Zealand and other Dollar Bloc Countries*, Reserve Bank of New Zealand Discussion Paper 2000/10.

Edison, H.J. (1993): *The Effectiveness of Central-Bank Intervention: A Survey of the Literature after 1982*, Special Papers in International Economics, 18, July 1993, Princeton University.

Eichengreen, B. (2002): *Can Emerging Markets Float? Should They Inflation Target?*, University of California, mimeo, <elsa.berkeley.edu/~eichengr/website.htm>.

Evans, M.D.D./R. Lyons (2001): *Portfolio Balance, Price Impact, and Secret Intervention*, NBER Working Paper 8356.

Fatum, R./M. Hutchinson (1999): Is Intervention a Signal of Future Monetary Policy? Evidence from the Federal Funds Futures Market, *Journal of Money, Credit, and Banking* 31 (1), 54-69.

Faust, J./J.H. Rogers/J.H. Wright (2001): *An Empirical Comparison of Bundesbank and ECB Monetary Policy Rules*, International Finance Discussion Papers 705, Board of Governors of the Federal Reserve System.

Federal Reserve Bank of Kansas City (1996): *Achieving Price Stability, Proceedings of the symposium August 29-31, 1996*, Kansas City.

Federal Reserve Bank of New York (2001): *Treasury and Federal Reserve Foreign Exchange Operations April-June 2001*, <www.ny.frb.org>.

Fischer, A.M. (2000): *Do Interventions Smooth Interest Rates?*, CEPR Discussion Paper 2479.

Flood, R.P./M. Taylor (1996): Exchange Rate Economics: What's Wrong with the Conventional Macro Approach?, in: Frankel, J./G. Galli/A. Giovannini (eds.): *The Microstructure of Foreign Exchange Markets*, Chicago, 261-294.

Flood, R.P./A.K. Rose (1996): Fixes: of the Forward Discount Puzzle, *The Review of Economics and Statistics* 78, 748-752.

Flood, R.P./A.K. Rose (2001): *Uncovered Interest Parity in Crisis: The Interest Rate Defence in the 1990s*, CEPR Discussion Paper 2943.

Frankel, J.A./K.A. Froot (1990): Chartists, Fundamentalists, and Trading in the Foreign Exchange Market, *American Economic Review* 80 (2) 181-185.

FRIEDMAN, M. (1953): *The Case for Flexible Exchange Rates, Essays in Positive Economics*, Chicago.

FROOT, K.A./J.A. FRANKEL (1989): Forward Discount Bias: Is It an Exchange Risk Premium?, *Quarterly Journal of Economics* 104 (1), 139-161.

FROOT, K.A./R.H. THALER (1990): Anomalies: Foreign Exchange, *Journal of Economic Perspectives* 4 (3), 179-92.

GEORGE, E. (1998): Exchange Rates: An Intractable Aspect of Monetary Policy, *Bank of England Quarterly Bulletin*, 38 (2), 178-181.

GERLACH, S./F. SMETS (2000): MCIs and Monetary Policy, *European Economic Review* 44, 1677-1700.

GHOSH, A.R. (1992): Is It Signalling? Exchange Intervention and the Dollar-Deutschemark Rate, *Journal of International Economics* 32, 201-220.

GOLDBERG, P. K./M. M. KNETTER (1997): Goods Prices and Exchange Rates: What Have We Learned?, *Journal of Economic Literature* 35 (3), 1243-1272.

GOLDSTEIN, M. (2002): *Managed Floating Plus*, Policy Analysis in International Economics 66, Institute for International Economics, Washington, D.C.

GOODFRIEND, M. (1991): Interest Rate Smoothing and the Conduct of Monetary Policy, *Carnegie-Rochester Conference Series on Public Policy* 34, 7-30.

GOODFRIEND, M. (1999): Maintaining Low Inflation: Rationale and Reality, in: BLEJER ET AL. (EDS.), 8-14.

GOODHART, C. (1996): *Why Do the Monetary Authorities Smooth Interest Rates?*, LSE Financial Markets Group, Special Paper 81.

HALL, R.E./N.G. MANKIW (1994): Nominal Income Targeting, in: N.G. MANKIW (ED.): *Monetary Policy*, Chicago, 71-94.

H.M. TREASURY (1997): *The New Monetary Policy Framework*, The Chancellor of the Exchequer's Letter of 6 May 1997 to the Governor of the Bank of England, <www.hm-treasury.gov.uk>.

H.M. TREASURY (1998): *Exchange Equalisation Account: Accounts 1997-98*, < www.hm-treasury.gov.uk >.

HALDANE, A. (1999): Targeting Inflation: The United Kingdom in Retrospect, in BLEJER ET AL. (1999), 52-59.

HAUSMANN, R./U. PANIZZA/E. STEIN (2000): *Why Do Countries Float the Way They Float?*, Inter-American Development Bank Working Paper 418, May 2000.

HEIKENSTEN, L. (1999): *Monetary Policy and the Exchange Rate*, Speech at a meeting with the Riksbank's primary dealers, 19th April 1999, <www.riksbank.se>.

HODRICK, R.J. (1987): *The Empirical Evidence on the Efficiency of Forward and Futures Foreign Exchange Markets*, Chur.

HUANG, A./D. MARGARITIS/D. MAYES (2001): *Monetary Policy Rules in Practice: Evidence from New Zealand*, Bank of Finland Discussion Paper 18-2001.

HÜFNER, F.P. (2000): *The British Foreign Exchange Reserves Puzzle*, ZEW Discussion Paper 00-55.

HÜFNER, F.P./M. SCHRÖDER (2002): *Exchange Rate Pass-Through to Consumer Prices: A European Perspective*, ZEW Discussion Paper 02-20.

HUNG, J.H. (1997): Intervention Strategies and Exchange Rate Volatility: A Noise Trading Perspective, *Journal of International Money and Finance* 16 (5), 779-793.

IMF (2001): *Draft Guidelines for Foreign Exchange Reserve Management*, May 24, 2001, <www.imf.org>.

ISARD, P. (1995): *Exchange Rate Economics*, Cambridge.

ISSING, O./V. GASPAR/I. ANGELONI/O. TRISTANI (2001): *Monetary Policy in the Euro Area*, Cambridge.

KAHN, G.A./K. PARRISH (1998): Conducting Monetary Policy with Inflation Targets, *Federal Reserve Bank of Kansas City Economic Review*, 3rd quarter 1998, 5-32.

KAMINSKY, G.L./K.K. LEWIS (1996): Does Foreign Exchange Intervention Signal Future Monetary Policy?, *Journal of Monetary Economics* 37, 285-312.

KEARNEY, C./R. MACDONALD (1986): Intervention and Sterilisation Under Floating Exchange Rates: The UK 1973-1983, *European Economic Review* 30, 345-364.

KENNEDY, P. (1998): *A Guide to Econometrics*, 4th edition, Cambridge.

KIM, S. (2002): Monetary Policy, Foreign Exchange Intervention, and the Exchange Rate in a Unifying Framework, forthcoming in *Journal of International Economics*.

KIM, S.-J./J. SHEEN (2002): The Determinants of Foreign Exchange Intervention by Central Banks: Evidence from Australia, *Journal of International Money and Finance* 21 (5), 619-649.

KRUGMAN, P.R. (1987): Pricing to Market when the Exchange Rate Changes, in: ARNDT, S.W./J. D. RICHARDSON, *Real-Financial Linkages Among Open Economics*, Cambridge, 49-70.

KRUGMAN, P.R./M. OBSTFELD (1991): *International Economics: Theory and Policy*, 2nd Edition, New York.

KUTTNER, K.N./P.C. MOSSER (2002): The Monetary Transmission Mechanism: Some Answers and Further Questions, *Federal Reserve Bank of New York Economic Policy Review* May, 15-26.

KYDLAND, F./E.C. PRESCOTT (1977): Rules Rather than Discretion: The Inconsistency of Optimal Plans, *Journal of Political Economy* 85 (3), 473-491.

LAFLÈCHE, T. (1996): The Impact of Exchange Rate Movements on Consumer Prices, *Bank of Canada Review* Winter 1996-1997, 21-32.

LAFRANCE, R. (1997): *Background Paper: The Monetary Frameworks of Four Inflation-Targeting Countries*, Proceedings of a conference "Price Stability, Inflation Targets and Monetary Policy", May, Bank of Canada, <www.bankofcanada.ca>.

LEIDERMAN, L./L.E.O. SVENSSON (EDS.) (1995): *Inflation Targets*, London.

LEVY-YEYATI, E./F. STURZENEGGER (2000): *Classifying Exchange Rate Regimes: Deeds vs. Words*, Universidad Torcuato Di Tella, mimeo, <www.utdt.edu/~ely/papers.html>.

LEWIS, K.K. (1995): Puzzles in International Financial Markets, in: GROSSMAN, G./K. ROGOFF (EDS.): *The Handbook of International Economics* III, Amsterdam, 1913-1971.

LOTTI, L. (2000): *Forward-Looking Interest Rate Rules as a Tool for Central Bank Watching*, Banca Intesa Risk Management Working Paper 9.

LYONS, R. (2001A): New Perspectives on FX Markets: Order-Flow Analysis, *International Finance* Summer, 303-320.

LYONS, R. (2001B): *The Microstructure Approach to Exchange Rates*, Cambridge.

MARK, N.C./Y. WU (1998): Rethinking Deviations from Uncovered Interest Parity: The Role of Covariance Risk and Noise, *The Economic Journal* 108, 1686-1706.

MCCALLUM, B.T. (1996): *Inflation Targeting in Canada, New Zealand, Sweden, the United Kingdom, and in General*, NBER Working Paper 5579.

MCCALLUM, B.T./E. NELSON (2001): *Monetary Policy for an Open Economy: An Alternative Framework with Optimizing Agents and Sticky Prices*, CEPR Discussion Paper 2756.

McCarthy, J. (2000): *Pass-Through of Exchange Rates and Import Prices to Domestic Inflation in Some Industrialized Economies,* Federal Reserve Bank of New York Staff reports 111.

Meese, R.A./K. Rogoff (1983): Empirical Exchange Rate Models of the Seventies – Do They Fit out of Sample?, *Journal of International Economics* 14, 3-24.

Menon, J. (1995): Exchange Rate Pass-Through, *Journal of Economic Surveys* 9 (2), 197-231.

Meredith, G./M.D. Chinn (1998): *Long-Horizon Uncovered Interest Rate Parity*, NBER Working Paper 6797.

Mishkin, F.S./A.S. Posen (1997): Inflation Targeting: Lessons from Four Countries, *Federal Reserve Bank of New York Economic Policy Review*, August 1997, 9-110.

Mishkin, F.S. (2000): Inflation Targeting in Emerging-Market Countries, *American Economic Review* 90 (2), 105-109.

Mishkin, F.S. (2001): *From Monetary Targeting to Inflation Targeting: Lessons from the Industrialized Countries*, World Bank Working Paper 2684, October 2001.

Mishkin, F.S./K. Schmidt-Hebbel (2001): *One Decade of Inflation Targeting in the World: What Do We Know and What Do We Need to Know?*, NBER Working Paper 8397.

Murray, J./M. Zelmer/D. McManus (1996): *The Effect of Intervention on Canadian Dollar Volatility*, Proceedings of the conference "Exchange Rates and Monetary Policy" at the Bank of Canada, 1996, <www.bankofcanada.ca>.

Muscatelli, V.A./P. Tirelli/C. Trecroci (2000): *Does Institutional Change Really Matter? Inflation Targets, Central Bank Reform and Interest Rate Policy in the OECD Countries*, CESifo Working Paper 278.

Mussa, M. (1981): *The Role of Official Intervention*, Group of Thirty Occasional Paper 6.

Neely, C.J./P.A. Weller/R. Dittmar (1997): Is Technical Analysis Profitable in the Foreign Exchange Market? A Genetic Programming Approach, *Journal of Financial and Quantitative Analysis* 32, 405-426.

Neely, C.J. (2000): Are Changes in Foreign Exchange Reserves Well Correlated with Official Intervention?, *Federal Reserve Bank of St. Louis Review*, 82 (5), 17-31.

Neely, C.J. (2001): The Practice of Central Bank Intervention: Looking under the Hood, *Federal Reserve Bank of St. Louis Review*, 83 (3), 1-10.

Neely, C.J. (2002): The Temporal Pattern of Trading Rule Returns and Central Bank Intervention: Intervention does not Generate Technical Trading Rule Profits, *Journal of International Economics* 58 (1), 211-232.

Nelson, E. (2001): *UK Monetary Policy 1972-97: A Guide Using Taylor Rules*, CEPR Discussion Paper 2931.

Newey, W.K./K.D. West (1987): A Simple, Positive Semi-Definite, Heteroskedasticity and Autocorrelation Consistent Covariance Matrix, *Econometrica* 55 (3), 703-708.

Peiers, B. (1997): Informed Traders, Intervention, and Price Leadership: A Deeper View of the Microstructure of the Foreign Exchange Market, *Journal of Finance* 52 (4), 1589-1614.

Portes, R. (2001): *The Euro and the International Financial System*, CEPR Discussion Paper 2955.

Ramaswamy, R./H. Samiei (2000): *The Yen-Dollar Rate: Have Interventions Mattered?*, IMF Working Paper 00/95.

Rankin, B. (2000): *The Exchange Rate and the Reserve Bank's Role in the Foreign Exchange Market*, <www.rba.gov.au>.

RAGNARTZ, C. (1999): Interest Rate Risk in the Foreign Exchange Reserve – Duration Intervals for the Investment Portfolio, *Sveriges Riksbank Quarterly Review* 3/1999, 31-43.

REINHART, C.M. (2000): The Mirage of Floating Exchange Rates, *American Economic Review* 90(2), 65-70.

RESERVE BANK OF AUSTRALIA (1999): *Reserve Bank Board Report and Financial Statements 1999*, <www.rba.gov.au>

RESERVE BANK OF NEW ZEALAND (1999): Monetary Policy Implementation: Changes to Operating Procedures, *Reserve Bank of New Zealand Bulletin* 62(1), 46-50.

RESERVE BANK OF NEW ZEALAND (2001): *The Impact of Monetary Policy on Growth*, <www.rbnz.govt.nz>

RIKSBANK (2001A): *Currency Interventions Cannot Be Ruled out*, Press release 2001-06-14, <www.riksbank.se>.

RIKSBANK (2001B): *Separate Minutes from the Executive Board Meeting on 8 November 2001*, <www.riksbank.se>.

RIKSBANK (2002): *The Riksbank's Interventions in the Foreign Exchange Market – Preparations, Decision-Making and Communication*, Press release 2002-01-31, <www.riksbank.se>.

ROGER, S. (1993): *The Management of Foreign Exchange Reserves*, BIS Economic Papers, 38.

ROSENBERG, M.R. (1996): *Currency Forecasting: Methods and Models for Predicting Exchange Rate Movements*, Chicago.

SAACKE, P. (2002): Technical Analysis and the Effectiveness of Central Bank Intervention, *Journal of International Money and Finance* 21(4), 459-480.

SARNO, L./M.P. TAYLOR (2001A): Official Intervention in the Foreign Exchange Market: Is It Effective, and, if so, How Does It Work?, *Journal of Economic Literature* 39(3), 839-869.

SARNO, L./M.P. TAYLOR (2001B): *Purchasing Power Parity and the Real Exchange Rate*, CEPR Discussion Paper 2913.

SCHAECHTER, A./M.R.STONE/M. ZELMER (2000): *Adopting Inflation Targeting: Practical Issues for Emerging Market Countries*, IMF Occasional Paper 202.

SHERWIN, M. (2000): *Foreign Reserves: Some Observations in an Asian Context – Current Issues in Reserves Management for Asian Central Banks*, Speech to a conference of the World Bank Treasury, 9 May 2000, <www.rbnz.govt.nz>.

SJÖÖ, B./R.J. SWEENEY (2001): The Foreign-Exchange Costs of Central Bank Intervention: Evidence from Sweden, *Journal of International Money and Finance* 20(2), 219-247.

SHLEIFER, A./L.H. SUMMERS (1990): The Noise Trader Approach to Finance, *Journal of Economic Perspectives* 4(2), 19-33.

SPOLANDER, M. (1999): *Measuring Exchange Market Pressure and Central Bank Intervention*, Bank of Finland Studies E:17.

STERNE, G. (1999): The Use of Explicit Targets for Monetary Policy: Practical Experiences of 91 Economies in the 1990s, *Bank of England Quarterly Bulletin* August 1999, 272-281.

STEVENS, G.R. (1999): Economic Forecasting and Its Role in Making Monetary Policy, *Reserve Bank of Australia Bulletin*, September 1999, 1-9.

STOCK, J.H. (2001): Instrumental Variables in Economics and Statistics, in: SMELSER, N.J./P.B. BATES (EDS.): *International Encyclopedia of the Social and Behavioral Sciences* 11, Amsterdam, 7577-7582.

SUTHERLAND, A. (2001): *Inflation Targeting in a Small Open Economy*, CEPR Discussion Paper 2726.

SVENSSON, L.E.O. (1996): Comment on FLOOD/TAYLOR (1996): 'Exchange Rate Economics: What's Wrong with the Conventional Macro Approach?, in: FRANKEL, J./G. GALLI/A. GIOVANNINI (EDS.): *The Microstructure of Foreign Exchange Markets*, Chicago, 296-301.

SVENSSON, L.E.O. (1997A): Inflation Forecast Targeting: Implementing and Monitoring Inflation Targets, *European Economic Review* 41, 1111-1146.

SVENSSON, L.E.O. (1997B): *Inflation Targeting in an Open Economy; Strict or Flexible Inflation Targeting?*, Reserve Bank of New Zealand Discussion Paper G97/8, November 1997.

SVENSSON, L.E.O. (1997/1998): *Monetary Policy and Inflation Targeting*, NBER Reporter Winter 1997/98, 5-8.

SVENSSON, L.E.O. (2000A): The First Year of the Eurosystem: Inflation Targeting or not?, *American Economic Review* 90(2), 95-99.

SVENSSON, L.E.O. (2000B): Open-Economy Inflation Targeting, *Journal of International Economics* 50, 155-183.

SVENSSON, L.E.O. (2001A): *Inflation Targeting: Should It Be Modelled as an Instrument Rule or a Targeting Rule?*, NBER Working Paper 8925.

SVENSSON, L.E.O. (2001B): *How Japan Can Recover*, Financial Times, Personal View, September 25, 2001.

SVENSSON, L.E.O. (2001D): *What Is Wrong with Taylor Rules? Using Judgment in Monetary Policy Through Targeting Rules*, Princeton University, mimeo, <www.princeton.edu/~svensson>.

SVENSSON, L.E.O. (2001E): *Independent Review of the Operation of Monetary Policy in New Zealand*, Report to the Minister of Finance, <www.princeton.edu/~svensson>.

SVENSSON, L.E.O. (2002A): *The Inflation Forecast and the Loss Function*, CEPR Discussion Paper 3365.

SVENSSON, L.E.O. (2002B): *A Reform of the Eurosystem's Monetary-Policy Strategy is Increasingly Urgent*, Briefing Paper for the Committee on Economic and Monetary Affairs (ECON) of the European Parliament, <www.princeton.edu/~svensson>.

SZAKMARY, A.C./I. MATHUR (1997): Central Bank Intervention and Trading Profits in Foreign Exchange Markets, *Journal of International Money and Finance* 16(4), 513-535.

TAKAGI, S. (1991): Foreign Exchange Market Intervention and Domestic Monetary Control in Japan, 1973-89, *Japan and the World Economy* 3, 147-180.

TAYLOR, D. (1982): The Mismanaged Float: Official Intervention by the Industrialized Countries, in: M.B. CONNOLLY (ED.): *The International Monetary System: Choices for the Future*, New York, 49-84.

TAYLOR, J.B. (1993): Discretion Versus Policy Rules in Practice, *Carnegie-Rochester Conference Series on Public Policy* 39(0), 195-214.

TAYLOR, J.B. (2000A): Teaching Modern Macroeconomics at the Principles Level, *American Economic Review* 90(2), 90-94.

TAYLOR, J.B. (2000B): *Using Monetary Policy Rules in Emerging Market Economies*, Stanford University, mimeo, <www.stanford.edu/~johntayl/>.

TAYLOR, J.B. (2001): The Role of the Exchange Rate in Monetary Policy Rules, *American Economic Review* 91(2), 263-267.

TAYLOR, M.P./H. ALLEN (1992): The Use of Technical Analysis in the Foreign Exchange Market, *Journal of International Money and Finance* 11, 304-314.

TAYLOR, M.P. (1995): The Economics of Exchange Rates, *Journal of Economic Literature* XXXIII, 13-47.

WADHWANI, S. (2000): *The Exchange Rate and the MPC: What Can We Do?*, Speech to the Senior Business Forum at the Centre for Economic Performance, 31 May 2000, <www.bankofengland.co.uk>.

WILLIAMSON, J. (1996): The Crawling Band as an Exchange Rate Regime: Lessons from Chile, Colombia, and Israel; Washington, D.C.